The Economics of Social Policy

The Economics of Social Policy

A. J. Culyer

ASSISTANT DIRECTOR, INSTITUTE OF SOCIAL AND ECONOMIC
RESEARCH, UNIVERSITY OF YORK

DUNELLEN

New York

First published in 1973 by
Martin Robertson & Company Ltd.
17 Quick Street, London N1 8HL

This edition published by
The Dunellen Company Inc.
145 East 52nd Street, New York N.Y. 10022

International Standard Book Number 0 8424 0074 5
Library of Congress Catalogue Card Number 73 82264

Typeset by Santype Ltd (Coldtype Division) Salisbury Wiltshire
Reproduced and printed by photolithography and bound in Great
Britain at The Pitman Press, Bath

Contents

The complicated analyses which economists endeavour to carry through are not merely gymnastic. They are instruments for the bettering of human life. The misery and squalor that surround us, the injurious luxury of some wealthy families, the terrible uncertainty overshadowing many families of the poor — these are evils too plain to be ignored. By the knowledge that our science seeks it is possible that they may be restrained! Out of the darkness light!

A. C. Pigou

Enthusiasm for the ideal in faith, in hope, and in charity is the best of human possessions; and the world owes very much to those who have been thrown off their balance by it. But, on the other hand, a responsible student of social problems must accept mankind as he finds them; and must base his estimates on that which is practicable. He must nourish the ideal in his heart: but his actions, his conversation, and even his thought must be occupied mainly with the actual: he must resist every temptation to make a short cut to the ideal. For indeed a traveller in a difficult country, who makes for his ultimate goal by a straight course, is likely to waste his time and strength and perhaps to meet disaster.

Alfred Marshall

for Tom and Alex

Preface

One of the unsatisfactory features of many textbooks in the social sciences is that they are frequently packed full of contemporary numerical and historical — dated and dating — data. A book purporting to be an applied textbook cannot entirely avoid these things but I have attempted to minimise them. Substantial parts of the book expound the necessary theory that is to be applied and these parts will become obsolescent not with the mere passing of time but with the accumulation of knowledge. In selecting areas for application I have tried to pick material that both illustrates well the application of a technique or an intellectual approach and is representative of a *type* of problem that recurs throughout social policy. Since the purpose of the book is to explore both a method and how to use it, extensive passages of social history, or potential social history, are avoided without detracting too much, I trust, from its overall value. It is only partially true that the present cannot be understood without a knowledge of the past and for that part of the subject there are, after all, innumerable books, pamphlets, articles and official publications which describe social policy and its history but which rarely are the 'economics of' social policy.

I have tried to write a book that will be useful to those who have had only an elementary introduction to economics to show them how economics has been and can be used in what I regard as some of the most important aspects of social policy. It will also be useful, I hope, to mainstream economics students for whom the novelty will be less in the analysis than in its relatively unfamiliar application. Since the relating of economics to the world in which we live is easily the hardest thing economists have to learn — such is the way we teach the subject — if I have been only partially successful in this I shall be well satisfied.

In writing it, I have offended against the cardinal rule of textbook writers by trying to appeal more to students than to their teachers. In the area of social policy, where there are almost as many schools of thought as individual teachers and writers, this has to be done and in trying to navigate my own passage I have inevitably diverged from the methods and approaches of many colleagues. Nevertheless, I hope I have not been unfair to them, even when my disagreement is plain. In particular, I have studiously tried to avoid 'politicising' the subject even though this may be both fun to do for its own mischievous sake, useful to stir students into fundamental thinking as they form their own politics, and tactically helpful in compelling the attention of a generally conservative consensus beyond academia. Indeed, it is the belief that social scientists, *qua* social scientists, should abstain from such partisanship that underlies the whole of this book. Ethical absolutists can claim neither to be scientific nor to speak for society. I hope that my alternative way may prove to lie upon both firmer and more mutually agreeable ground.

York   A.J.C.
November 1972

Acknowledgements

Though this book is short my debts are huge. Many are amply indicated by the Further Reading appended to each chapter and no further confession of my intellectual debt is required. In other cases it is required, however. Armen Alchian, Alan Peacock, Alan Williams and Jack Wiseman have all either taught me and/or taught with me – I am not sure which process has been the more powerful influence but their innovatory intellects, belief in the relevance of microeconomics in constructing a better world and their pioneering work in showing how economic notions can be usefully applied and revised in the reality of policy-making have been nothing short of an inspiration. Their vision provided a background without which the book could never have been written and I can only hope that my own inadequacies have not distorted it irredeemably. Michael Cooper suffered long hours in our joint teaching of undergraduate specialists at Exeter (as did the undergraduates, I fear) as I sought a unifying thread in social policy analysis while he, with marvellous instinct, saved us from pursuing an indefinitely large number of dead ends. Alan Maynard read occasional drafts with patience and a kindly but critical eye. His suggestions have immeasurably improved it. Tony Atkinson generously read through Part II. For his corrections, his extra insights and his encouragement I am profoundly grateful. The students both undergraduate and graduate who tolerated my personal ineptitude have earned my personal gratitude for helping me to understand my own mind better and making me able, I hope, more effectively to share it with others. In particular, for reading various parts of it and for not pulling their punches the following graduate students from York are all my creditors: Peter Agar, Ron Akehurst, Jon Baldry, Steve Barg, John Cullis, Phil Jacobs, Pete Myers, Malcolm Rees and Peter West. Some of these are already well-launched in their academic careers and will doubtless soon contribute to the obsolescence of the book. To all members of the Public Sector Studies Programme and the Health Economics Research Programme at York I owe a great debt: the intellectual environment created by these research programmes is enormously stimulating.

None of these people has seen the final version and in any case I have not always followed their teaching or advice. Thus, while none can escape responsibility for having made me what I am they must be absolutely absolved from the imperfections of my work. These are mine and mine alone.

For their extraordinary patience and efficiency in the speedy transformation of a scrawly manuscript into beautiful successive typescripts my thanks (and admiration) to Barbara Dodds, Barbara Pateman and Rosie Shaftoe. Freda Smith has earned my special gratitude for having typed — and retyped — the greater part of it. I am grateful that she is still smiling — and still my secretary! Eva Heavens, ISER's operations chief, helped to get deadlines met and, with consummate tact, kept me from monopolising the clerical staff entirely. Her services can be taken for granted far too easily but without her nothing would be possible. With her, anything — almost — is.

Finally, for Siegi and the children all the externalities were adverse. A husband and father whose nose is in his manuscript even on the *Romantische Strasse* can scarcely hope to compensate them adequately. I can only promise: he will try.

A.J.C.

PART I

Prelude

1 Introduction

Social policy is so intertwined with contemporary political issues and associated in people's minds with idealism, ideology and party politics that it is fitting that we begin this book with a statement about how we intend to use economics in policy analysis. This is the task of the present chapter.

Economists commonly divide their activity into two kinds – 'normative' economics and 'positive' economics. In the first, value-judgements about what in general ought to be done in society are made and inferences are drawn from these basic ethical assumptions for specific, recommended, courses of action. The second is value-free in the assumptions of the analysis and positive economics is intended to be entirely predictive of observable social events. Positive economics, however, requires value judgements concerning the method to be adopted. For example, a value-judgement about what constitutes a refutation of someone's theory, or a value-judgement about what is a 'good' theory. These value-judgements belong, however, to a different level of discourse from those required in recommending public policy. Indeed, positive economics cannot recommend any policy. It can only point out the observable consequences of this or that policy.

In this book, both normative and positive economics, in these senses, will be used. The reader should be alert to them. For example, 'socialist governments always reduce retirement pensions' is a positive statement (but false). 'Conservative governments are more concerned about efficiency than equity in social policy' is a positive statement (that needs better definition if its truth is to be tested). 'University education is the right of every person over the age of eighteen' is a positive false statement. 'University education ought to be available for every eighteen year old' is a normative statement whose truth or falsehood cannot be established with reference to objective facts alone.

Some of the *methodological* value-judgements of this book are as follows. Statements that predict social events whether large or small, important or trivial, should always be designed so that they are, in principle, refutable by reference to events in the world. A theory that predicts correctly 51% of the times it has been tested is better than tossing a coin. A theory that predicts correctly 60% of the time is better than one that is only 51% right. A theory whose assumptions are unambiguous and whose implications are derived clearly from them is better than one for which either one or both of these things is not the case. All of these involve a particular view about the philosophy of science.

The normative foundations in the analysis of social policy are a different set, relating to what is good for society, rather than what is good in science. They are so important, and so much confusion exists about the economic approach, and why it is what it is, that we shall discuss them at some length, for they will be taken for granted throughout the rest of the book which builds extensively upon them.

The ethical underpinning

How, in social science, are we to go about deciding what social policy is *good* social policy? In the extreme, each reader will have his own notion of what is desirable and one approach would certainly be for policies to be evaluated according to the author's own preconceptions of how things ought to be. This will not be the course adopted in this book. To do so would be to write a tract and to do so would also be less general than an alternative. Indeed one of the emphases running right through this book will be that one should avoid identifying the *social* interest with one's own.

An appropriate ethical rule for social science when it is evaluative is to ask whether any policy — actual or proposed — looks as though it is in the social interest. If it is, then we judge it good. If it is not, we judge it bad. But to be able to make such judgements we need, of course, to be able to identify the social interest. This sounds like something of a tall order but fortunately economists have devised a method by which it is possible — sometimes — to be able to do it.

The first basic value judgement we shall have to make is that no one person's — or group's — values shall be paramount. That is, for example, we shall not let Conservative values override Socialist values; nor soft-hearted values the hard-hearted; nor generous values the mean. We shall not attempt, in short, to assert any categorical absolutes. On the other hand neither shall we assert some wishy-washy compromise that possibly corresponds to nobody's idea of what is good. We shall judge any course of action to be good if those who are affected by it *agree* that it is good.

The notion of agreement, or of consensus, is at the heart of modern normative economics and arises, paradoxically, out of the nature of economics as the study of conflicts between individuals – or more specifically, out of the study of the resolution of conflicts. Just as individuals can conflict over who gets what scarce resources exist, so they conflict, of course, about concepts of social justice. But if the effected persons can agree that things are better with a proposed course of action than without it, then we shall assert that things actually will be better, that the course of action proposed is a good course to take (not necessarily the best, for there may be even better alternatives) and that the social interest would be advanced further by taking it than by doing nothing.

Agreement is naturally more likely to happen if negotiation takes place. An employer would doubtless think it excellent if a worker worked for him at £5 for a 50 hour week. Since the worker is unlikely to agree with this, no deal ought, on our criterion to take place – nor, indeed is it likely to! If, however, they can negotiate with one another, or simply offer probably agreeable terms, it is highly probable that they will be able to reach some mutual agreement. If so, we judge that an improvement in their welfare has taken place. The only guide, in general, that the economist allows to indicate such improvements in social welfare is when individuals voluntarily agree to arrangements.

What can we say if someone is forced to do something involuntarily? We cannot say that it is *not* in the social interest, for we do not know: the person who did the coercing may benefit a lot and the person who was coerced may only have lost a little, or alternatively the coerced party may have suffered a tremendous set back. We have no observable or measurable way of comparing the private welfare of individuals. We cannot say that coercion is in the social interest. Nor can we say it is not. All we can say is that if the affected parties agree to the change we judge an improvement in social welfare to have taken place. If they agree not to make the change we may also say that it ought not to take place since it would diminish social welfare.

It is worth pointing out some other value assumptions of this approach. First, note that we are assuming that welfare is a subjective experience about which some idea can be objectively got only from observing individuals' behaviour. Second, we are basing our ethical norm firmly upon the *individual*. We shall not judge any action to be good unless those who are harmed by it — if any — receive what they regard as at least an adequate compensation. No one may legitimately simply impose his own preferences — no matter how high-sounding they may be — upon anyone else. In this book, as elsewhere in the economic literature, this criterion for an improvement in social welfare (naturally a good thing) is termed the *Pareto criterion*, after the Italian economist and sociologist Vilfredo Pareto. Such improvements are termed *Pareto improvements* in social welfare. They are improvements simply because no one opposes them. Though many may have alternatives that *they* prefer, unless they can get others to agree we cannot judge them to be improvements for, since some disagree, we have no objective basis for evaluation.

Pareto, like Weber, was anxious to minimize the subjective and personal ethics of the observer in policy matters, with the ethical norms of society being taken as data rather than being altered or overruled for the sake of the analyst's own subjective opinions. When any one member of society believes that social welfare would be increased by a particular course of action he is expressing *his own* view about what is best for society. But society is, of course, composed of many individuals, with many views about what is best. A single individual has only his own subjective concept of social welfare — this is not the same thing as the information required to state that a particular course of action actually, or even potentially, increases social welfare. Thus, while we must concede that it is not possible to eliminate all normative considerations from problems of policy prescription, Pareto indicated a way in which they can be made a good deal less subjective than otherwise they might be. To that extent, social science is the more scientific. Unfortunately, Pareto was considerably less objective in his sociology than in his economics which is why, perhaps, he is today more highly regarded by economists than by sociologists.

The reader will doubtless think the Pareto criterion a very weak ethical view. Indeed it has to be since we shall not assert any one ethical system to be superior to any other. The Paretian approach is essentially tolerant of all ethical systems and it is this generality that makes it attractive in social science which, like all science, seeks generality rather than specificity. It is also highly suited to the normative analysis of social policy in democratic and democratic socialist societies. But though it is a weak criterion, it is probably far more powerful than those who are unacquainted with it imagine. In this book we shall use it to analyse a large range of social problems of current interest, from the problem of poverty to the problem of law and order.

A related concept is that of the *potential* Pareto improvement, which is much used in cost-benefit work. This criterion says that any change is *potentially good* so long as the improvement in the welfare of those who gain from a change is more than sufficient to compensate those who lose. Of course, we can never know whether it *actually* was an improvement unless the compensation actually takes place. Nevertheless, in many practical problems it is useful to identify potential improvements even though we cannot recommend them as actually good ones.

This approach is an unusual one in the study of social problems, for it insists that neither the author nor economics has a monopoly of righteousness − unless you think ethical tolerance to be righteous! It is an approach that 'depoliticises' academic study of social policy and, as a result, both gives insights where more partisan approaches give none and also enables one to take a more detached look at some of the very vexed intellectual skirmishing that customarily preoccupies a great number of writers in the social policy field. These are not negligible advantages.

Now the concept of welfare used here is not, of course, that used in the expression the 'Welfare State'. We shall not attempt any definition of this latter, beyond observing that it consists of a set of social policies operated by government. For some, the Welfare State is an outward and visible testimony to the fact that man is a moral being with a compassionate soul; that he cares about his fellows and is not an unscrupulously grasping and selfish creature. A substantial part of this book accepts the factual element in this proposition as being true and much of our analysis is built upon it. However, our interpretation of the proposition is that the Welfare State is a *means* by which compassion and an individual's identification with the corporate body of his fellows are implemented and is *not an end in itself*. This is an admittedly partial approach. It implies, for example, that the kind of zero user-charge provision sometimes encountered in the Welfare State is to be evaluated not in terms of its intrinsic merits but in terms of what it enables us to get done. The Welfare State, according to our view, is *instrumental* – a means to moral ends – not a universal object with moral significance of its own. Thus, those who would include among the problems of the Welfare State whether it debilitates the individual and erodes initiative (latter-day Samuel Smileses) or whether a glorious counter example to the materialism and triviality of a sick society is not being eroded by the very forces it seeks to vanquish, will find much to disappoint them in these pages. Profoundly important though this kind of question is – some of them may be far more important than many of the questions to which we shall address ourselves – they are beyond the ability of social science fully to comprehend. The student of social policy will have to draw upon his own ideology in examining these problems. It would be an unpardonable crime were we to attempt to lend the scientific authority of social science to promoting a personally ideological *Weltanschauung*. To nourish ideals, to have faith, hope *and charity*, are the finest human attributes. We owe too much to the noble souls of history to doubt this reassuring truth. But the student of social policy must subdue his enthusiasm. He must accept mankind as he finds it.

The application of economic analysis where idealism and ideology may be prominent in one's thoughts provides a fundamental emotional difficulty for the student of social policy to overcome. The uncompromising attitude of economics to means and ends may also prove difficult. Contrary to a popular view, in economics *only* the ends can ever 'justify' the means. Specific ends may be mutually incompatible and specific means may be more or less consistent with a given end. These, indeed, are the very stuff of social science. But only the ends can ever warrant particular means. Indeed, it is hard to see that anything else could possibly be the case. The major problem arises when some ends are beyond the ability of social science in general, or economics in particular, to comprehend. In such cases one must honestly confess that the social science – or economic – solution to a social problem is only a partial one. We will have gone as far as we can.

The problems to be tackled

What then are the problems to be tackled? They can be divided into three. First, we seek to establish a way of knowing what, in specific instances of social policy, should be done. Second, we seek to devise methods of analysis that will help the people who make decisions about social policy to make better decisions. Third, we seek to develop an institutional framework that encourages these decision takers to take decisions that are more certainly in the social interest and not in any sectional interest (especially their own).

From 1951–1970 unemployment benefit in the U.K. (for married couples with two children) plus the family allowance rose from 36% of after tax income for an employed man (with wife and two children) to over 48%. Was this too much, too little or just right? The number of families with incomes below the poverty line was not more than 12% in 1963 and was at least 3½% in 1969. What is the best way of tackling this problem? In 1970, out of 6.4 million persons over 65 years of age, 93,000 were cared for in local authority homes and 573,000 received home nursing. Are these numbers too small or too large? Are their relative proportions about right? In 1971 the average doctor in the British National Health Service had 2,460 patients on his list and 4,000 out of over 19,000 had lists in excess of 3,000. Is there a doctor shortage? Will there be one in fifteen years' time? In 1970/71 total expenditure on the National Health Service was just under £2,000 millions, of which about £183.5 millions were raised by the specific tax known as the National Health Service Contribution. Is this overall figure too small or too large? How would one tell? What is the point of retaining the NHS contribution? From 1961 to 1970 the proportion of pupils still at school at the age of 17 rose from 9.0% to 17.1%. Should this trend be encouraged? If so, how? In 1970 over 9 million persons owned the dwellings they lived in (over double the number of owner occupiers in 1950) and nearly 6 million dwellings were rented from local authorities (again more than double the 1950 number). What subsidies do these two sets of people get from the state? Are they sensible subsidies? In 1969 over 6 million metric tons of sulphur dioxide was poured into the air. What consequences would flow from a total prevention of this pollution? Ought it to be stopped? Moderated? By how much? In 1970 crimes known to the British police rose to 32.2 per thousand population from 16.2 in 1951. 38.5 % were cleared up (compared with 40.6% in 1951). Are police resources deployed in the most efficient way? What *is* the most efficient way?

These are the sorts of problem falling squarely into the first category. A substantial portion of economic analysis has been devoted to inventing methods by which such problems could, in principle, be solved. Much of this type of analysis is qualitative rather than quantitative. For many purposes qualitative analysis is all that is required. For example, it can be used to supply decision takers in government departments with 'shopping lists' of considerations that analysis says are relevant to any particular problem (e.g. output budgeting). Such analysis can also satisfy our urge to *understand*, to explain, phenomena. For example, it helps to explain why university education has been principally the preserve of the children of middle class parents despite state aid in providing it for any who have the potential to benefit.

The second category of problem implies the development of quantitative techniques whereby the parameters of the models invented by social science can be estimated and variables measured. Economic planning models such as forecasting models, cost-benefit analysis and linear programming are some of the techniques that have been developed to meet this need. With their aid it becomes possible to compare the relative advantage of, say, spending an additional £100,000 on primary or secondary education, to calculate the social costs and benefits of increasing the price of school meals, to estimate the future supply and demand of doctors or to derive the valuations that policy makers currently (implicitly) place upon, say, the value of a road accident death prevented when they are deciding what and how many road improvements to undertake. In short, the quantitative methods enable students of social policy and the responsible decision makers alike to identify not only whether we get too much or too little of some things relative to others but *how much* less or more we ought to get.

Helping decision takers to take better decisions is informed by the specific analysis of actual problems and it enables *general* rules and concepts to be laid down and used repeatedly in different contexts. Concepts such as 'social cost', 'externality', 'transfers', 'shadow prices', and 'discount rates' are purely theoretical ideas which require a means of relating them to real events. It is necessary to make them operational — usable in specific instances. Although this book is in no sense the rubric for a 'compleat policy maker', it does lay down the foundations and explores the major problems, as well as giving adequate references to those works that are in the nature of a rubric.

The final set of problems, concerning the actual behaviour of decision takers, is the least developed area in the economics of social policy and involves us in inventing theories of the behaviour of public decision takers in order both to enable us the better to interpret some of the data we observe and also to design institutions that work in the social interest. It would be of little avail to invent the techniques of qualitative and quantitative analysis if we lack confidence that public decision takers would actually use them or behave in a way that was consistent with the public interest. Some people seem to begin by *assuming* that decision takers in the private or public sectors work systematically either for or against the social interest (regardless of their individual motivations) but it is obvious that the validity of this assumption (whichever it may be) must be subject to testing.

Suppose, for example, that you have evidence that a public decision taking body has been systematically allocating resources in an arbitrary, inefficient and unfair way. Would decision takers in the private sector be any the less arbitrary, inefficient or unfair? Why or why not? What system of sticks and/or carrots might make public and private decision takers act more in conformity with the social interest? In calculating the cost functions of institutions such as hospitals the assumption is required that whatever the unit cost level attained by any individual institution that unit cost level is the lowest technically attainable given current technology and current output rates. But why should unit cost at each observed output, or at each size of the institution, be the lowest technically attainable? What incentives are there for decision takers in hospitals to minimise costs? To answer all these questions we need some pretty well worked out theories of organisational behaviour, not prejudiced assertions or unsupported assumptions. Moreover, since it is with questions such as these that we come, perhaps, nearest to the scientific questioning of what are, for many people, matters upon which their political beliefs provide a ready answer, it becomes doubly important to accept the social scientist's self-denying ordinance by dismissing 'ideology'. He must become a kind of schizophrenic, keeping his existing political conceptions separate from his academic enquiries, though there is no reason why the two compartments of his mind should not fructify one another. For example, his politics may suggest the areas of academic study that interest him most and they may make him persevere the more in defending scientific results that he 'likes' and criticising those he 'dislikes'. In this way, so long as the politics provides *only* the motivation for, and not the method of, discourse, the search for truth may become more effective, for there are some people for whom the mere desire for truth is a subsidiary ideal compared with sustaining their political prejudices. Conversely, one's dispassionate economic analysis may inform and mould one's politics. In the emotionally difficult areas one need not cease being a political animal but should seek to keep the mode of discourse, one's mode of thinking and one's standards of scholarship above the debating chamber level of self-justification, advocacy of personal viewpoints and sustenance of personal positions. There is, or should be, little room for 'self' in the social scientist.

Thus, as well as there being important allocation and investment problems in the Welfare State and in the broader area of social policy there are also many important problems concerned with the organisation of social policy and with developing methods of analysis and approach to social policy. Each of these problems can be, and ought to be dealt with in the economics of social policy. In this book we shall try to give each an equiproportionate share of the space.

People's rights

One feature of the Paretian approach, broadly outlined above, which frequently gives rise to confusion is the economist's characteristic attitude to claims made that certain individuals have rights. What a person means when he says, say, that everyone has a right to, say, a decent livelihood is not that everyone actually has a *legal right* to it but that he thinks that everyone *ought* to have the legal right to whatever the observer thinks is decent. This is, of course, a perfectly legitimate statement of two personal value-judgements. It is not, however, a statement of fact. Nor is it the kind of ought-statement that the Paretian system permits us to make, unless everyone *agrees* that they ought to have the right. Since making the right effective usually implies that others will lose — at least some will lose some of their wealth — it is far from a foregone conclusion that this value statement commands genuine general assent. Of course, it may do, for although some persons may lose in financial terms they may also gain in terms of other sources of personal satisfaction. If that were generally the case, then even the weak Pareto criterion agrees that they ought to have the right. If they do not agree, while we cannot say they should have the right neither can we say they should not. We simply cannot tell. Doubtless some passionately believe that they ought and others that they ought not. Economics, however, has no means of identifying the best moral approach to human rights. We can only allow in everyone's opinion, without fear or favour, and judge those specific changes upon which agreement can be reached to be changes that are unambiguously in the social interest.

Social man

Economic man is frequently regarded as some kind of amoral (if not immoral) calculating machine. As a matter of fact, the economic postulates relating to the behaviour of individuals in society (see chapter 2) assume neither that individuals are selfish nor that they make calculations. What they do state is that in choice situations, individuals respond in predictable ways. Since predictability is the foundation stone of *all* social science this can scarcely be regarded as a distinguishing feature (let alone an undesirable feature) of economics. There is, however, a certain propaedeutic value in discussing this popular misconception in more detail.

Perhaps the *popular* misconception about 'economic' (i.e. choosing) man derives from the formal differences in appearance between sociological and economic treatises. The fact that the lay public can more readily understand the more descriptive passages in applied sociology may be one source of the misconception. An empirical technique that, at the moment, lacks quantifiable indicators of many of its theoretical variables (compared, say, with the economists' national income data, concentration ratios, etc.) compels it frequently to fall back upon painstaking descriptions of case studies which give a superficial appearance of dealing with a more complete man than can ever be contained in anybody's theory. Since, however, the scientific status of any discipline derives from its *theoretical* foundations, this impression is only falsely given by the respective *empirical* methods of the various disciplines.

Perhaps the confusion derives from a belief that economic man is interested only in money and things carrying a money price. While there is no reason why one should not apply economic analysis only to monetary phenomena – if one wishes – there is nothing in economics which places this limit on its application. Economics has a perfectly general theory (though not a perfect theory!) of human action. Indeed, in this book we shall, as already indicated, use an essentially economic approach to incorporate highly relevant social parameters as endogenous variables in the economic system (for example, political institutions). We shall also apply the analysis to apparently 'non-economic' phenomena such as crime and tenant eviction.

Yet another possible explanation for the mistrust of 'economic' man lies in his frequent association with classical Utilitarianism, according to which individuals sought to maximise some objective thing called utility and made 'rational' (granted this objective) calculations about how best to reach their goals. Such a vision of 'economic' man is, indeed, unpleasant and unduly simpliste. Such monsters have no place in this book nor in any other contemporary works on economics.

Man as a chooser, however, remains at the core of this book. Our theory of choice, moreover, encompasses all choice problems. For example, it certainly encompasses the choice problems faced by a completely selfish man (if such persons exist) but it can also deal with the man who gives away his all to others. The latter still faces a choice problem: to whom shall he give what? How much shall he give each? Shall he work harder to earn more to give away? Shall he give it away privately or shall he organise a charity? Shall he vote for higher taxes so that the State can give more away? Shall he give it with strings attached? Shall he give it in kind or cash? Such questions by no means exhaust the range of choice problems facing economic man as the contemporary economist defines him. But they have little in common with the popular misconception.

In short, the economic paradigm does not commit us to any particular ethically loaded definition of the individual. The *model* of individual behaviour to be used will be explicated in the following chapters.

If the fundamental model of man that economists use is an ethically free constellation of assumptions that does not mean, of course, that the behavioural implications of the model cannot be evaluated in ethical terms. For example, it is perfectly possible to express ethical judgements about 'selfishness' or 'generosity' as these are exhibited by behaviour. It is also possible to specify concepts of what is socially *desirable* and to recommend policies on the basis of whether or not the behaviour of individuals under alternative institutions contributes or not to the approved objectives. This approach should be distinguished from one in which one identifies what is socially *desired* (a more factual matter) and explores behaviour under alternative institutions for consistency with the Pareto criterion. There is nothing intrinsic in the economic approach that commits us to any particular ethical norms. Nor indeed does it require us to adopt ethical norms at all. In this sense, the core of economic analysis is value-free. We may inject values if we feel so inclined but we are not obliged to. If we do inject an ethical scheme others are entitled to reject it but, in so doing, they do not reject the implications of pure economic analysis, for they are at liberty to employ the same analysis with alternative ethical judgements, though we have argued that the Paretian ethical approach has substantial advantages over others.

One kind of value-judgement will *not* be made in this book, however. At no time shall we discuss the morality of individual *motivation*. Motives will be taken as given — as data in the system. When we judge, it will be *behaviour* that is judged. We shall evaluate policy in terms of whether it enables people to behave in the way prescribed by the Paretian system. This will include such questions as whether a social policy enables them to gain employment, live in security, have good health and a sound education; whether it enables them to give expression to generous instincts and whether it gives them freedom without restricting the freedom of others. These involve value-judgements to be sure, but at root they are not highly controversial ones.

This emphasis on the ethical aspects of social policy should not detract from the fact that substantial parts of the economics of social policy are positive rather than normative. As well as prescribing, there is a substantial amount of explaining to do as well. As will be seen, the two will normally go hand in hand.

FURTHER READING

Three classics worth reading are:

V. Pareto, *The Mind and Society* (ed. by A. Livingston and trans. by A. Bongiorno and A. Livingston), New York, Harcourt and Brace, 1935 (especially chapter 12).

V. Pareto, *Manual of Political Economy* (trans. by A. S. Schweir, Ed. by A. S. Schweir and A. N. Page), New York, Kelley, 1971. The 'Pareto criterion' is explicitly stated at chapter 6, para. 33 and in the Appendix at para. 89.

M. Weber, *The Methodology of the Social Sciences* (trans. and ed. by E. Shils and H. Finch), Glencoe, The Free Press, 1949.

and an excellent assessment of Pareto is:

V. J. Tarascio, *Pareto's Methodological Approach to Economics*, Chapel Hill, University of North Carolina Press, 1968.

For some modern writings in the 'Paretian' tradition:

K. J. Arrow, *Social Choice and Individual Values*, (2nd Edition), New York, Wiley, 1963.

D. Black, 'On the Rationale of Group Decision-Making', *Journal of Political Economy*, Vol. 56, 1948.

H. R. Bowen, *Toward Social Economy*, New York, Rinehart, 1948.

J. M. Buchanan, 'Positive Economics, Welfare Economics and Political Economy', *Journal of Law and Economics*, Vol. 2, 1959.

R. A. Dahl and C. E. Lindblom, *Politics, Economics and Welfare*, New York, Harper, 1963.

For scientific method in general, consult:

T. S. Kuhn, *The Structure of Scientific Revolutions*, Chicago, 1962.

K. R. Popper, *The Open Society and Its Enemies*, London, Routledge and Kegan Paul, 1945.

K. R. Popper, *Conjectures and Refutations,* London, Routledge and Kegan Paul, 1963.

and for positive economics:

L. Robbins, *An Essay on the Nature and Significance of Economic Science,* London, Macmillan, 1932.

M. Friedman, 'The Methodology of Positive Economics', in *Essays in Positive Economics*, Chicago, University of Chicago Press, 1953.

J. Melitz, 'Friedman and Machlup on the Significance of Testing Economic Assumptions', *Journal of Political Economy*, Vol. 73, 1965.

2 The Fundamental Economics of Social Policy

In this chapter the basic economic analysis required for subsequent examination of social policy is presented. Like bikinis, this chapter covers only the bare essentials but these form the basis for the whole of the rest of the book. Some additional complications and limitations are discussed later in the contexts in which the theory will be applied. The Further Reading contains some references for those wishing for greater sophistication.

The economic approach is about choices. The majority of choices that are made, by individuals, managers, administrators, are in practice *marginal* choices. That is, they are choices between a little more of this or a little more of that rather than all or none of this or that. For example should another 10p be added to the retirement pension? Should it be added to the marginal rate of income tax? Should another ward be added to the Bradford 'A' Hospital Management Committee's bed complement? Should the output of primary school teachers be increased by 5 or 6% a year? Should the probability of death by road accident be reduced by 5 or 10%? Should police constables' salaries be increased by £100? Should the noise level in York's Coney Street be reduced from 75 perceived decibels to 70? Should the level of air pollution in asbestos textile factories be reduced from 12 fibres per cubic centimetre to 10? Should Joe Smith take a higher wage, higher risk or a lower wage, lower risk job?

In setting out the basic economics of choice a highly simplified paradigm will be used initially. Subsequently, some of the simplifications will be dropped, especially those that prevent its effective application to social policy, but not all. The task of incorporating social policy into a really complex microeconomic model of general equilibrium will not be undertaken in this book. Fortunately, however, a

17

great many problems can be handled quite satisfactorily without such complexities.

The fundamental assertion that is made and upheld without exception[1] in this book is the following law:

> *The more any individual has in a given time period of any entity that he regards as desirable, other things remaining the same,*[2] *the lower its marginal value to him.*

To illustrate this, consider an individual with 24 hours a day at his disposal who must choose when to go to bed and when to set his alarm clock (i.e. he must choose how to divide his day between sleeping and waking). Figure 2.1 illustrates his choice problem. MV_S shows how the

Fig. 2.1.

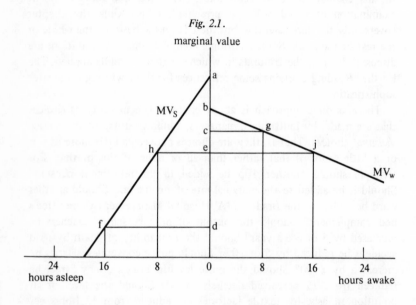

value of extra minutes sleeping falls as he takes more, MV_W shows how the marginal value of waking time falls as he has more. We suppose, purely for diagrammatic purposes, that the MV curves are straight lines, though all our assertion actually commits us to is that they slope downwards. Suppose the individual whose preferences (on a particular day) happen to be those shown in Figure 2.1. were to be told to sleep for 16 hours and to wake for 8. The marginal value of sleep would be

Od and the marginal value of waking *Oc*. The total value of sleep would be the area below *af* and the total value of waking the area below *bg*. To see why, recall that the *MV* curves show the marginal values of additional units of the desired entity. Thus, *Oa* is the value of one minute's sleep. A point on MV_S slightly to the left of *a* indicates the value of an additional minute's sleep. The two together give the total value of two minutes' sleep. With 8 hours' sleep, the *total* value is the area below *ah* and the *marginal* value of eight hours' sleep is given by the height of *h* above the axis.

The total value of sleeping and waking is the sum of the areas below *af* and *bg* when he sleeps for 16 hours and wakes for 8. We now introduce a second assertion:

Every individual chooses entities so as to maximise their value to him.

We can now definitely assert that our individual will *not* choose to sleep 16 hours by reasoning as follows: if he gave up 8 hours' sleep he would lose the area under *fh*. By the same token, he would gain 8 hours of waking time valued at the area under *gj*. This latter area is larger than the area under *fh* therefore the total value of 8 hours asleep and 16 hours awake must be greater than that of 16 hours asleep and 8 hours awake. Therefore he will choose the former rather than the latter.

In fact, the choice of 8 hours' sleep is the best possible choice for our individual, for at this rate of sleeping, the marginal value of sleeping equals the marginal value of being awake. The total value of time spent in these two primitive activities is maximised. This the reader can demonstrate for himself on the diagram by comparing the value of a minute more (or less) of sleep with that of a minute less (or more) awake. We have a general rule:

Every individual will choose entities in such quantities in each period of time that their marginal values are equal. When marginal values are equal the individual maximises his benefit from the entities in question.

Before going further let us pause to ask a fundamental question. We have spoken of values, total and marginal, but *in terms of what* are we valuing sleep. etc? In the early days of marginalist economics the answer would have been that we are measuring everything in terms of 'utility'. Now, a century later however, the answer would be that these values are expressed in terms of some other desired entity, or what is referred to as a *numéraire*. For example, if over the time period in question the individual has a fixed stock of peanuts, we could be measuring the value of sleep, waking hours, *etc.,* in terms of the peanuts a person would give up for extra amounts of these things. To imagine things being had for peanuts is a great deal more satisfactory than measuring the strength of a preference by 'utility' but it has some tricky aspects of which one, above all others, is worth special attention.

The tricky feature is this: what happens if the amount of peanuts one will give up does not depend only on the hours asleep or awake but also on the amount of peanuts one has left? The answer is that the equi-marginal rule that says all marginal values are equalised does not change at all. It is still generally valid. The association of total values with areas under the curves is, however, no longer generally valid for if any amount other than an insignificant proportion of the total peanut flow is given up, the curves showing the marginal value of sleep will reflect not only the diminishing marginal value of sleep but also the *increasing* marginal value of peanuts (in terms of sleep, *etc.*). In short, a measuring rod is of little use if it keeps changing its length!

There are two principal ways out of this difficulty. One is to assume that the total flow of the numéraire entity is large relative to the notional quantities surrendered to obtain more of something else. For this reason money income is frequently used as the numéraire when, if total expenditure upon any commodity is a small proportion of total money income, the measures of total valuation may be good enough approximations to the truth for most practical purposes. The other method, when this assumption is not plausibly tenable, is to adopt a technique that specifically allows for the simultaneous variation of *all* marginal valuations when measuring total values. This requires more advanced analysis but, fortunately, most of the practical problems of concern in this book will not, as we shall see, require us to develop this analysis. We shall however relax the assumption of a constant marginal value for the numéraire when it seems likely to cause serious distortions.

In general, we assert the following:
(a)   the marginal value of all desired entities falls as the rate of consumption increases, other things being equal
(b)   the marginal value of each entity is less than its total value
(c)   valuations may be conveniently expressed in 'monetary' terms with the unit of account as, say, peanuts but more con- veniently, pounds and pence

(d)   because the marginal value of each desired entity falls as more
        is had, one entity may be substituted for another
(e)   normally, many goods will be chosen.

Now consider the marginal valuation curve in terms of *money* for
any desired entity, x. If x has a price attached to it, the individual will
adjust his rate of acquisition of x until its MV is equal to its price.
Beyond that point, MV will be lower than price (though still positive)
so that the individual will lose more than he will gain by acquiring
more. Up to that point the individual will always gain a positive net
marginal benefit equal to the difference between MV and price. The
higher the price, the less will be acquired. The lower the price the more
will be acquired. A purely abstract, but logical, theory has been turned
into a *refutable* theory. The implication that MV equals price implies
the so-called 'law of demand':

*The higher the personal cost of obtaining any entity, the less will be
acquired in any period of time.*

It also implies that the prices voluntarily paid by individuals to gain an
increment of a good, or receivable to compensate for the loss of a good,
provide an objective measure of MV. This result is of profound
importance in economic policy. It forms the basis, for example, of
much cost-benefit analysis.

With all this the reader is probably already familiar. Let us turn,
before introducing the special complications appropriate in the analysis
of social policy, to the equally familiar 'law of supply'. We assume first
that the ownership of all enterprises engaged in production is shared
out among shareholders who have a great deal of knowledge about the
nature of the firms they own, can readily sell and buy shares, and
whose one ambition in life (as shareholders) is to make as much money
as possible. Under these circumstances all enterprises will seek to make
the highest possible profits. Second, we assume that at going prices, all
firms can sell as much of their output as they wish. These two
assumptions imply that the firm will always produce at a rate at which
price is equal to the lowest marginal cost of that output. To produce
less would mean that an expansion would yield more in additional
revenue than cost; to produce more would yield higher additional costs
than additional revenue. Only when (rising) marginal cost is equal to
price is the current period's profit maximised.[3] Thus, since price is set
equal to the marginal cost of output, at each price the rate of supply is
determined – the marginal cost curve *is* the supply curve. In general,

the marginal cost curve is assumed either to rise eventually with the rate of supply due to the 'law' of diminishing returns, or to be approximately constant.

Under the market conditions specified, a single *market-clearing price* for x will emerge determined by the intersection of the horizontal sum of every x-producer's supply curve and the horizontal sum of every x-demander's marginal valuation curve. Market forces drive the price to the point at which, for demanders, MV = price and, for suppliers, MC = price. We may infer that under competitive conditions, $MV = MC^4$. Alternatively, a central planner with sufficient knowledge about MC's and MV's could calculate a 'shadow price' at which demand equalled supply and could instruct producers to produce and consumers to consume accordingly.

Pareto Optimality

The word 'efficient' as it is popularly used, frequently means that a given activity is being performed at a given rate *at the least cost.* The economic concept of efficiency is, however, wider than this and runs as follows:

A society has allocated its resources efficiently when no input and no output can be transferred to some alternative use without making at least one person worse off, even if the welfare of others is improved.

Clearly this definition includes the least cost notion of efficiency, for if a given output of anything could be obtained at less cost, then someone can gain without anyone losing. For example, less inputs could be used in that activity and devoted to increasing output elsewhere. But it also says more than this, for it specifies that even if every good is obtained at least cost, these goods must be so distributed among the members of the society that no redistribution may take place among them that benefits some without harming others. Suppose, out of a stock of an available good, one person places a higher marginal valuation upon his share than another places upon his. Economic efficiency exists only when the marginal values are equal, for otherwise there will be some sum of money that the person with the high MV will give the person with the low MV, and which lies in between the two MV's, that will persuade the latter to surrender some of the good to the former so that both may gain with no one losing. The person surrendering some of the good must be compensated by a price at least equal to his *MV* if he is voluntarily to exchange with the other. The person acquiring the more of the good will value the addition not less than the price he must pay. Only when *MV*'s are equal is there no further scope for *mutually* beneficial redistribution – one person may gain but only at the expense of another. Clearly, when *MV*'s are different as between individuals they will normally, in their own interests, seek to exchange with one another.

A situation in which there is no further scope for mutually beneficial exchange of goods, in which everything that is produced is produced at its lowest marginal cost and in which marginal cost is equal to marginal valuation is a *Pareto optimum*: an economically (or socially) efficient allocation of resources in which no one's welfare can be improved without harming someone else. Related to this, and of great practical importance, is the notion of a *Pareto improvement,* when at least one person's welfare is *raised* without harming anyone else, although the notional optimum may not be attained. Clearly, there are many cases in the world with which we are familiar when some people benefit at the expense of others. Are such cases efficient? The answer, according to the Pareto criterion is that *they may be but we cannot tell.* The Pareto criterion does not tell us that such allocations are *bad,* only that we cannot tell if they are good. The reason for this is important and should be well understood. It is as follows. If one individual takes some good from another individual, assuming the good to be efficiently produced and allocated, then the former gains and the latter loses. We could say that social welfare had also improved if we could specify *how much* benefit the one had gained and *how much* the other had lost. Unfortunately, unless the loser voluntarily *gives* something to the gainer, or else the gainer voluntarily compensates the loser enough for the loser voluntarily to surrender the good, we cannot make this comparison, for welfare is a subjective experience and is unique to each individual. Only when individuals voluntarily agree to perform certain actions can we be sure that their welfare is increasing – but even then we cannot tell how much one gains relative to another. Nevertheless, if no one loses and someone gains we can safely say that social welfare has increased. Conversely if no one gains and someone loses we can safely say that social welfare has fallen. When some gain and others lose without compensation for their loss we cannot, unless we are prepared to place *our own valuation* upon the gains and losses of others, say anything at all about changes in social welfare.

The objection to a third party, such as a student of social policy, placing his or her own valuation on the gains and losses of others is, as we have seen, that it is fundamentally ascientific. If observer A and observer B place *different* values on the gains and losses, we have no means of selecting the correct one. All that we have is a subjective evaluation of someone else's subjective experience! As we shall see, this scientific 'impossibility' of making interpersonal 'utility' comparisons has proved an obstacle in social policy evaluation, especially where redistribution of income is important, and a number of attempts have been made to overcome it which will be investigated later (Chapter 4). Meanwhile, however, we do not attempt to go beyond the restrictions imposed upon us by the Pareto criterion.

Although it is restricted, the Pareto criterion is far from useless. For one thing, it is good for enthusiastic students of social policy to discover the limits to which they may (as social scientists) go.[5] The concept of economic efficiency is also, however, famous for the production of some famous *qualitative* results. A major result of this kind is that a competitive market will, like an 'invisible hand', guide resource allocation (given an initial income distribution) to a Pareto optimum. Under competition with costless markets where all goods are priced, and where certain other conditions are satisfied, the price system is such that the forces of supply and demand create a unique price in every market where the quantities demanded and supplied are equalised. At this price, as we have seen, the market is cleared — everyone has as much as he wants of each thing at the current price. The price is the amount he must pay to someone else in compensation for parting with some good so that no one is, on balance, worse off as a result of any exchange. This system gets everything produced efficiently, produced in the right quantities and distributed to those who derive most benefit from it (given an initial distribution of income). Or does it?

If the world were really as we have so far assumed we would, as scientists, have to agree that it did, though we need not agree that it was a just as well as an efficient system. But the world is not, of course, quite like this. In practice lots of things happen to make the ideal described above absolutely unattainable. In the real world the future — and much of the present — is uncertain. Substantial costs have to be incurred to acquire and evaluate information, to arrange and enforce agreements, and so on. All these have been left out of the competitive paradigm. In practice one must allocate the resources used in these processes in an efficient way. In the real world the social framework in which we live is beset by monopolies, falling rather than rising marginal costs and countless other phenomena that vitiate any simple conclusion about the market. Sometimes society tries to correct some of the more obvious imperfections but even then one cannot be certain that the cure is better than the disease. Sometimes society, recognising that the market is rather inept at revealing the social interest, substitutes government allocation for market allocation. Unfortunately, the political process is also rather inept at revealing the social interest (for example, with simple majority decision rules, 51% of the people can overrule the preferences of 49%). Nevertheless, some people would maintain that it is easier to attain a Pareto optimum or make Pareto improvements with Socialist planning than with markets and argue their case for socialism on these grounds more than on any other. Others argue similarly for capitalism! In this book we shall be concerned a great deal with making comparisons between these two methods of allocation, one centralised, one decentralised. One may rest assured, however, that they are each imperfect. The student of social policy has to find the least imperfect method of approaching a relatively efficient allocation of resources. The task of devising modifications to existing social institutions so as to improve social welfare, or to invent entirely new ones, is fortunately exciting and difficult; we may thereby perhaps be compensated for the knowledge that the ideal is beyond our reach!

In this book, three respects in which the simple competitive supply/demand approach is inadequate will consistently crop up. This trio of complications contains the following: external effects of individual or collective actions; public goods and bads; and the problem of uncertainty and ignorance. Let us discuss each in turn.

Externalities

Let us assume for the moment that no complications exist. We would then say that if Mr. A's marginal valuation of bread were equal to the marginal cost of providing it then the result would be efficient. Remember that Mr. A's marginal valuation (call it MV^A) is his own private valuation — it is an *internal* valuation. If we drew a diagram such as Figure 2.2. we would say that social welfare was at a maximum (if nothing else changes) if he obtained OQ^* bread per year.

Fig. 2.2

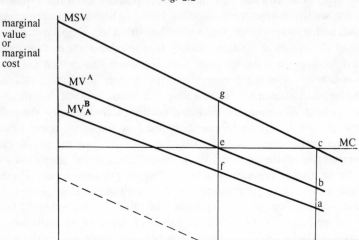

Now let us introduce the first kind of complication. Suppose that there exists someone else (Mr. B) who, in addition to caring how much bread he himself gets, also cares how much Mr. A gets. There is a sense, of course, in which *everyone* cares how much everyone else gets, for the more everyone else gets the less there is for oneself. This effect is, however, transmitted readily through the price mechanism and has helped to determine the competitive price. The kind of concern that our Mr. B has is different from this: we suppose that, in his opinion, Mr. A does not get enough to eat. Mr. B has a preference about Mr. A's bread consumption. Bread consumed by Mr. A benefits, in other words, not only Mr. A *but also Mr. B.* Let us suppose that the marginal value placed by Mr. B on Mr. A's bread consumption (call it $MV_A{}^B$) falls in the usual way. It may look something like the $MV_A{}^B$ curve in Figure 2.2. Thus, when Mr. A is consuming OQ^* bread he obtains a marginal (internal) benefit of Q^*e *and Mr. B obtains a marginal (external) benefit of Q^*f.*

If Mr. B were to consume another loaf (per year) his additional benefit would be just slightly less than Q^*e and Mr. A's would be just slightly less than Q^*f, but together their additional benefit would be greater than the marginal cost of producing the additional loaf. Clearly then, social welfare would, according to the Pareto criterion, be increased if Mr. A ate more bread. In fact, with this externality, the

Pareto optimal, or efficient, allocation of bread to Mr. A is OQ^P rather than OQ^*, for at OQ^P the additional benefit to both A *and* B (marginal *social* valuation or *MSV*) is just equal to the marginal cost of obtaining the additional benefit. With external benefits, therefore, our original rule for allocational efficiency must be modified. Instead of having

$$MV^A = MV^B = MC$$

we must now write:

$$MSV^A = MV^A + MV_A^{\ B} = MV^B = MC$$

Marginal *social* valuation of A's consumption should be equal to that of B's consumption and equal to marginal cost.

This concept of external benefit is of crucial importance in social policy. As we shall see, it provides one of the major reasons why, for example, education and health are subsidised by the State for, with external benefits, too little may be consumed. For the moment, however, let us pause to note three things about the (qualitative) result we have obtained.

First, the mere fact that Mr. B receives an external benefit from Mr. A's actions is not sufficient in deciding whether social welfare might be increased by arranging some means (a subsidy, perhaps) by which Mr. A can be persuaded to engage in more of the externality generating activity. The external benefit must be a *marginal* external benefit at Mr. A's current rate of activity. If, for example, $MV_A^{\ B}$ were the dashed line in Figure 2.2. though Mr. B would benefit from Mr. A's consumption, Mr. A is still consuming the right amount. Note, furthermore, that even at the efficient rate of consumption, Mr. B derives a positive marginal external benefit ($Q^P a$) but this does *not* imply that Mr. A ought to get more. *A Pareto-relevant marginal external benefit exists only where the sum of internal and external marginal values exceeds marginal cost.* Today, when 'externalities' have begun to become an incantation in popular journals and newspapers and where a divergence between social and internal benefits[6] is held to warrant a whole range of government – or private – compensating actions, it is as well to emphasise that the relevant divergence is between social benefits *at the margin* (i.e. the sum of internal and external marginal benefits *at the margin*) and marginal costs.

Second, note that the Pareto criterion will evaluate a move from Q^* to Q^P as a good one only if the externally affected parties (in this case, Mr. B) subsidise the additional consumption. In our example, the minimum Mr. B will have to pay is ecb, the sum of the differences between A's MV of additional units and the price he will have to pay over the range Q^*Q^P, which B would be prepared to pay since he derives an additional external benefit of Q^*faQ^P. If a third individual, Mr. C, does not care about Mr. A's bread consumption, it is no use Mr. A and Mr. B getting together to force Mr. C to pay for the subsidy (even though if there were only three people they would have a majority) for Mr. C would lose some benefit without being compensated and we have no means of telling whether the extra benefit accruing to Messrs A and B exceeds the loss they impose on Mr. C.

Third, we may ask, if Mr. B stands to benefit from helping Mr. A to eat more bread, why the 'invisible hand' has not already forced him to do so − if A and B can mutually benefit by a move from Q^* to Q^P, why on earth might it be necessary to get, say, the government to subsidise bread production? Why have A and B not already taken advantage of these potential gains? The answer is that sometimes they do. A great deal of charity has always existed without government intervention. But there are also good reasons why individuals may not have an incentive to reap the potential gains and these arise especially when there is a large number of externally affected parties. We shall return to these reasons below when we discuss public goods.

We have discussed divergences between social and internal benefits. It is a relatively easy matter to do the basic analysis of the case where there is a divergence between social and internal cost. Let us suppose that no one cares how much bread other people eat. We return to a situation in which the optimum is where the *horizontal* sum of internal marginal valuations rather than the vertical sum equals marginal cost. Once again we are back at OQ^* bread consumption in Figure 2.3.

Now let us suppose that, although he pays for all his normal inputs in bread production in an entirely proper way, the baker emits a quantity of smoke from his ovens. The more he bakes the more they smoke. The more the smoke the more frequently neighbours must wash etc. Spring-cleaning, with OQ^* bread production, takes place in Summer, Autumn, Winter, as well as Spring. (We shall be be dealing with far less trivial cases later in the book). The baker, of course, does not incur these costs, he merely imposes them on others. Let MC^P represent the producer's internal marginal cost, as before. Let MC^R represent the (external) marginal cost imposed on the rest of society. Thus, at OQ^* bread production, marginal values are everywhere equal at Q^*e, but marginal costs are Q^*e incurred internally by the baker *plus*

Fig. 2.3

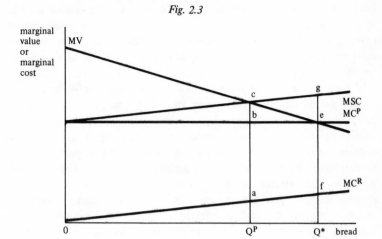

eg incurred externally by his neighbours – a total *marginal social cost* of *Q*g*.

If the baker reduced his output by a loaf a year, the sum of these marginal costs (marginal social cost) would fall while marginal benefit would rise – a net social gain would take place. The astute reader will immediately recognise that the optimum will be at *OQ^P*, with less bread being baked, where the marginal benefit to all bread consumers is just equal to the sum of internal and external marginal costs i.e. marginal social costs. Thus, instead of having

$$MV^A = MV^B = MC,$$

we must now write:

$$MV^A = MV^B = MC^P + MC^R \ [= MSC]$$

Once again, all the warnings concerning the interpretation of external benefits apply to external costs. Moreover, do not fall into the common trap of identifying external costs with social costs. Social costs (unless we exclude the baker from society, which he will justly resent) are the *sum* of internal and external costs. To identify social with external costs is to ignore internal costs, which is as silly as ignoring external costs.

Before turning to the interesting problems of public goods which have been promised an investigation, two final warnings are in order in relation to the policy inferences to be drawn from the existence of externalities of either kind — benefits or costs. Where Pareto-relevant marginal externalities exist there will either be too little of an activity (in the case of benefits) or too much of it (in the case of costs). First, this does not imply that in the case of an external benefit the good or service should necessarily be given away free. Nor, in the case of an external cost does it necessarily imply that the activity ought to be banned altogether. Second, externality relationships are (like all relationships) reciprocal. Consider, for example, the imposition of an external cost by some productive activity that creates pollution. We may presume that the polluter has (by default possibly) the right to pollute and he therefore imposes external costs on others. Suppose, however, that we changed the system of rights so that neighbours have the right to a pollution-free life. Then *they* impose an external cost on our original polluter. From the *allocation* point of view it frequently does not matter who has the right. The important thing is that the right be exchangeable so that if the factory has the right neighbours can compensate him for reducing pollution and increasing thereby his internal opportunity costs. Conversely, if neighbours have the right, the factory can compensate them for accepting some level of pollution. In general, with private property rights that can be exchanged, externalities tend to be internalised (i.e. compensated so as to produce some efficient rate of the activity) or else it is inefficient to internalise them — the social costs of arranging property rights may be too great. Most of the problems we shall meet in the externality field derive from the absence of exchangeable private property rights — frequently they are not feasible. It is ironical that much criticism has been made of private property and capitalism for creating massive externalities whereas most externalities can easily be seen to be created in situations where private property and capitalism either do not or cannot be expected to obtain. However, as we shall see later when we investigate the role of government, it is sometimes more efficient to internalise externalities through formal planning procedures. The essential economic problem of the government's role is to establish its and the market's appropriate range of activities, as determined by the contribution made to social welfare. We shall not prejudge this issue by, for example, false assumptions about the efficacy of universal private property on the one hand or the efficiency of the 'socialist conscience' on the other.

Public goods and bads

Let us begin by reviewing the kinds of goods discussed so far. We began with private goods whose characteristics are two-fold: (a) the benefit a person derives from them depends upon how much *he* has, and (b) the more he has of any good the less someone else must have. We then investigated *externalities* whose characteristics are also two-fold: (a) the benefit a person derives depends upon how much *someone else* has, and (b) the more of a good he has the less someone else must have. *Public goods* form a third category with the following characteristics: (a) the benefit a person derives depends upon how much of the good *exists in society*, and (b) the more a good is produced for him the *more* there is for everyone else. In this section we explore the consequences of this type of good (or bad). Some examples of public goods (though they are not all 'pure' public goods) include: defence, national parks, immunisation against communicable disease, fire engines and good ideas. Some examples of public bads are: smog, poverty, criminals, asbestos dust and bad ideas.

Most goods and bads are mixtures of public and private. For example, if an additional fire engine is added to the stock, every property owner in the area will gain as the probability of fire spreading to his home falls and as the probability of serious damage also falls – but if another person builds a house and moves into the area he will diminish, even if only by a little, the protection available to everyone else by raising the probability of an outbreak of fire and hence the probability that the fleet will be attending to him just when someone else may need it.

With public goods, everyone need not have the same *quantity* as everyone else. To use the fire engine example, households nearest the fire station get more protection than those living some distance off. Moreover, even if they did receive the same quantity, they would not normally place the same value upon it because individuals' tastes differ. The case where everyone has an identically equal amount of a public good is usually termed a 'pure' public good case. Whatever the quantity of a public good produced individuals' marginal valuations will, as a rule, be different. One characteristic of publicness is thus that *marginal valuations cannot be brought into equality*. This in turn implies that we are not concerned with the efficient allocation of public goods between individuals once the goods are produced (the analogue to this problem becomes, where relevant, the problem of where to site the .ire station). Instead we are faced with the problem of how much of them to create. If Mr. A valued an additional unit of some public good at £5, Mr. B valued it at £10 and Mr. C at £15, then the total increase in benefit from providing the extra unit (in a three person world) would be £30. Clearly, if it cost less than £30 to create the extra unit, it ought to be provided according to the Pareto criterion. This gives us the general rule for the optimal production of a public good: it is where the sum of all internal marginal values (marginal social value) is equal to marginal cost:

$$MSV = MV^A + MV^B + MV^C = MC$$

Using our by now familiar diagrammatic technique, optimal production is OQ^P in Figure 2.4, where the sum of the marginal values is Q^Pe

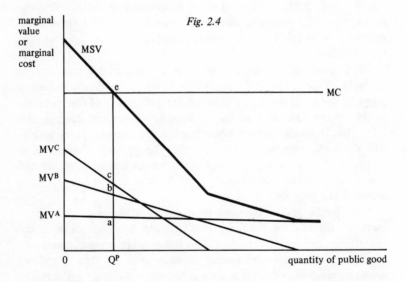

Fig. 2.4

and is equal to marginal cost but, in this case, no single person's marginal valuation is ever alone sufficient to warrant any production at all because for everyone, internal valuations are always less than cost at the margin. This situation is very commonly the case with public goods and bads: few people, if any, have sufficient wealth, and value defence enough, for it to be worth their while providing it for themselves individually and, even if they did, they would not provide as much as *should* be provided to maximise social welfare. Few people, again, have sufficient wealth or interest to make, by themselves, any significant dent in the poverty problem. With public goods, individual action is seldom either desirable or desired by individuals themselves. Instead, they clearly have an incentive to act *collectively* to create public goods and destroy public bads.

Collective action, democracy and the free rider problem

In the practical world the existence of public goods and externalities affecting many people creates two enormous problems which are closely related to one another. The first is deciding how much to provide, e.g. how much pollution to abate, how much to rectify income deficiencies, how much public health service to provide. The second is how to pay for it. The problems can be well enough illustrated by a simple example. A small township of 500 persons contains an orphanage for forty children. There is a general feeling in the village that it would be nice to provide the children with a touring holiday. Each day of the tour will cost £25 plus a progressive allowance for every extra day the driver and supervisors spend away from home being driven potty by the children. Thus a one day holiday costs £25, a two day holiday £55, a three day holiday, £90, a four day holiday £130, etc. The problems for the community are (a) how long a holiday to give the children and (b) how to pay for it. Let us suppose the 500 members of our community to be divided into two types of person. 200 of them are very kindly people valuing each additional day touring at a (constant) 15p. (For simplicity we assume away *diminishing* marginal values). The remaining 300, while kindly, are less kindly and/or poorer. They value each additional day at 10p. Finally, let us assume that there is a general presumption that the total costs of the tour will, in the end, be divided equally among the inhabitants. We note in passing that if the children are to get any holiday at all it *has to be* by the *collective* action of the villagers. Individual initiative is not enough even to provide a single afternoon's coach trip.

A village meeting is called and as is the wont in such community-spirited places, everyone turns up. The meeting has the job of deciding, democratically of course, what to do. The chairman of the meeting, being used to giving a lead, suggests that the children be given a day out in the coach at a cost of £25. That implies a per capita charge of 5p. per villager and receives everyone's unanimous support (the more generous people each valuing it at 15p. and the less generous at 10p.). Obviously someone will suggest that the chairman's proposal is a bit on the mean side. Why not two days? Cost per person is 11p. (marginal cost, 6p.), again everyone supports the idea. Similarly, everyone will support a three day holiday which will cost each person 18p. and consensus is obtained up to a six day holiday costing 45p. each. One of the more generous villagers now proposes a seven day holiday, costing each member of the meeting an additional 11p., or 56p. in all. Suddenly the happy unanimity with which everyone agreed that previous proposals were miserly disappears. This time the matter is actually put to a vote and 200 people approve the motion; 300 vote against. The meeting has decided that a six day holiday is what the children shall have.

Let us now assume that the village, as a whole, is more kindly than had been supposed before. Suppose now that 300 instead of 200 value additional days at 15p. and that 200 instead of 300 value them at 10p. It can readily be foreseen that the meeting would, under these circumstances, vote for an eleven day holiday, for the 300 will outvote the 200 when a seven day holiday is proposed, but not one will vote for a holiday in excess of eleven days.

We may compare these results with what our theory tells us ought to be the length of the children's holiday. This is, one may recall, the holiday such that the sum of all 500 marginal valuations is equal to the marginal cost of an additional day touring. A little heavy arithmetic soon tells us that the ideal length of the children's holiday, according to the views of the whole village, is eight days when the sum of the marginal valuations (£60) is equal to the additional cost of the eighth day. (Alternatively it is nine days if 300 rather than 200 are relatively generous). Can it be that collective action in general, and democracy in particular, has failed so disastrously to attain the ideal?

It has to be admitted that even in our rather perfect democracy described here (where everyone voted and there was no deliberate misleading of anyone by anyone else) the result has turned out to be unsatisfactory. It is also salutary to learn, however, that collective, or political, mechanisms for decision taking can be imperfect in much the same way as individualistic, or market, mechanisms (though it is, perhaps, less surprising when one realises that any institution is manipulated by individuals for their own ends, good or bad). Note that, in the case of the village we have described, the argument that at least collective action produces *some* holiday for the children is not necessarily a good one, for it need not be the case that the community benefit from the holiday that is too long exceeds that of no holiday at all. Note also that our democratic procedure does not make any allowance for the benefit received by the children. All that counts is *their welfare as perceived by the villagers.* The villagers could, if they wished, give the children full voting rights in the village meeting (it would make no difference in the case we have discussed, but imagine the consequences of majority voting if the children outnumbered adult villagers or even exceeded the numerical difference between the two groups of villagers!) Alternatively we could, if we wished, include children in our definition of the 'society' whose welfare is to be maximised and thus include their marginal valuations in the efficiency criterion. In fact, however, we do not normally do this in human societies. The only welfare that counts as far as children are concerned is their welfare as perceived by others (parents, teachers, social workers, the population at large, *etc.*) which is how we have treated them in our example.

A general conclusion we reach is that majority decision rules tend, if people with strong feelings have a majority, to devote too many resources to producing public goods and if they have a minority to devote too few resources to such activities. There is a conceivable way out of this difficulty. Suppose a six day holiday had been decided. The less generous majority will not vote for any longer holiday unless the additional costs are borne entirely by the more generous minority or, alternatively, that the minority compensate the majority for the higher costs they will incur. It is quite conceivable that a scheme could be devised whereby each individual would agree to an eight day holiday, *provided that the marginal cost to him never exceeded his marginal benefit.* In this way, a political consensus similar to the consensus of the 'perfect' market would dictate an eight day holiday. But it clearly requires a 'perfect' political mechanism — which is, unfortunately, just about as rare as the 'perfect' market — so that the relatively generous (or rich) compensate the relatively mean (or poor) for extending the holiday beyond the point the latter prefer.

The principal reason for this imperfection of the collective decision process, apart from the great costs sometimes incurred just in reaching *any* decision, is known as the *free rider problem.* Markets frequently fail to function efficiently because of this problem, and so do collective decision-making organisations. The problem is this: although everyone stands to gain by getting together and acting collectively, each individual will gain *even more,* as he sees it, if he misleads everyone else about his true preferences. Thus, if one villager pretended not to care at all about the provision of a public good such as the children's trip, with a little luck, the rest of the village may organise it and he would – inescapably – benefit from it without having to contribute a penny. In short, as well as the children, he gets a '*free ride*' at the expense of everyone else. Obviously, if everyone tries to act as a free rider, nothing will get done at all. This is one reason why the contribution scales are usually agreed in advance, so no one can be a free rider. The trouble is that this prevents the adjustments to the cost-sharing agreement that are necessary for the ideal to be attained.

There are quite a large number of other methods devised to overcome the free rider problem. One is to fence off the public good so that non-contributors can be excluded from enjoying it. This is possible with some public goods (such as light waves from cinema screens, theatres and television sets) but not others (such as lighthouses, or the benefits of defence and poverty eradication). Another is to tie in some private good benefit with subscription to public goods production. This is, in fact, a very common technique and can be seen in operation when people who support good (public) causes can be seen sporting badges letting the world know about their good deeds, or when subscribers to the National Trust (which lobbies on our collective behalf) get free admission to National Parks. Finally, and most important, members of the community may make a prior agreement that all will contribute to produce public goods. Acceptance of compulsory taxation is implicitly such an arrangement – a sort of social contract. Of course, none of these methods *guarantees* the efficient production of public goods. What we emphasise, however, is the great difficulty of ensuring an efficient rate of their production under *any* kind of institutional framework. We shall be returning to these problems many times in the course of this book and later, when we come to deal with social indicators, output budgeting and cost-benefit analysis, some methods will be suggested by which the government may improve decisions about public goods production.

Uncertainty

The third and final complexity that we shall need to tack on to the basic analysis concerns the evident existence of uncertainty and ignorance. A great deal of social policy is, of course, justified by, and devoted to ameliorating the effects of uncertainty and ignorance. Lack of perfect knowledge about both the present and the future arises for the simple reason that all information is costly to acquire. Indeed, much information, even of a probabilistic kind, may be impossible to acquire.

In general, any individual, when confronted with a situation or choice, the outcome of which is given but uncertain, may do two things about it. First he may seek to acquire more information and thus reduce his uncertainty. For example, a person seeking a job would normally be well-advised to discover − if he can − how likely it is that he will be laid off or made redundant. Secondly, he may seek to avoid some of the consequences of the risks he faces by insuring against them. For example a person may, as well as taking measures to reduce the probability that he might need a surgical operation in hospital, insure against that contingency so that some of its consequences (e.g. the costs of treatment) are borne by someone else.

Both these alternatives have in common the fact that they are costly − information is costly to acquire and one cannot pass on the risk of loss to someone else without compensating him for it. Our preceding analysis would suggest the nature of an efficient treatment of uncertainty, if we assume that, as uncertainty is reduced or its consequences shifted to others, additional reductions or shifts have a declining marginal value. These efficiency conditions are first that the marginal value of extra information be equal to its marginal cost and second that the marginal value of risk shifting be equal to its marginal cost. The latter principle implies in particular that the marginal value of risk shifting ought to be proportional to the risk − the cost of insuring against the consequences of a disaster with a 50% probability should be greater than those of insuring against that disaster if it has only a 25% probability, for those who accept the risk are accepting a higher expected loss of their own wealth or welfare − a higher additional cost.

The treatment of uncertainty (which we assume to be a 'bad') is thus on all fours with the treatment of other allocation problems. Two things in particular, however, are of great importance. The first of these is that information is a public good − if someone discovers that every worker in an asbestos mine has a 10% chance of dying of asbestosis before the age of forty the fact that one worker has this information does not reduce the amount of information available to everyone else. Moreover, it is frequently the case that there are *economies of scale* in information collection – the unit costs, for example, of large agencies collecting a wide variety of data relating to unemployment are likely to be lower than those of numerous small agencies each doing little bits. An obvious consequence of these two factors is that it is frequently desirable for individuals to act collectively in the provision of information, usually via the government. The scale economy argument does not itself suggest governmental information discovery and dissemination but it does, at least, suggest that the government will not be a more costly method of doing it.

The second implication that is of importance relates to insurance. Imagine that one is considering insuring against one's house burning down and that cover is obtainable at a constant marginal cost in £10 lots, with the cost equal to the amount insured multiplied by the probability of fire (e.g. we assume no transaction costs for insurance agencies). In Figure 2.5. we see that the efficient choice with marginal

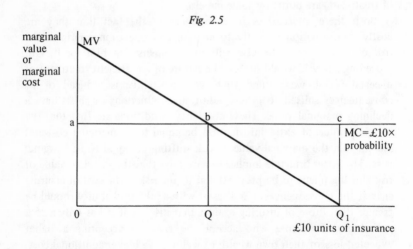

Fig. 2.5

benefits shown by MV is OQ insurance, for beyond this point, even though the individual values additional cover up to OQ_1 (the value of the house), he is not prepared to acquire it on the terms voluntarily acceptable to those who are providing it – that is, often it is socially efficient according to the Pareto criterion for individuals to bear some of the consequences of risk themselves. Thus, if the house burns down, the individual will receive £10(OQ) and he will have to pay a premium of £$OabQ$. He has exchanged the probable loss $OacQ_1$ for the certainty of a loss of $OabQ$ plus the probable loss of $QbcQ_1$. Once insured, however, things may change, for now that he has shifted some of the risk, he has less of an incentive to take care his house does not burn, for many of the costs will no longer fall on him but on the insurance agency. The objective probability of fire therefore rises and insurance agencies, attempting to anticipate this increase in the probability of *their* loss, ought, for efficiency, to charge higher premiums than they would in its absence or to add clauses to the contract which deter the insured party from increasing the risk. We shall meet this problem of *moral hazard* (as it is quaintly known) later in the course of this book.

We have looked at some of the implications that the existence of uncertainty has for our basic analysis. Let us finish by stating some of the things that it does *not* imply. It does *not* imply that individuals are stupid or cannot make sensible choices. It does *not* imply that uncertainty in itself prevents the attainment of an optimum. It does *not* imply that risk and uncertainty can be abolished. It does *not* imply that it is socially non-optimal for some individuals who dislike risk still to bear some. It does *not* imply that somebody who knows the probabilities best ought to make decisions for those who know them less well.

With the basic equipment of this chapter we are now in a position to tackle a large variety of the problems of social policy. In later chapters we shall relate this analysis to the use of cost-benefit analysis in social policy, to social indicators, to the running of individual social services, to their financing, to the role of the public and private sectors, and to other types of problems in social policy. We shall also make modifications to this basic analysis. We turn now to the economics of a basic problem in social policy: the measurement and analysis of redistribution.

NOTES

1. One alleged exception to be investigated in a later chapter is the problem of drug addiction which some believe implies rising marginal valuations. Addiction is discussed in chapter 11.
2. Much discussion has taken place among economists concerning precisely which are the 'other things' to remain constant. For simplicity, in this book we are using a 'Marshallian' framework. For a discussion of this, and other alternatives that could be adopted, see A. J. Culyer, 'A Taxonomy of Demand Curves', *Bulletin of Economic Research*, vol. 23, 1971.

3. Strictly speaking we should allow for the fact that producers make production decisions that have consequences over a period of time and that individuals to receive goods and services also do not use them up immediately. To allow for this and make the analysis more realistic would take us into more complicated analysis than we really need and would not, in any case, affect most of our conclusions. In cases where the implications of decisions through time are important, as in social investment decisions, we shall allow for it explicitly. (See Chapter 7).

4. The explanation why *every* individual's *MV* for any desired entity is the same, which these statements imply, is given in the next section.

5. As an illustration, consider the argument one sometimes hears that people tend to be too myopic – they discount the future too much because events then will, for example, mainly impinge upon future generations of largely different people. Such an argument often crops up in questions concerning the protection of the environment. The basic problem is not a conflict of interest between future generations and the present one, since it is impossible for the interests of unborn generations to be represented today. The conflict is usually between different opinions among members of the present generation about the value *they* place upon preserving the environment (*etc.*) for the future. Those who say that others are too myopic seem to be implying that some elite possessing a distinguishing characteristic such as great intelligence, prudence, sense of history, sensibility, race, colour, or whatever, should decide. (Perhaps they mean that *they* alone should decide.) The Pareto framework requires us to reject this sort of argument. Beware of jumping from the fact that one disapproves the values and decisions of others to the inference that the decisions are not socially preferred. *You* are not *society*!

6. The terms 'social' and 'internal' are used in this book rather than 'social' and 'private' used by some other writers since *all* benefits are privately experienced. The key distinction is whether the benefit is internally or externally generated. Social benefit is thus the sum of all internal and external benefits (it is, by definition, the sum of all private benefits).

FURTHER READING

A good general introduction to welfare economics is Part One of: R. Millward, *Public Expenditure Economics,* London. McGraw-Hill, 1971.

Three classics on the externality problem are:
J. M. Buchanan and W. C. Stubblebine, 'Externality', *Economica*, vol. 29, 1962.
R. Coase, 'The Problem of Social Cost', *Journal of Law and Economics*, vol. 3, 1960.
O. A. Davis and A. B. Whinston, 'Externalities, Welfare, and the Theory of Games', *Journal of Political Economy*, vol. 70, 1962.

An excellent introduction to public goods is:
J. M. Buchanan, *The Demand and Supply of Public Goods*, Chicago, Rand McNally, 1968.

The best (and original) sources on collective action are:

J. M. Buchanan and G. Tullock, *The Calculus of Consent*, Ann Arbor, University of Michigan Press, 1962.

M. Olson, *The Logic of Collective Action*, Cambridge, Mass., Harvard University Press, 1965.

On normative economics and socialism see, for example,

M. Dobb, *Welfare Economics and the Economics of Socialism*, Cambridge, Cambridge University Press, 1969.

A. P. Lerner, *The Economics of Control*, New York, Macmillan, 1964.

PART II

Redistribution of Incomes

3 The Measurement of Redistribution

A fully comprehensive treatment of redistribution in modern societies ought properly to start with the analysis of what determines the pre-tax/subsidy distribution of income and wealth among families. This, for reasons of space rather than any issue of principle, will not be covered in the present book. Moreover we shall not be concerned with the redistribution of wealth, but rather with personal incomes.[1] This latter approach is adopted primarily because of the nature of the data with which we shall be dealing but the procedure is, in principle, undesirable because of the close connection between income and wealth. It can also lead us seriously astray in our interpretations if we concentrate on the redistribution of incomes received during a time period (usually a year) for even a person who owns little physical capital may have *human* capital (the value of an individual's skills and any other attributes that are embodied in his person) of considerable value with a relatively low flow of current incomes in the time period considered. For example, it is generally the case that annual incomes of educated employees in employment rise steadily to a peak at the age of 55 but may begin (at the age, say, of 21) at a lower level than less trained or educated manpower of the same age. Suppose, now, that a prime concern of social policy was to reduce the inequality of economic power between individuals (for families). By looking *only* at current earnings one might conclude as a result that incomes ought to be redistributed from the older to the younger individuals with similar job qualifications, and from the less educated to the more educated for younger persons of similar ages. Both inferences would be *false*, because on average the human *wealth* of the young is greater than that of the old with similar job qualifications and the human wealth of the young educated person is greater than that of the young less educated person.

45

Ideally, one should take *expected lifetime earnings*, suitably discounted in the case of future earnings to allow for the lesser value people place on future income relative to the here and now, as one's unit of measurement.[2] Unfortunately, in practice this is at present not possible. In using current income data, whether earned or 'unearned', the reader is therefore warned about the inherent dangers in making inferences about the direction of the desired distribution. Present value calculations of future earnings, however, could also mislead even if they were possible since lower income groups are far more constrained in the extent to which they can borrow against future income.

A second set of difficulties arises in connection with the kind of redistribution considered. In modern societies, the redistribution of incomes is an exceedingly complex business. Flows from individuals into the budget of government can occur through income and wealth taxation, through indirect taxation, through the sale of government produced goods and services, through inflation[3] and through several other means as well. Similarly, the benefits provided by the government go to special pressure groups (eg. farmers, intellectuals); to special interest groups (the sick, the old); to *everyone* out of necessity in the case of mostly public goods (such as defence, law and order). In short, resources are collected from and distributed to a motley collection of individuals, both horizontally and vertically with respect to income classes. Moreover, the form in which resources are redistributed, though mostly in money on the revenue side, takes the form of both money and of goods and services in kind on the expenditure side. Clearly the task of identifying the individuals who contribute and who receive, and the respective amounts contributed and received, is a formidable one.

A third set of difficulties relates to the concept as well as the measurement of the changes that occur in the economic position of individuals as a consequence of redistribution. In any society, either a set of redistributive results occurs or it does not. If it does, one naturally seeks to assess what its effects have been and to do so one needs to know what the distribution of incomes would have been if the redistribution that took place had not taken place. But this is by no means a simple task. One of the functions of government, as has been seen above, is to provide public goods and these certainly have redistributive impact. But the pre- and post-redistribution comparison is not as simple as imagining that currently publicly produced public goods were previously produced in the private sector. It may not be possible for them to be produced in the private sector, or not on the same scale. But if this is so, then redistribution cannot be considered to take place out of a constant total community income — redistribution cannot be considered apart from production. Suppose this problem had been solved somehow, and suppose also that a definition of 'income' to be used had been decided upon, one would still require first, a theory and measurement of the effects of taxes and, second, a theory and measurement of the effects of expenditures. A highly simple numerical example can illustrate the kind of problem still involved (and also imply how much harder are the problems to be met in the real world).

Consider a two person community in which, after redistribution has taken place, Mr. A has £2,000 income and Mr. B £1,000. The redistribution, we shall suppose, has taken the form of £500 taken in income tax from A and given as an income deficiency payment to B (that is, we assume (a) that the 'government' operates costlessly (b) it balances its budget (c) it has no other functions). It would almost certainly be false to say that Mr. A is £500 worse off and Mr. B £500 better off as a result of the redistribution. It will almost certainly be false to say that total income after the redistribution (£3,000) was the same as the income previously available for redistribution. If the £500 tax on A is to imply that his income would be £2,500 had no redistribution taken place, then it must be assumed that his choice of amount of work to do to earn the income is independent of what he expects to take home. On the face of it, that is unlikely. But if he works less for the same wage after the tax than he would have without tax, then he is (a) losing *more than* £500 to Mr. B (though he is only paying £500); (b) gaining some benefit by not working as much as he did before, thereby reducing his loss; (c) reducing his contribution to the total value of physical output in the economy. Conversely, consider B. If we are to infer that his no-redistribution income would have been £500 we must also be assuming that his choice of working hours is independent of money receipts. Suppose, however, that after the redistribution he also works less than he would have if no redistribution took place, then he is (a) gaining in net terms less than the £500 transferred from Mr. A; (b) gaining more leisure than he would have otherwise have had; (c) reducing his contribution to national output.

Similar problems relate, of course, to other forms of taxation. The redistribution effects of £500 taken from A and given to B as an income deficiency payment will, it is to be expected, vary according as the £500 is removed from A by income tax, wealth tax, excise tax, a reduction in educational expenditures on A's children, *etc*. Moreover, in complex societies, there is a large number of complicated interrelation-ships among the decisions made by a single individual and also between the various individuals in the society. With benefits that are given in kind, there is a problem of valuing their worth to those who receive them. Enough has surely been said, however, to convince the reader of the great complexity of the analysis and measurement of redistribution.

Fourth, there exists the problem of providing an *explanation* for why the redistribution that takes place does take place – the positive problem of explaining why the people who contribute do so, why these who benefit do so, and why the flows of money and goods and services take the forms and have the sizes they do. Related to this is the *normative* problem of evaluating redistribution – prescribing how it should be and formulating means of attaining the desired objectives. As we shall see, both these problems can become very complex. They are, of course, of consummate interest.

Finally, there remains the problem of defining the basic units of analysis – income and the unit receiving the income. The definition of income most commonly employed by economists is that it is 'potential consumption' in the sense of the value of consumption that is possible in any time period without reducing the value of his wealth. This definition has the advantage of measuring the total potential increase in a person's wealth during the time period (if he consumed nothing it would be his actual increase), or his 'economic power'. It has, however, the disadvantage of not corresponding to the Inland Revenue definition which, for example, excludes capital gains.

As far as the income-unit is concerned, the natural unit to take is that within which incomes are shared. The basic unit is naturally the nuclear family of adults and their children but the question arises as to how far to include other household members (where a household is defined as in the Family Expenditure Survey as persons 'living at the same address having meals together and with common housekeeping') such as married children, elderly persons, or lodgers living with the nuclear family. If the fundamental concern in redistribution or poverty is with 'economic power', the choice would seem to depend upon the extent to which incomes were actually shared within households. If they were not shared very extensively, poverty amongst, e.g. the elderly will be understated by using the household as the unit. In general the best definition seems to be the nuclear family. Intrahousehold 'transfers' outside the nuclear family should therefore be treated as separate sources of income for those additional household members.

In these three chapters concerned with income redistribution, the discussion will be divided up as follows. In the remainder of this chapter we survey some of the available evidence on the redistribution of incomes. In the next chapter we survey some normative and positive theories of redistribution. In the third chapter we turn to the problems of income redistribution and social policy — to evaluating current British policies of income redistribution (and, especially, anti-poverty policy) and some proposals for change and reform that have recently been made.

In investigating empirically the redistributive effects of the government at the most general level, the effects of *all* government activities would be considered. For example, ideally one would include an assessment of the distribution (by family income class) of expenditure on defence, roads, agriculture, museums and art galleries. Alternatively, even though all these government activities have — and are sometimes intended to have — redistributive effects, one might take a narrower view and assess the redistributive effects of 'social policy', in which case, of course, one faces the problem of defining the activities that are held to constitute 'social policy'. We shall provide examples of both approaches together with some discussion of the assumptions made in each case to derive the estimates and an assessment of the results. The more comprehensive approach is illustrated by a recent American study, and the more restricted approach by a recent British study.

Income redistribution in the U.S.A. 1960

In his study of U.S. Redistribution in 1960, Irwin Gillespie used a variety of income concepts for measuring the changes in the economic position of families. The concept of income used in the results reported here is hypothetical income *in the absence of a public sector*, comprising family money income plus capital gains and retained earnings, *part* of corporation profits tax, *part* of the employer's social security contribution and imputed rental values of owner-occupied homes, plus own produce consumed by farmers, less all personal transfer payments. In common with other empirical students of income redistribution, Gillespie ignored the logical difficulties in assuming that abolition of the public sector does not affect the private sectors ability to produce the same goods, but some of the dangers inherent in simple arithmetical manipulations were met, so far as possible, by including *parts* of corporation tax and employer's social security payments. Thus, some studies have indicated that the effect of the imposition of corporation tax is partly to raise prices (shifting some of the burden of the tax on to consumers), and partly to reduce shareholders' incomes. Consequently, Gillespie allocated an estimated one third borne by consumers to taxpayers according to the distribution of consumption expenditure by income class and the rest to taxpayers according to the distribution of dividend earnings by income class. One half of the employer's social security contribution was distributed among wage earners and the other half (through its effect on prices) was distributed among taxpayers according to consumption by income class. Individual income tax was assumed to fall entirely on the individual paying tax; excise taxes were assumed to be passed on entirely to consumers and sales taxes were assumed to be shifted to consumption goods less food product purchases.

On this basis, the percentage figures in rows 3, 4 and 5 in Table 3.1 were derived, showing that both federal, but especially state and local, taxation is in general remarkably regressive − the proportion of income taken in tax falls as incomes rise. The regressivity arises mainly from the highly regressive incidence of social security contributions and indirect taxes. Frequently, however, a regressive tax structure is *unavoidable* at the lower end of the income distribution. For example, a family living entirely on income transfers (which are excluded from our income base) will pay some tax (e.g. sales tax on purchases of consumer goods), which could be an *infinite* proportion of base income! Consequently, it is sometimes misleading to look only at the progression of the tax side of the budget − an overall view must be taken, including expenditures.

Benefits from public expenditures were valued at cost[4] and divided up among the various income classes as follows: highway expenditures were allocated among consumers of passenger travel, consumers of transported goods and non-users (such as adjacent property owners); education expenditures among the families of pupils and students according to the stage of education completed; public health and housing expenditures were allocated according to presumptions about who benefited from them, for example, immunisation expenditures (which are largely public goods) were allocated according to family distribution, and sewage control by a weighted average of owner-occupied and rented housing units; social security benefits were allocated according to the distribution of the income classes of recipients; agricultural support expenditures according to the estimated

TABLE 3.1: *Percentage Income Paid in Tax, Received in Benefit and Net Change, U.S.A. 1960*

	Under $2,000	$2,000 to $2,999	$3,000 to $3,999	$4,000 to $4,999	$5,000 to $7,499	$7,500 to $9,999	$10,000 and over	Total (weighted)
				Family Money Income Brackets				
1. Families	14	9	9	11	28	15	14	100
2. Family Money Income	2	4	5	8	28	20	33	100
Tax Payments:								
3. Federal	37.8	42.0	33.6	28.1	20.8	15.7	26.6	23.9
4. State & Local	26.2	25.1	18.0	17.4	12.4	7.1	5.3	9.8
5. Total	64.1	67.2	51.6	45.5	33.2	22.8	31.9	33.7
Benefits:								
6. Federal	174.7	56.4	34.6	22.0	17.1	15.7	15.3	20.9
7. State & Local	126.1	52.9	25.7	18.3	12.2	8.5	5.4	12.8
8. Total	300.8	109.3	60.3	40.3	29.3	24.2	20.7	33.7
9. Net change in base income	+236.7	+42.1	+8.7	-5.2	-3.9	+1.4	-11.2	0.0

Source: Gillespie, *op. cit.*, Tables 3, 5, 6 and 11.
Note: items may not add to totals due to rounding.

51

incidence of these benefits, for example, partly to consumers (a negative gain), partly to farmers (positive gain), partly to the nation (as the value of surplus production) and partly to taxpayers (another negative gain). General expenditures (such as national defence) were allocated according to the distribution of base income. The possibility that in a society with no public sector, the private sector might increase the rate of its own transfer expenditures was ignored.

The net result of the various calculations implied by the foregoing produced the distributions shown in rows 6, 7 and 8 of Table 3.1, which are quite strongly progressive in their effects (in the sense that benefits fall as a proportion of income as the latter increases). The net effect on redistribution of governmental activities is shown in row 9, from which it appears that the redistribution was progressive up to incomes of $4.999; regressive from $4,000 to $9,999; and progressive from $7,500 on. The main redistribution would appear to occur from the richest 14% of families (having 33% of total family money incomes) to the poorest 23% (who had 6% of total money incomes). A striking oddity is that not only was the net incidence of redistribution regressive in the $5,–10,000 brackets but that those 15% of all families, with 20% of all money incomes, in the $7,500–$9,999 bracket actually received net *gains* from redistribution.

Total tax collections in 1960 amounted to $134,147 millions with expenditures of $133,595 millions. The existence of this small *budget surplus,* with not all collections being disbursed, implies that the post-redistribution distribution of incomes was lower (at least over some ranges) than it would have been with a balanced budget. Had the surplus been distributed proportionately would the post-redistribution distribution over all income classes simply have been shifted upwards? Would a similar effect have occurred if the excess taxes had not been collected, on a proportionate basis? The answer depends upon the effect that budget surpluses and deficits have upon the price levels of different commodities subject to tax and the level of employment which changes earned incomes for different classes, an analysis of which is beyond the scope of this book, but which can be found in most intermediate textbooks of macro-economic policy. In general, however, one would not expect a mere vertical shift of the post-redistribution distribution. One would expect it even less in view of the improbability that the surplus would have been spent in the same proportions as the original distribution.

Before discussing the meaning and significance of the results obtained by Gillespie we shall examine a recent study of redistribution in the United Kingdom. We shall then be in a position to compare the methods and results of each.

Income redistribution in the U.K. 1969

The concept of income used by the British Central Statistical Office in its studies of redistribution is different from that used by Gillespie and is derived from the Family Expenditive Survey of about 7,000 households. Income is the sum of incomes in cash and kind before the deduction of taxes and before the addition of those state benefits which are included in the analysis. It excludes all of the employers' social security contributions (treated as an indirect tax), all corporation tax and capital gains. Income in kind included consists primarily of an imputed value of income from housing for people in rent-free accommodation.

The assumptions implicitly made about the incidence of taxes and benefits were rather extreme and were as follows: income tax was assumed to fall entirely upon the individual taxpayer; employers' social security contributions entirely upon consumers; indirect taxes on final and intermediate goods were assumed to be passed on fully in higher prices (and thus to consumers).

On this basis the percentage figures in row 3 of Table 3.2 were derived showing again, even more markedly than the U.S. data, the general regressiveness of the total tax structure.

On the benefit side, a far more restricted set of items of expenditure was included in the C.S.O. study, viz., family allowances pensions and other cash benefits such as educational scholarships; imputed values of state education services, the National Health Service and welfare foods, and indirect benefits such as housing subsidies. The cash benefits were what respondents stated the households received over a twelve month period. Benefits in kind were valued at cost according to the type of education being received and according to the number of persons receiving it in each household. Benefits from the N.H.S. were also valued at cost to the health services and were allocated among households according to (a) children born during the period (b) number of children (c) adults below retirement age and (d) adults over normal retirement age; (a) being based on the current cost of maternity services, (b) (c) and (d) according to rough estimates of the extent to

TABLE 3.2: *Percentage Income Paid in Tax, Received in Benefit and Net change, U.K., 1969*

	under £260	£260 to £314	£315 to £381	£382 to £459	£460 to £558	£559 to £675	£676 to £815	£816 to £987	£988 to £1195	£1196 to £1447	£1448 to £1751	£1752 to £2121	£2122 to £2565	£2566 to £3103	£3104 and over	Total (weighted)
								Household Base Income Brackets								
1. Households	15	1	2	2	2	3	4	6	8	11	13	12	10	6	7	100
2. Household base income	.7	.2	.3	.4	.6	1.0	1.8	3.4	5.7	9.8	13.5	15.2	15.3	11.4	20.6	100
3. Tax Payments	168	65	53	52	46	43	42	41	39	39	38	37	37	37	40	40
4. Benefits	742	175	135	111	88	65	48	39	30	24	18	14	13	11	7	23
5. Net change in base income	+574	+110	+82	+59	+42	+22	+6	−2	−9	−15	−20	−23	−24	−26	−33	−17

Source: Central Statistical Office, *op. cit.* Table 2(i).
Note: items may not add to totals due to rounding.

which different age groups make use of the service. School meals and other welfare foods were allocated according to the number of children and the cost was calculated net of household contributions. Housing subsidies (the difference between current expenditure by local authorities on housing and the rents paid by tenants) were estimated separately for each local authority dwelling in the sample.

The aggregate effect of these benefits as a proportion of base income is shown in row 4 of Table 3.2 and again indicates the strong progressivity of benefits. The net redistributive effect is shown in row 5, showing a quite strong progressive element in the net redistribution – rather stronger than the American data appear to indicate – with the richest 35% of households (having 62.5% of total base incomes) losing, in net terms, 26% of their base income and the poorest 20% (having 1.5% of total base incomes) gaining, in net terms, an addition of 45% on theirs.

It is striking to notice the discrepancy between the totals of rows 3 and 5 in Table 3.2; apparently 40% of total base income went in tax but only 23% came out in the form of benefits. Although at this time a budget surplus did exist, a major reason for this enormous difference (for the U.S. data, the difference was so small that it was rounded out in Table 3.1) is that while the calculations embrace the bulk of the tax side of the budget, a substantial part of the expenditure side is omitted. According to the sample data, total tax collections in 1969 from the households sampled were £4.26 millions with total benefits of £1.74 millions.

This raises the question of the desirable scope and coverage of measures of redistribution. The American study attempted to embrace the entire budget to assess the overall redistributive impact of the government's activities. The British study, however, attempted only to cover the redistributive effects of 'social services' defined narrowly on the one hand and taxation defined broadly on the other.

There are clearly good reasons why one may be concerned to assess the overall impact of government policy on the distribution of incomes. The chief of these is that it is the net result that all policies, taken together, for individual families that is normally the object of concern in redistribution. One may also, however, be concerned to assess the redistributive impact of policies that are *designed* to be redistributive or which are defined as falling within the sphere of 'social' policy. The area of 'social' policy has smudgy edges (if it has any at all) which will tend to vary from commentator to commentator and does not, accordingly, commend itself. The identification of policies that are, in part or in whole, designed to be or regarded as redistributive is, perhaps, less difficult. The best approach, on this view of the purpose of the exercise, would probably be to examine each policy individually to discover the extent to which it contributes to redistribution and whether it is progressive or regressive. What the C.S.O. study has done, in effect, is to combine all policies which are thought to have – or which *ought* to have – strong redistributive effects, and to assess their joint effect. It concentrates on the *deliberately* redistributive effects of the *State*. Redistribution in its broadest sense might properly include transfers that take place in the private sector, especially if the redistributive effects of 'social' policy are being considered (which might include, for example, private and occupational pension schemes).

For some purposes it may be desired to construct a 'social welfare budget' in which the redistributive effects of the social services (or 'social' policy) are examined in connection with the means that are used to finance them *and only them*. The social welfare budget implies, since most taxation is general and not earmarked for specific spending purposes, that some assumptions must be made about the proportion of tax proceeds being devoted to the categories of spending being considered. An obvious assumption of this sort is to suppose that social services are financed out of total taxation (net of earmarked taxes) in the same proportions that their costs (net of earmarked receipts) occupy in total expenditure. Presumably, the social welfare budget would be balanced or unbalanced as the total budget was balanced or unbalanced. Alternatively it could be adjusted to balance, with the rest of the government's budget bearing the whole of the overall surplus or deficit.

These conventions will, in general, depend upon convenience and ease of calculation on the one hand and the purpose of the exercise on the other. To summarise, a number of plausible approaches to the scope of any redistribution study might be taken:

1. The redistributive effect of the entire budget, as in Gillespie's U.S. study, may be examined.

2. The redistributive effect of individual taxes or benefits may be investigated.

3. The redistributive effect of 'social' policy could be investigated, with 'social' presumably including the private sector.

4. The redistributive effect of redistributive policies as such could be investigated.
5. The redistributive effect of the social services could be studied which would deal only with the state schemes.
6. The redistributive effect of a national 'social welfare budget', as outlined above, could be calculated.

The C.S.O. study reported here does not fall readily into any of these six categories, mainly because it is not clear what objective is being aimed at (4 or 5 appear to be the nearest approximations). The original idea of J. L. Nicholson (who pioneered a set of studies of which the one reported here is merely the latest at the time of writing) was to examine 'the extent of the redistribution of income resulting from the various forms of taxes and social service benefits in the United Kingdom.'[5] The criteria for inclusion in the study are, unfortunately, not given.

Because of the differences in the scope of various studies it is essential to be wary of drawing comparative conclusions about the relative extent of redistribution between areas or through time where different approaches have been adopted. For example, the redistributive effect of policy in the U.K. in 1969 appears, from Table 3.2, to be greater than that in the U.S.A. in 1960 appears from Table 3.1. This conclusion is not warranted (even though it may be correct). In fact, there is a number of reasons why the C.S.O. study may exaggerate the extent of redistribution in the U.K.

Criticism of the C.S.O. study

A number of distortions can arise from the limited scope of the C.S.O. study of redistribution in the U.K. in 1969. Some of the most important of these are due to the nature of the Family Expenditure Survey upon which it was based. The use of a survey technique might be expected to yield more relevant information on redistribution than, for example, the statistics of the Board of Inland Revenue which are collected for administrative, rather than policy, purposes. Unfortunately, however, the Family Expenditure Survey was *not* designed for redistributive studies (it was originally designed to collect information for the construction of price indices). As a result, capital gains, for example, are excluded from the definition of income. There may also be greater scope for the under-reporting of incomes than is suspected to exist with Inland Revenue data especially in the case of the self-employed and part-time employees. These effects almost certainly mean that the proportion of income lost by the relatively rich households is overstated. There was some approximate correction for the severe under-reporting of expenditure on tobacco and alcohol.

A second set of problems arising from the F.E.S. (and, indeed, any sample survey) lies in the errors that arise in grossing-up the results, or generalising them for the whole community. Some of the earlier F.E.S. data, which were based on a smaller sample, had substantial biases in them due to non-response alone. For example, mean income was probably about 6% too low and the highest incomes about 14% under-estimated (this quite apart from the effect of under-reporting income). Even with the currently enlarged sample, the numbers of households in some income groups are very small (for example, 36 in the less than £260 bracket) and the sample, though stratified regionally, for population density (in rural Scotland) and according to rateable values, is not stratified according to incomes.

The unit for analysis in the C.S.O. studies is the *household*, which is not as perfect as the *family* unit, for more than one family may dwell in the same household and, as we have seen, this definition can overstate the extent of redistribution. It has been reported that over 28% of households in 1964 consisted of groups other than single persons or families of more than one person. Moreover, only *private* households are included in the F.E.S. survey, which thus excludes people living in institutions. Since one may suppose that interest in redistribution is concentrated chiefly on family units, and that families (including single persons) living in institutions (eg. hotels, homes for the aged) may be of specific interest in redistribution policy because they are not representative of the population at large, comparisons based upon the F.E.S. household unit should be interpreted with caution.

Some of the assumptions made about the incidence of taxes have been discussed above. An important distortion arises also, however, from assumptions made about the incidence of benefits, especially benefits from housing, and there are substantial reasons for supposing that the subsidies to tenants of local authority housing and to owner-occupiers are very much more than the national amounts attributed in the C.S.O. studies. The chief distortion would occur in the case of owner-occupiers whose mortgage interest payments are deductible against income tax. Thus, for example, the owner-occupier paying interest on a mortgage at £250 per year who was also paying tax in 1969 at the standard rate of 8/3 received a subsidy of over £103 a year. These subsidies, which substantially benefit the relatively rich, are completely omitted from the C.S.O. studies, as is also the implicit subsidy arising from the exemption of owner-occupiers from capital gains tax on the appreciation of house values and the exemption from income tax on the imputed rent on their houses (i.e. the rent which notionally they could receive if they were not themselves 'consuming' the income from ownership of the capital asset, a house).

The method of allocating cash benefits is also open to criticism. National Insurance and other cash benefits amounted in 1969 to 24% of all government expenditure. The method of allocating these benefits was to count the receipts of those actually receiving them. But generalising from here to a statement about overall redistribution may be hazardous. The assumption behind the C.S.O. studies is that generalisation is broadly safe on the grounds that households of a given composition and in a given income range will have broadly comparable 'expectations' with broadly comparable probabilities of being unemployed, being in retirement, etc. But the criteria for receipt of benefits are dependent upon many factors other than income levels (eg. being unemployed, retired, having more than one child, giving birth), thus, averaging the experience of a sampled household to all households of that composition and income range is fraught with dangers. Since the distribution of cash benefits is much greater for the lowest income groups than for others, the averaging procedure used in the C.S.O. studies, it has been alleged,[6] tends to understate the amount of redistribution. Whether or not this is the case depends, of course, upon whether the households sampled (of given composition and income) are numerous enough to form a representative collection. In fact, the C.S.O. study shows a very strong falling away of cash benefits as one passes through higher income brackets, which is what one would expect and suggests that even though distortions may be present they are not so great as to produce any extremely perverse results.

In the light of the technical criticisms of the C.S.O. study it would appear probable that the degree of redistribution which it suggests is greater than that which actually takes place and probably more in line with the more sophisticated Gillespie results. By making an alternative set of assumptions about base income, the unit of measurement and the scope and incidence of taxes and benefits, Adrian Webb and Jack Sieve re-estimated 1964 data of redistribution and found that, on their assumptions, redistribution between *families* of different income classes was less progressive than the C.S.O. data suggest. Moreover, by concentrating on family, rather than household, income they found that although there was noticeable redistribution to the lowest income *households*, poor *families* with children are not so effectively helped as this might suggest.

An offsetting influence is, however, the limited expenditure coverage of the C.S.O. studies. We may accept a likely overestimate of the extent of redistribution using the expenditure categories discussed but, nevertheless, an implicit budget leaving 60% of taxes unallocated (and 60%, moreover, only of those taxes actually considered) cannot be considered a very sound basis for making any firm statement about the redistributive effects of the government's budget *as a whole*. If what one is interested in is redistribution of incomes *per se*, there can be no substitute for assessing the incidence of *all* government income and expenditure patterns, as Gillespie attempted to do, even though the conceptual (let alone empirical) problems involved in so doing are enormous and, as yet, unsolved.

There remains widespread concern that vertical redistribution is in fact far less than may appear from the C.S.O. studies. Similar views have been held concerning the American situation. Many people, on both sides of the Atlantic suspect that an effect of the total budget, or of social policy in its broadest sense, upon redistribution is certainly to redistribute *some* income from the rich to the poor, but at the same time to redistribute the bulk of transferred resources among the middle income groups. Until, however, more satisfactory methods have been devised by which the true incidence of taxes and benefits can be separated from their impact (which requires close study of individual taxes and items of expenditure, including transfers within the private sector) and a more comprehensive approach to the problem is adopted than that used in the British studies, the results derived to date have to be treated with great caution. Here, therefore, there is substantial scope for further research in the economics of social policy. The ferocious difficulties that exist in practical measurement of the theoretical ideal should be challenging rather than taken either as statements of the impossible or harsh criticisms of the pioneering studies described here and others listed in the Further Reading at the end of this chapter.

A widespread belief that much redistribution takes place within the middle income brackets is currently also associated with the view that the very poor receive relatively little benefit from redistribution and the emphasis has even shifted away from the effects of redistribution *per se* towards specific policies towards the very poor. Policy is also, of course, concerned with *horizontal* redistribution (among families with similar incomes but differing needs) as well as the *vertical* redistribution discussed in this chapter. Before turning, however, to the question of poverty, which forms the bulk of the subject matter of chapter 5, let us investigate some of the theories that have been put forward to explain why redistribution takes place and to justify it. Chapter 4 therefore discusses some 'social philosophies' of redistribution.

NOTES

1. British policy has in practice been far more concerned with the taxation of wealth rather than with its redistribution but this is not the main reason for excluding a discussion of it in this book.
2. The relation between income and wealth is $W = Y/r$, where W is the value of wealth, Y is income as a perpetual annuity and r is the rate of time discount. The relationship between W and current income in the ith year (y_i) is:

$$W = y_1/(1+r) + y_2/(1+r)^2 + y_3/(1+r)^3 + \ldots$$

3. An illuminating discussion of the effects of inflation upon redistribution is by A. A. Alchian, "Inflation and Distribution of Income and Wealth" in *The Distribution of National Income*, quoted in the further reading. Alchian argues persuasively that inflation *per se* does not discriminate among social or economic classes of persons (though the manner in which it is generated may do so) but that it discriminates against *all* net monetary creditors.

Fig. 3.1

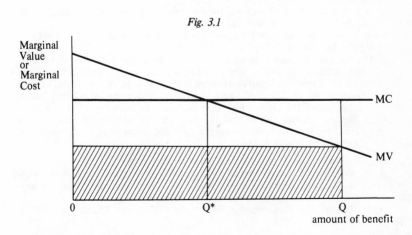

amount of benefit

4. This may produce either an under or an overestimate of the value of benefits in kind depending on (a) the charges, if any imposed on recipients (b) the other costs – such as congestion on roads – they may incur in obtaining the benefit, and (c) how much benefit in kind they receive. In Figure 3.1, let MV be the social marginal valuation curve of some benefit, let MC represent the marginal cost of providing the benefit. To the left of OQ total value exceeds total cost; to the right total cost exceeds total value. OQ^* is the ideal amount of benefit to provide, hence with ideal benefits, normally valuation at cost understates the total value of the benefit. In terms of exchange value, valuation at cost yields the correct answer if the correct amount is provided. But if, say, OQ were provided, value in exchange (the shaded area) is less than cost.

5. J. L. Nicholson, cited in the Further Reading, p. 121.

6. Especially by Adrian Webb and Jack Sieve, cited in the Further Reading.

FURTHER READING

A useful selection of modern literature on the *distribution* of incomes is the following:

A. B. Atkinson, 'On the Measurement of Inequality', *Journal of Economic Theory*, Vol. 2, 1970, for an interesting, but technical, discussion of measures of equality and inequality.

E. H. Phelps-Brown and P. E. Hart, 'The Share of Wages in National Income', *Economic Journal*, June 1952.

M. Kalecki, 'The Distribution of the National Income', in W. Fellner and B. F. Haley (eds), *Readings in the Theory of Income Distribution*, London, Allen and Unwin, 1950.

M. W. Reder, 'Alternative Theories of Labor's Share., in M. Abramovitz *et al. The Allocation of Economic Resources*, Stanford, Stanford University Press, 1959.

M. Friedman, 'Choice, Chance and the Personal Distribution of Income', *Journal of Political Economy*, Vol. 61, 1953.

G. J. Stigler, *The Theory of Price*, (3rd Ed.) Chicago, University of Chicago Press, 1966, pp. 288–311.

J. Marchal and B. Ducros, (eds) *The Distribution of National Income*, London, Macmillan, 1968. This volume includes empirical data for several countries as well as theoretical analysis. Especially useful is M. W. Reder, 'The Size Distribution of Earnings' (pp. 583–617). There are also some useful discussions of the papers which are reported in the book.

G. S. Becker, *Human Capital and the Personal Distribution of Income*, Ann Arbor, Institute of Public Administration and Department of Economics of University of Michigan, 1967.

On redistribution *per se*, the following may be consulted:

A. B. Atkinson, 'Poverty and Income Inequality in Britain', in D. Wedderburn (Ed), *Relative Deprivation, Inequality and Class Structure*, British Association, (forthcoming 1973). An excellent introduction to the whole field.

A. M. Carter, *The Redistribution of Income in Post-war Britain*, New Haven, 1955.

R. M. Titmuss, *Income Distribution and Social Change*, London, Allen and Unwin, 1962.

A. R. Prest and T. L. Stark, 'Some Aspects of Income Distribution in the U.K. since World War II', *Manchester School*, vol. 25, 1967.

A. T. Peacock and P. R. Browning, 'The Social Services in Great Britain and the Redistribution of Income' in A. T. Peacock (ed), *Income Redistribution and Social Policy*, London, Cape, 1954. This is the *locus classicus* of the 'social welfare budget' approach to redistribution.

W. Irwin Gillespie, 'Effect of Public Expenditures on the Distribution of Income', in R. A. Musgrave (ed), *Essays in Fiscal Federalism*, Washington DC, Brookings, 1965, pp. 122–186. This is the source for the American data in Chapter 3.

J. L. Nicholson, 'Redistribution of Income in the U.K. in 1959, 1957 and 1953', in C. Clark and G. Stuvel (eds) *Income and Wealth Series X*, London, Bowes, 1964. This provides the methodological basis for the C.S.O. studies in redistribution.

Central Statistical Office, articles on the impact (or incidence) of taxes and social service benefits on different groups of households, in *Economic Trends* for November 1962, February 1964, August 1966, February 1968, July 1968, February 1969, February 1970 and February 1971. The last of these forms the source data on the U.K. in Chapter 3.

For criticisms of these C.S.O. studies consult:

A. R. Prest, 'The Budget and Interpersonal Distribution', *Public Finance*, Vol. 23, 1967.

A. T. Peacock and J. R. Shannon, 'The Welfare State and the Redistribution of Income', *Westminster Bank Review*, August 1968.

A. L. Webb and J. E. Sieve, *Income Redistribution and the Welfare State*, London, Bell, 1971.

The economic literature, both empirical and theoretical, on the initial impact and final incidence of taxation and benefits is enormous. For a good survey of the theory on the tax side consult:

A. Williams, *Public Finance and Budgetary Policy*, London, Allen and Unwin, 1963.

P. Mieszkowski, 'Tax Incidence Theory: the Effects of Taxes on the Distribution of Income', *Journal of Economic Literature*, Vol. 7, pp. 1103–1124.

The flavour of empirical work can be tasted by reading some literature in the recent controversy over the incidence of Corporation Tax:

M. Krzyzaniak and R. A. Musgrave, *The Shifting of the Corporation Income Tax*, Baltimore, Johns Hopkins, 1963.

J. G. Cragg, A. C. Harberger and P. M. Mieszkowski, 'Empirical Evidence on the Incidence of the Corporation Income Tax', *Journal of Political Economy*, Vol. 75, 1967.

R. J. Gordon, 'The Incidence of the Corporation Tax in U.S. Manufacturing 1925–1962', *American Economic Review*, Vol. 57, 1967.

H-J. Krupp, 'Econometric Analysis of Tax Incidence', in A. T. Peacock, (ed), *Quantitative Analysis in Public Finance*, New York and London, Praeger, 1969.

For an excellent discussion of the conceptual problems on the expenditure side and of the logicality of 'conjectural history', consult:

Alan Peacock, 'The Treatment of Government Expenditure in Studies of Income Redistribution', in W. Smith (ed), *Essays in Honor of Richard Musgrave* (forthcoming 1973).

4 Normative and Positive Theories of Redistribution

As has been stated in Chapter 3, we shall not be concerned in this book to examine the various theories that have been put forward to account for the *distribution* of incomes and how social policy can affect income distribution (for example, with regard to encouraging and controlling the activities of trade unions and employers' associations) rather than how it can operate by *re*distributing incomes already received by individuals. Instead, we concentrate upon the latter aspect of the State's activities: upon the question of redistribution of *incomes* in general and upon the problem of poverty, or income deficiency, in particular. In this chapter the methods in which redistribution and poverty have been incorporated into economic analysis will be explored. In the next chapter the policy problems concerned with methods of redistribution and methods of abolishing poverty will be investigated.

As with all social phenomena, one may adopt two stances: one normative, the other positive. The normative approach to income redistribution asks what distribution do we want and how shall it be achieved. The positive approach seeks to explain why the redistribution that occurs takes place and how it would alter if certain changes were to be made. The approaches to be considered here will be positive or normative in these senses. A thread of continuity will be that the basic unit for analysis in each case will be the individual. Thus, in the normative analysis, the touchstone of what is good will be taken to be the individual preferences of the members of society, not some (mythical) omniscient outside observer or some group of benevolent (or otherwise) dictators. In the positive analysis, it will be taken for granted that the behaviour of individuals acting alone or in concert determines the social policies that are actually adopted. Such, at least, would seem a reasonable presumption in societies describing themselves in broad terms as 'democracies'.[1]

As we have seen in the previous chapter, a great deal of the redistribution that takes place in modern societies such as Britain or the U.S.A. is not merely a redistribution of money income, nor is it necessarily a vertical redistribution from the rich to the poor. To begin with, however, we shall suppose that the purpose of redistribution is to transfer money from the rich to the poor. Subsequently we shall investigate some theories attempting to explain why the direction of flow need not be from the rich to the poor and finally we shall extend the analysis to incorporate non-monetary transfers.

Normative Analysis of Redistribution

Equality and utilitarianism

One normative approach to the problem of deciding an appropriate interpersonal (interfamilial) distribution of money income is primarily of historical interest only but since it can still be found, often only implicitly, in some modern writing, we shall give it some attention.

For Utilitarians such as Bentham and Sidgwick, the objective of society was the maximisation of the sum total of individuals' utilities. With an appreciation of the 'law of diminishing marginal utility' (which stated that each addition to a person's money income per year yielded less utility than the previous addition, though the total continued to rise) coupled with an assumption that all individuals are fundamentally alike in their preference and their capability of enjoying the good things of life, a normative argument for egalitarianism can be made to follow on quite naturally from the utilitarian approach, though it will not follow automatically by market processes.

The egalitarian argument can be shown quite easily in a simple diagram such as Figure 4.1. On the vertical axis is measured the marginal utility of money income. On the horizontal axis we have the size of money income. The curve MM' shows how for two individuals, Mr. A and Mr. B, the marginal utility of money income falls as income

Fig. 4.1

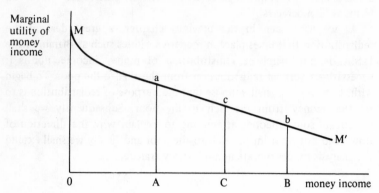

increases. Now suppose that Mr. A has *OA* income and Mr. B has *OB*, ie. Mr. B is the richer of the two, Mr. A's marginal utility is *Aa* which is higher than Mr. B's *Bb*. The sum total of utility in our society of two individuals is *OMaA* plus *OMbB*. The utilitarian argument for an equal distribution would run thus: that by removing *BC* income from B and giving it to A, B will lose less than A will gain, since B's marginal utility is lower than A's throughout this income range. With equal incomes of *OC*, each has the same marginal utility of money income and the sum total of utility in society is maximised, being equal to twice *OMcC*, which must be larger than *OMaA* plus *OMbB*.

In its strict form, the argument for absolute equality depends crucially upon an identity of tastes for money income among the population. (Alternatively, one could argue that they *ought to be treated* as identical.) But a weaker form will still hold even when tastes differ. In Figure 4.2 for example, Mr. B, the rich man, has a marginal utility curve that is everywhere higher than Mr. A's. A possible reason for this is that his great wealth has enabled him to appreciate Cordon Bleu cooking and opera, tastes which Mr. A has not had the opportunity to acquire.

According to this less radical utilitarianism, with different tastes, equality is not required in order to maximise the sum total of individual utilities. One still requires that the marginal utilities of each individual's income be the same but this is now achieved with a transfer of *BB'* from B to A — inequalities are reduced but not eliminated.

At this point the reader will doubtless be aware of a possible perversity in the argument: what if the marginal utility of income for the rich man (B) is *higher* rather than *lower* than that of the poor man?

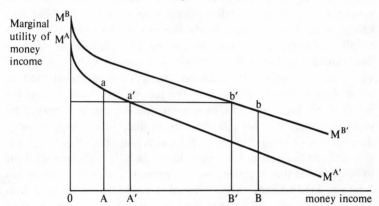

Fig. 4.2

This seems to be a perfectly possible contingency. If the rich man were to say that he got more utility from the ability to buy an additional Rolls Royce than the poor man from an additional pair of clogs, who could gainsay it? But if this were the case, then income should be transferred from the poor man to the rich man! The egalitarian argument of this school of thought thus depended upon the assumption of similar preferences.

The utilitarian view of distribution survived in essentially the form presented here until after the first World War. For example, Pigou, in his classic, *The Economics of Welfare,* which first appeared in 1920, wrote, 'It is evident that any transference of income from a relatively rich man to a relatively poor man of similar temperament, since it enables more intense wants to be satisfied at the expense of less intense wants, must increase the aggregate sum of satisfaction'.[2] Similarly Dalton, in *Some Aspects of the Inequality of Incomes in Modern Communities* also appearing in 1920, wrote, 'Put broadly, and in the language of common sense, the case against large inequalities of income is that the less urgent needs of the rich are satisfied, while the more urgent needs of the poor are left unsatisfied ... this is merely an application of the economists' law of diminishing marginal utility ...'.[3]

There are, of course, many objections to utilitarianism, both scientific and ethical. For our purposes, however, the chief of these relates to the possibility of making comparisons of the quantity of utility that different individuals receive at the margin. One difficulty lies in the use of the word 'utility' among earlier economists. It was, for example, frequently identified with 'satisfaction'. But this raises problems of meaning, for while it may make sense to talk about zero utility, as an abstract idea, it clearly does not make a great deal of sense to talk about zero satisfaction. One may be able to talk about 'more' or 'less' satisfaction, but it clearly cannot be measured in the same way as we measure distances. More fundamentally, however, what kind of sense does it make to say that one person has more utility (or satisfaction) than another? Clearly *some* meaning can be conveyed by such statements. It is not ridiculous to say that, 'John is happier today than he was yesterday' or that, 'John is happier than Fred', but it is very difficult to say *how much more* happy he is. It is also very difficult to be quite sure that in making such judgements one has not interpreted John's or Fred's behaviour quite mistakenly, and the relative happiness of two persons with different incomes is usually harder to observe than their relative happiness with their Christmas presents.

Since people's tastes do undoubtedly differ and therefore their marginal utilities of money income will differ (even if they have the same income) the absolute equality of incomes cannot be defended on utilitarian grounds. Similarly, since utility is not an observable quantity and the relationship between it (or satisfaction) and a man's income is not at all clear, all we can say is that *we think* that John is more satisfied than Fred – and John need not be the richer man. It also seems impossible to make the interpersonal comparisons of utility with anything like the degree of accuracy we would need to evolve a redistribution policy. Nor have we any reason to suppose that satisfaction varies systematically for all people in society in the way such a basis for policy would require. Even if we allowed that one poor man received less satisfaction than one rich man, it would be unsurprising to find another poor man who was more satisfied than either of them.

As a result of these, and other, considerations it is hardly surprising that the utilitarian case for redistribution of incomes from the rich to the poor has been cast into limbo. Which is where we shall leave it and advise our readers to do the same.

The uncertainty argument for equality

In his classic book *The Economics of Control*, Abba Lerner attempted to overcome the objections raised above by putting forward the following theorem: if it is impossible, on any division of income, to discover which of two individuals has a higher marginal utility of income, the utility of income will *probably* be maximised by dividing income equally.

Lerner's argument, like the previous one, can easily be illustrated in a simple diagram. In figure 4.3 $M^A M^{A'}$ is A's marginal utility of income curve, as before, and $M^B M^{B'}$ is B's but is read from right to left instead of left to right. The two individuals have, we suppose, differing tastes and therefore different marginal utility curves. We do not know unfortunately, however, where they lie in respect to one another. Suppose that they are actually as in Figure 4.3. What we do know for a

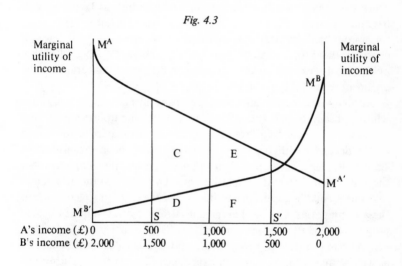

Fig. 4.3

fact are their respective money incomes. Suppose these to be £500 for A and £1,500 for B, as at point S. Then by transferring £500 from B to A, each has a post-redistribution income of £1,000. B will have lost area D of utility but A will have gained areas C plus D: total utility will have increased in net terms by area C. But, of course, we cannot be sure that A's curve *is* $M^A M^{A'}$ and that B's is $M^B M^{B'}$. Since interpersonal utility comparisons cannot be adequately made, it is just as likely that the curve $M^A M^{A'}$ is B's curve and that $M^B M^{B'}$ is A's! If that were the case, then by replacing all A's in the diagram by B's and all B's by A's we now begin at S'. In transferring £500 from B to A, B loses areas E plus

F while A gains only area F — a net loss of utility equal to area E. By an assumption that we are equally likely to be wrong about which marginal utility schedule belongs to whom, there is a 50% chance of a net gain of C and 50% chance of a loss by area E. Since C must be larger than E, the probability is that an egalitarian distribution will increase total utility. To maximise the probable sum total of utilities requires that income be equally distributed.

Note that the Lerner theorem does not tell us whether, once the redistribution has taken place, there has been any *actual* utility gain to society as a whole, for we are still ignorant about the shapes and relative heights of marginal utility functions. All one can say is that *if* net gains were made they are larger than *if* net losses had been made. Thus there can be no absolute certainty of gain but, as Lerner himself has said, 'if I were offered 11 cents for every "head" in return for 10 cents for every "tail" on 100 million tosses of an unbiased coin, I would consider the probability of gain certain enough.'[4] Since all social policy decisions are taken under conditions of uncertainty the argument seems fairly powerful.

Although the Lerner argument has many attractions, it is also not without disadvantages. It continues to assume, like utilitarianism, that utilities can be added up (even though it does not require us to observe them). Secondly, although it grants that the utility people receive is not statistically dependent upon their relative incomes, it still requires that the utilities of different people be commensurable. Third, it assumes that one is *equally* uncertain about a loss as one is about a gain. Each of these assumptions is somewhat metaphysical: we can test none of them not even indirectly by their implications. Of the first it may be said to be highly improbable, for even if the utility received from X be known as well as that from Y, common experience suggests that the utility of X *and* Y together may be greater or smaller than the sums of their independent utilities. This is as true of an individual's personal view of different income distributions (for example, A may derive utility from the fact that B has more, or less, income than he has) as it is of shoes and shoe laces or of bangers and mash.

The really fundamental objection to the Lerner argument is, however, that the assumptions and implications upon which it rests are untestable. The assumption of equal ignorance might be acceptable if we could, *ex post facto*, test for the utility consequences of any redistribution. But since even Lerner admits that we cannot, we remain ignorant. As Ian Little has said of the Lerner theorem, 'from complete ignorance nothing but complete ignorance can follow.'[5] The Lerner approach is similar to the identification of *potential* Pareto improvements in social welfare. It is useful to the extent that potential gains can be identified but we can never know if any were actually reaped. But unlike the potential Pareto improvement, we could not use compensation to test the reality of the potential gains.

The 'new' welfare economics approach

The 'old' welfare economics, with which this chapter has so far dealt, attempted to give a fully integrated treatment of both allocative and redistributive efficiency. With a common professional consensus among most economists that the strong version of utilitarianism had grave short-comings which the influential (re)discovery of 'indifference curve' analysis did not, the whole meaning of 'utility' changed though, awkwardly enough, the name did not. Henceforth 'utility-maximisation' was simply to mean choice according to a ranking of preferred alternatives. Its metaphysical content was completely expunged as it became behaviourist. One consequence of this revolution in the economics of individual behaviour was that matters of allocative efficiency became completely separated from matters of distributive justice.

The new welfare economics described the necessary conditions that must be met for an optimum allocation of resources, some of which have already been described above in chapter 2. The optimal allocation of resources, such that no individual can be made better off without at least one other becoming worse off, depends however upon the initial distribution of money income. Consequently, there exists a variety of optima, choice amongst which will depend upon the associated (resultant) income distribution, and each of which is such that no changes could be made without harming somebody. The new welfare economics placed an embargo upon interpersonal comparisons of utility in defining the optima but was compelled to introduced explicit comparisons of this sort when it came to selecting the *optimum optimorum* – the optimal allocation with the best income distribution of all the various optima. But redistribution of course, would mean some people *are* made worse off in order to make others better off. As a rather odd way out of recognising the incompatibility of these twin criteria (one for allocation and one for distribution of real income) a 'social welfare function' was sometimes invoked to determine the best distribution, with the preferences of some omniscient mythical observer in it. This observer had to be a kind of superman, because the distribution problem in the new welfare economics largely ceased to be the distribution of *money* income. Superman was invoked in order to judge the ideal distribution of utilities — or *real* income.

The reason for employing the notion of Superman was, of course, the alleged 'impossibility' of interpersonal utility comparisons coupled with a professional modesty that made most economists reluctant to impose *their own* notion of correctness in distribution. In practice, of course, Superman amounted to the government, so, essentially, economists of this school of thought were abrogating any right on their parts to say whether any particular income distribution was better or worse than any other but at the same time affirming that a good distribution was necessary for the maximisation of social welfare. Somehow, someone else had to decide.

The new welfare economics, therefore, was almost entirely empty of relevant analysis of income distribution problems.

Pareto-optimal redistribution

Until very recently, welfare economics remained emasculated in this regard. The next significant development derived from a brave facing-up to the fact that it is *individuals* in society who have preferences about income distributions, despite the fact that it is governments who primarily intervene in making a distribution policy. Consequently, it seemed not unreasonable to include within the choice set of each individual a set of choices to be made about transfers. In short, individuals 'derive utility' from alleviating poverty or in assisting those families who have what they regard as special needs. Thus, both vertical and horizontal equity could be brought under the same methodological umbrella as allocational efficiency. One could describe an 'efficient' redistribution policy. The Paretian approach to income distribution is based not on, 'what utility does A get from his income and B from his' but on, 'what utility does A get from his *and* B's income and what utility does B get from his *and* A's.'

The argument can be illustrated in a diagram similar to the neoclassical utilitarian diagrams, but crucially different in its interpretation.

Fig. 4.4

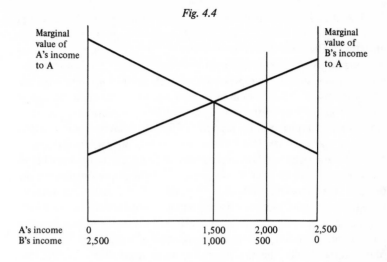

In Figure 4.4, marginal valuations are shown on the vertical axis and the incomes of two individuals along the horizontal axis, MV^A is A's marginal valuation of his own income and MV_B^A is A's marginal valuation of B's income.

Suppose that A has £2,000 income per year and B £500. At the predistribution level of incomes A's marginal valuation of his own income is *ab*. His marginal valuation from knowing that B has an income of £500 is *ac*. To increase his own utility he will therefore transfer some of his income to B. In our diagram, his welfare is maximised when he has transferred £500. At this point the marginal utility from a pound's worth of his own consumption equals the marginal utility (to him) of a one pound increment in B's income. Thus, for social welfare to be maximised, the transfer *ought* to be made. Distributional efficiency obtains where, for A, $MV^A = MV_B^A$. The analysis gives explicit recognition to the fact that many people are (a) concerned about the welfare of others and (b) generous. If MV_B^A, (A's marginal utility from B's income) were everywhere zero, he would be indifferent to B's welfare and therefore neither concerned nor generous. If it had positive values but lay everywhere to the left of *a below* MV^A, A would be concerned but not actually generous – he would not care *sufficiently* to make the transfer. In both these cases a 'corner solution' exists at which $MV^A > MV_B^A$ and it is inefficient to make the transfer.

Does the Pareto-optimal approach to income distribution imply that society ought to adopt a progressive, proportional or regressive tax structure? The conclusions worked out by Harold Hochman and James Rodgers, who pioneered this approach and applied it in an N-person setting rather than the two-person expository model employed here, are that the answer depends upon both the shape of the size distribution of income *and* the responsiveness of each person's 'demand' for transfers (to others) to changes in income differentials. Assuming identical preferences at each level of income with an income distribution that is skewed to the right (a higher proportion of families have incomes below the average income than above it) and with a responsiveness of the demand for transfers such that the size of the preferred transfer increases in proportion with the initial income differentials, the Pareto optimal pattern of redistribution is effected through *progressive* taxes on income. Even if the demand for transfers is independent of the size of the differentials, the tax structure, while somewhat complex, also ought to have marked progressive characteristics.

Thus, the Pareto criterion can be used to assess the goodness even of income distributions. The test of a socially beneficial redistribution is that it should be voluntarily undertaken, for we take voluntary behaviour to be behaviour that is not against the interest of the person or persons concerned. Usually, however, some judgment (but not a value judgment) will have to be exercised to decide the *fact* of voluntariness and this is sometimes quite difficult with collective actions. Essentially, however, the Pareto criterion can be used to evaluate *efficient* redistributions. There will usually be a set of efficient redistributions and, moreover, the set will vary according to the initial distribution from which one starts.

An efficient redistribution is not, nevertheless, the same as a *just* or a *fair* one. To take an extreme example, the starting point may be one where one person owns *all* society's wealth and he is, moreover, totally ungenerous. In this case, the initial distribution would be an efficient one, for no transfer could be made that would not harm this extraordinarily rich man. But it is not likely to be viewed as a *just* distribution – even by the extraordinarily rich man.

One method for testing the justice of distributions of income and wealth has been suggested by the moral philosopher John Rawls, which is based on a variant of the Pareto criterion used in a kind of 'social contract'. The question asked is: what general principles would be jointly agreed by the members of a community in appraising the justice of the institutions and rules that regulate their conduct *independently* of whatever present position they may occupy in society? Rawls suggests that a consensus would be likely to be reached on three basic principles which together constitute the criteria for a 'fair' or 'just' framework. (Note the emphasis on consensus). The three principles are:

(i)   Each person engaged in an activity or affected by it has an equal right to the most extensive liberty compatible with a like liberty for all.

(ii) No inequality is just unless it is *to the advantage of* the most unfortunate individual. Thus, if the removal of some inequalities would, in the process, harm the interest of the less well placed individuals, it would not be a just removal, i.e. inequalities must work to everyone's advantage.

(iii) Inequalities deriving from positions or offices held in society should be equally available to all to compete for on the basis of their ability.

These principles, which at the *general* level it is highly likely indeed that we would all accede to, can take us further than the straightforward application of the Pareto criterion which takes the pre-redistribution distribution of income as given, for it is now possible to evaluate it in terms of social justice. In constitutional democracies where principle (i) is generally practised (it is, indeed, a Paretian assumption), principles (ii) and (iii) frequently are not. It is not hard to instance cases where, quite certainly, incomes could be redistributed from the rich without harming, for example, the long term employment prospects of the relatively poor, nor is it hard to instance cases of unfair competition in all walks of life.

Redistribution can thus be justified that may actually harm some members of society, and such redistribution would be warranted on grounds of justice (which is not, of course, the only criterion. There are other criteria too, such as whether the social structure is liberal, conducive to invention, or productive of variety). Further redistribution may then be justified on the narrower interpretation of Paretian efficiency. Note, however, that the broader framework of justice, like the narrower one of efficiency, in redistribution, does not imply or prescribe a *uniquely* just and efficient distribution of income. Nor does it imply any particular form of ownership of resources.

Positive Analysis of Redistribution

Positive theories of income redistribution, ie. those theories that attempt to *explain* why the redistribution that takes place does take place, may be divided into three. The first is a positive version of the Paretian system outlined above based on generosity and is due to Harold Hochman and James Rodgers. The second is based on the selfish proposition that in a democracy the poor use their votes to effect transfers to themselves from the rest of society and is due to Anthony Downs. The third is more eclectic, drawing on elements of the other two theories and is due to Gordon Tullock.

Redistribution through generosity

The Hochman-Rodgers positive theory of redistribution is based upon the foregoing normative analysis. Individuals in a democracy are assumed to be utility-maximisers, where the sources of utility for any individual are not necessarily selfish. For example, it is the key to their theory that one individual may derive utility from an increase in another person's income. The theory also requires that the democracy in question is a 'perfect' democracy in that no decisions can be made that harm anyone. In short, a *consensus* is required for any action, such as redistribution, to be taken – each citizen has a veto. This is, of course, a rather extreme departure from the majority decision making rules that characterise the democracies with which we are most familiar, and it is one that is relaxed in the other positive theories we shall discuss. Nevertheless, it is interesting to see how much can be obtained that is consistent with the world we know, even though this assumption (ruling out coercion) is somewhat extreme. In addition, the theory assumes that the larger one's income, the lower the ratio of its marginal utility to the marginal utility one derives from the existence of another person's income. Thus, it is quite clear that the existence of *altruism* is implied, an individual derives utility not only from his own income but also from others' – the more income they have the more utility the altruist must necessarily gain.

Thus the greater the income possessed by a (generous) person, the greater the differential between his income and that of the lowest income classes and the lower the ratio of his marginal valuation of his own income to his marginal valuation of the lowest income classes' incomes. As a consequence, in a world in which individuals have approximately the same preferences at each level of income, the greater the income differential the greater the amount of the transfer that the relatively rich will want to make to the relatively poor. This in turn implies that the observed calculation of 'fiscal residuals' (the differences in the value of transfers received and taxes paid) will decline as one moves progressively up through various income classes. The evidence on actual redistribution is broadly consistent with this implication, though the estimation of the residuals is extremely hazardous. Thus, for the U.S.A. in 1960, persons in the highest income class according to the data of chapter 3, with an average income of £15,000, financed most of the redistribution that actually took place; persons in the middle income brackets seemed, more or less, to break even: those in the lowest brackets received definitely positive net monetary gains from the redistributive process. There is, however, a particular oddity which the theory does not account for, namely 15% in the $7,500 − 9,999 bracket (second from the highest bracket) who received small but positive net money gains.

It therefore seems that the Hochman-Rodgers theory, which specifies the pattern of an optimal redistribution, succeeds in explaining *observed* distributions only approximately. An obvious reason why this may be so is that the consensus assumption upon which the model is based is violated in practice and, moreover, that this violation of the assumption affects outcomes in a significant way. We turn later to an alternative model based upon a majority decision rule rather than consensus. Clearly, in practice, the consensus assumption can only be an approximation to the truth. In modern (large) democracies it is quite obvious that majority-type decisions may imply a substantial divergence from the consensus assumption, according to which any change hurts (in utility terms) nobody. In practice, political decisions do evidently harm some people. Some theories incorporating this possibility are discussed below. Nevertheless, it remains the case that the unrealistic consensus assumption may be sufficiently accurate for the results of the theory to be interpreted as a plausible explanation of reality − if, of course, they are not inconsistent with the facts. In particular, we might note that the *smaller* the political unit effecting the redistribution, and the easier it is for individuals to move from one unit to another, the more the consensus assumption holds true. One would accordingly expect the Hochman-Rodgers theory to apply more effectively in, say,

Switzerland, where the cantons are primarily responsible for income taxation and expenditure than in, say, the U.S.A.

Another important insight offered by the Hochman-Rodgers approach relates to the valuation of public expenditures received by individuals. As we discovered in chapter 3, the convention is to value benefits provided in kind at cost of provision and thence to infer that this is the value (or a minimum value) of the benefit received. The Pareto approach to redistribution invites the question 'value to whom?' It is quite conceivable for the personal valuation placed upon, say, free education by the children of the poor, to be less than the cost of provision. The Hochman-Rodgers explanation of why the education is provided is that there are *externalities* which benefit the educated well-to-do when poor children receive schooling, which is why the rich are prepared to provide it. If, in the spirit of Hochman-Rodgers, we assume that ideal amounts of education are provided, the benefit of the redistribution accrues to two sets of individuals: the poor *and* the rich at one at the same time − both place a value on the redistribution. If the poor would not have consumed education in an ideal amount without free provision, it follows that their marginal valuation of schooling is less than its marginal cost. The remaining differential of cost over benefit accrues to the relatively rich. There are thus two elements which make in-kind provision less progressive than the arithmetic of chapter 3 indicates. First, the value of benefits in kind *to the poor* may be less than the cost used as a proxy and second, the rich also benefit. Two implications follow from this:

1. The voluntary consensus view implies that in terms of *real income* (utility) *all* gain from redistribution, so the net distribution of *real income* may not be different after the redistribution of resources from the distribution previously prevailing. It may even move in favour of the rich! Redistribution of real income to benefit the poor can only be guaranteed if coercion is applied to the rich so that they are forced to do what they would otherwise not do.

2. In terms of the private valuation of beneficiaries and the private costs of tax payers the redistribution may be overstated because the former will usually be less than the cost data used as a surrogate for benefit received. There is a strong case for ignoring external valuations in *measuring* redistribution (but not in *explaining* it) because our concern is normally with the private value of resources received and lost rather than their social

value – the rich, egalitarians, liberals are concerned about the well-being of the poor rather than the well-being that the rich derive when the poor are made better off. But if this is true, then the use of cost data as measures of benefits is of dubious value. Direct enquiry would be one method of eliciting the various values placed upon such benefits but it too runs into great difficulties, not least of which is the incentive individuals would have to conceal their true valuations if they believed that the results might be used to shape future social policy.

The general predictions of the Hochman-Rodgers model are not wildly inconsistent with the results of chapter 3 (though they suggest some further questions about their validity). Unfortunately, the theory does not specify, for example, how progressive the net benefit structure will be (beyond the prediction that it will be progressive) for this depends entirely upon knowledge of people's preferences regarding income redistribution and, as we have seen, there is at least one inconsistency.

Redistribution through selfishness

The economic theory of democracy invented by Anthony Downs has implications for income redistribution and approaches the 'positive politics' of the problem from the opposite end to Hochman and Rodgers. Instead of the phenomenon of redistribution being explained primarily by the generous impulses of the relatively rich, Downs' explanation is couched in terms of the relatively poor using their political power to obtain transfers from the rest of society. Coercion is introduced.[6]

Downs' economic theory of democracy assumes that politicians who comprise the leadership of political parties seek office solely to enjoy the income, prestige and power that go with running the government apparatus. The policies of rival political parties are therefore seen strictly as a means of gaining votes in elections – 'they do not seek to gain office in order to carry out certain preconceived policies or to serve any particular interest groups; rather they formulate policies and serve interest groups in order to gain office.'[7] The Downs hypothesis implies that the government always acts so as to maximise the number of votes it will receive at the next election, as will its rival opposition parties (though, of course, one is unlikely to hear politicians admit as much). The citizens in Downs' theory are viewed as utility maximising individuals who vote for whatever party they believe will provide them with the highest utility from government action (these sources of utility need not be narrow and selfish: citizens may approve of governmental acts that may penalise them economically in order to help others. For the moment, however, we assume selfish citizens.). The Downs model has many fascinating implications and seems to explain many contemporary phenomena. Our concern, however, is with its implications for income redistribution.

The pre-tax distribution of income in most countries is such that a few persons have large incomes and large numbers have relatively small incomes. One way for a government to gain votes is therefore through redistribution, by depriving a few persons of income (thereby alienating them) and transferring it to many others (thereby gaining their support). A redistribution towards equality is therefore predicted as a consequence of democratic politics.

Three complicating factors in the Downs theory prevent the attainment of perfect equality. The first is that taxes and transfers have side-effects (for example, on willingness to work) that are believed to reduce the total (pecuniary) wealth of the community. Since citizens believe in this effect and are averse to wealth reductions, they tend also to be averse to *complete* equality. As a consequence, vote-maximising governments will not go for complete equality. Secondly, because the future is unknown, low income persons may hope one day to be rich themselves and this subjective probability (no matter how small the objective probability) will tend to make them prefer *some* degree of inequality. Finally, in an uncertain world, even in a one man, one vote democracy, the relatively rich have more political power, for they can use their wealth to create it, by affording time to organise pressure groups, by buying mass media communication, and so on. All three of these effects act as countervailing forces to the natural tendency of democratic governments to redistribute incomes from the rich to the poor. Indeed, the last effect may be so strong as to overwhelm the natural tendency altogether, though in general this would not appear to be the case, for all the countervailing effects derive from the existence of uncertainty and ignorance (about for example, the future and the probable consequences of various government programmes). Only when uncertainty and ignorance are higher than is commonly found in literate democracies would one expect the countervailing effects to be overwhelming.

Thus, the fundamental explanation of redistribution in a democracy according to the Downs theory is that it pays governments in terms of votes to transfer from the relatively few rich to the relatively many poor. Insofar as the relatively few rich are also persons of charitable instincts, the theory will tend to apply with even greater force.

According to the American data of chapter 3, the bulk of redistribution is from the richest 14% of families to the poorest 23%. These relative proportions are consistent with Downsian theory, though the fact (if it is a fact) that a majority of families loses from redistribution would appear to be inconsistent with it. The fact that, according to the C.S.O. study, a majority loses through redistribution clearly cannot be held as evidence against the Downs theory since the coverage on the benefit side in that study is restricted to a few social services only. But in the American data it is rather inconvenient for the Downs theory (at least in its simplest form presented here) that only 32% of the lowest income groups receive net gains when one would have predicted a percentage greater than 50. The 32% is not, however, inconsistent with Hochman-Rodgers. Thus, on balance, and recognising that the evidence is extremely thin, it appears that their hypothesis of generosity performs rather better than the Downs hypothesis of selfishness, which is a rather pleasing result for economists tentatively to assert.

The positive politics approach

Gordon Tullock's positive theory of income redistribution is based, as are the previous theories we have outlined, upon a stylised conception of the democratic process but has more in common with the Downs theory than with Hochman-Rodgers in assuming that politicians behave in broad correspondence with the wishes of a *majority* of the electorate. The Downs theory postulates that the n percent of families with the lowest incomes (where $n > 50$) are able to use their majority to take incomes from the top $(100 - n)$ % of families. Tullock asks, however, why we should not postulate that the *top n % ($n > 50$* again) should not remove some of the incomes from the bottom $(100 - n)$ % of families, since in at least the simple versions of these models only the number of votes cast is relevant in determining the redistributive − or any other − policy of governments. Consequently, one would expect the middle $(2n - 100)$ % of voters to control actual policy choices. For example, if a simple majority were sufficient for a policy decision, $n = 51$ and the middle 2% of voters would be able to effect a redistribution from either end towards themselves – in general, there would be a presumption that redistribution would tend to favour the middle income classes.

Several modifications to this very simple prediction can be made while remaining within the simple overall view of the democratic process. The chief modification arises out of the obvious fact that the relatively rich have more money. As a result of this, the higher the number of rich persons included in any coalition intending to transfer money from the rest of the population the smaller the amount of money that can actually be transferred – the cost of admitting a rich person to the coalition is higher than than the cost of admitting a poor person. Consequently, it is most likely for coalitions aiming at higher redistribution to contain persons none of whose incomes are higher than any person's not in the coalition – the dominant coalition is likely to consist of the poorest n % of the population. Remembering, however, that the middle $(2n - 100)$% are the 'marginal coalition members, the question arises of how the coalition of n voters will share the spoils taxed off the remaining $100 - n$?

If n is 51 and we suppose that 'the poor' constitute the bottom 20 percentiles of the income distribution, this 20% is only about 40% of the dominant coalition. Of course, if more than 51% of voters were needed to support a policy before the government felt sufficiently confident to implement it, then the poor would constitute an even smaller percentage of the dominant coalition. It thus appears that the middle and lower-middle classes (defined in terms of the family income distribution) would dominate the dominant coalition, so while one would predict that some redistribution would go to the poorest people, the theory suggests that the lower-middle and middle income brackets would fare best. The upper-middle and upper, income classes would not gain at all from redistribution – they would lose from it.

The broad pattern of redistribution suggested by Tullock's theory is thus, that the flow would be from the best off to the worst off, but that the lower-middle percentiles would tend to gain more than the very worst off.

Two factors might work to moderate these tendencies. First, to the extent that middle income groups are generous, the relative shares of the gains from redistribution among the dominant coalition will shift in favour of the really poor. Second, if the broad pattern of redistribution is as the theory implies, one would expect individuals at the *extremes* of the distribution to want to form a coalition. This would be in the interests of the very rich, for the really poor could by such an arrangement obtain more transfers and at the same time, by terminating transfers to the middle groups, the rich would also be better off. It would also be to the advantage of the poor, who would receive more under such an arrangement and hence be persuaded to leave the dominant coalition. The paradoxical result is thus obtained that the poor may recognise that their interests are more coincident with those of the very rich than with those nearer to them in income.

The data, such as they are, do not appear to support the Tullock prediction that the bulk of the gains will accrue to lower middle income groups, though they are consistent with the modified version. Even in the absence of generosity, it may be that the interests of the rich in minimising the burden of the inevitable redistributive tendency of democracy are coincidental with the interest of the poor in maximising receipts.

Finally, we may note that neither the Downs nor the Tullock theory is based upon the necessary existence of charitable instincts on the part of any section of the population, though neither approach necessarily rules out such motives which, of course, form the whole basis of the Hochman-Rodgers approach. Common to all three theories, however, is the assumption that the relatively poor are not averse to gaining through the redistribution of incomes. Although ignorance and the costs of acquiring information can be, and have been introduced into such analyses, the possibility that the poor prefer not to receive handouts through the state or via any other means has not been incorporated. In practice, as we shall see, one of the problems of obtaining a desired (by someone) redistribution lies in the reluctance of at least some of the poor to benefit from it. To the extent that this is true, one would *not* expect the poor to be as strongly interested in a coalition with the very rich as may otherwise be the case. Moreover, neither would they be expected to form a very vocal minority even of the dominant coalition. Both effects intensify the fundamental redistributive implications of the basic Tullock hypothesis which is not supported by the evidence to date. Tullock does provide, however, a theoretical explanation for the widespread view among empiricist students of social policy that most redistribution takes place among the middle income groups even though systematic evidence on this point is still lacking. Given the data difficulties emphasised it is clearly premature to reject or accept decisively any of the theories that have been discussed. On current evidence, the Hochman-Rodgers hypothesis appears to do best by a short head but further refinement of both methodology and data may turn up something better than casual evidence that is more consistent with one of the other theories. As we find so often in the economics of social policy, there are many fascinating beginnings but few firm conclusions. It is a highly research-able area indeed!

Equality or minimum standards?

The redistribution arguments with which this chapter has thus far been concerned have had it in common that the poor and the rich are both objects of policy – redistribution is from the relatively rich to the relatively poor not only because the former have more to transfer but because the relative positions of the two groups is itself important. The political argument (deriving from the principles of Liberalism) for this more or less symmetrical treatment, is that great inequalities of purchasing power also imply inequalities in political power. Redistri-bution is thus seen not only as the likely *consequence* of democratic politics (as the positive theories discussed above imply) but also as a probably *necessary condition* for democratic politics to exist.

As we shall see in the next chapter when problems of policy are discussed, relative equality is only a part of the problem, albeit the more general part, for in societies where the greatest inequalities have been removed, the emphasis has tended to shift away from the question of relative inequality towards safeguarding the economic well-being of those in the lowest percentiles of the income distribution. In this context, the question of guaranteeing minimum standards for all citizens – the avoidance of poverty – acquires prominence. Policy interest becomes less concerned with how progressive the tax structure is or should be and more concerned with how many people or families fall below a certain standard and what that standard should be. The search for a technological definition of subsistence has proved futile and the poverty line used officially has itself varied over time and varies between countries. In fact, the minimum standard cannot be defined with value-judgments.

The economics of minimum standards can conveniently be explored using a variant of Figure 4.4 above, as in the accompanying Figure 4.5. Let us suppose that A, a rich man, has £2,500 a year and B a poor man,

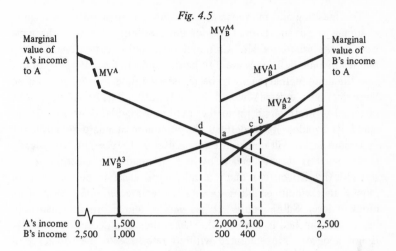

Fig. 4.5

has no income at all. If we exclude the possibility that Mr. B. may steal from Mr. A, or may use the state to expropriate income from him, (which, whether or not it is ethically unsound is, as we have observed, rare in practice) we ask how will the minimum standard for Mr. B. be determined? The answer, not surprisingly, turns out to depend crucially upon what is meant by a 'minimum standard'. According to one view, the minimum standard of guaranteed income is determined by what is regarded as being necessary for a 'decent' life for Mr. B and his family. What is 'decent' will depend upon Mr. A's views on this subject rather than Mr. B's, but Mr. B will, of course, normally be able to influence Mr. A's views by bringing various facts to his attention, or by having pressure groups operating on his behalf (for example, the Child Poverty Action Group) bring them to his attention. According to this view, we suppose that A's marginal valuation of reductions in B's income deficiency falls steadily as the deficiency is removed but, once the decent minimum is attained, that A places no value on further transfers to B. Given such a minimum A will value attaining it but will not wish to go beyond it. $MV_B{}^{A1}$ is such a marginal valuation curve, with £500 per year being regarded by A as the decent minimum for B. Given the configuration of the two curves MV^A and $MV_B{}^{A1}$ in Figure 4.5 we may say two things. First, the minimum income of £500 *ought* to be guaranteed to Mr. B. Secondly, we may safely assert on the positive side that (assuming that the free rider problem is somehow solved and that the political system works efficiently) it actually will be guaranteed.

The meaning and relevance of the minimum standard are not quite as simple as this, however. Consider the possibility that with the *same view of the minimum* Mr. A's marginal valuation curve for rectifying Mr. B's income deficiency were to be that indicated by $MV_B{}^{A\,2}$. In this case the amount that ought to be transferred (and that would be if no 'imperfections' existed) would be only £400. Mr. A would not be prepared to bring Mr. B up to the 'minimum standard'. This difficulty could be avoided if we defined the minimum standard to mean the maximum Mr. A will contribute (viz. £400 in this case) but this clearly is not what is usually meant by the minimum. At one time it was thought (by Rowntree) that the minimum ought to be that sum of money that would enable a person to operate *physiologically* at an efficient level. Subsequently, it has become much broader than that, but is still couched in terms of the 'necessities' of a decent existence — if not a decent life — defined without reference to the balancing of subjective gains *and losses* on the part of Mr. A. Consequently, the possibility arises of a minimum standard — even a generally recognised minimum standard — that no one save Mr. B, will want to achieve. We shall meet the empirical counterpart of this analytic problem in the next chapter when we come to discuss the poverty line.

Finally, consider two other possibilities. $MV_B{}^{A\,3}$ has it as an implication that the amount by which B's poverty is to be alleviated is £500 — the same as in the case of $MV_B{}^{A\,1}$. In this case, however, Mr. A values further transfers to B (up to £1,000) but will not actually transfer more than £500 because it is not 'worth' it to him. $MV_B{}^{A\,4}$ has it as an implication that, whatever the subjective costs to A, B will get his £500 — but not more. In this last case, we might say that B was, in A's eyes, *absolutely* in need — he should have the £500 regardless of its cost.

Sorting out which of these four possibilities is the true meaning of the minimum is clearly not easy. Let us dismiss $MV_B{}^{A\,4}$ as a likely possibility, for it is very odd in implying that A's desire to help B is the same no matter how high the cost to A and no matter *how* badly off B is. $MV_B{}^{A\,1}$ is also somewhat odd, in that it implies that A would continue to transfer the same £500 even if the last *thousand* of his own income had no value to him at all! The most plausible possibilities must, by this process of elimination, be $MV_B{}^{A\,2}$ and $MV_B{}^{A\,3}$ — but in neither of these cases is the 'minimum' agreed the minimum that will be met — or that should be met. In fact, the kinks in the *MV* curves have neither positive nor normative significance. The degree to which poverty is alleviated will be determined not by what is 'decent' for a man and his family, but by whatever the community, in the light of its desire to help and what it must forego to do so, decides. This conclusion will be of great help in disentangling the vexed problems to be met in the next chapter concerning the relevance for social policy of the poverty line.

Another important implication emerges from this. To the extent that concern is with the poor in particular rather than with equality in general, and to the extent that $MV_B{}^{A1}$ and $MV_B{}^{A4}$ are unlikely descriptions of A's concern for B, the amount that A will make available to alleviate B's poverty will depend, given his preferences in this regard, upon the costs of doing so. If, for every £1 sacrificed by A only 50p goes to B, A will give more and B receive less than if B received the full £1. We may see this readily on the diagram, for now £1 buys only one half as much poverty alleviation. Thus when A has lost £500, B has gained only £250 and A's marginal valuation of the income in his own use is given by a and his marginal valuation of his income received by B is b. Clearly, b is greater than a, so by transferring more to B's use from his own A will gain. In fact, he will continue to gain until his marginal valuation in each use is once more equal, i.e. at d and c. Thus with uniformly declining marginal valuations (which seems not unrealistic) the greater the administrative and other costs of making transfers, other things equal, the more will be given and the less received. This has the convenient implication that both the A's and the B's in the real world will seek to make transfer as efficient as possible. But it also implies that tax relief on charitable donations will reduce the value of donations while at the same time increasing the value of receipts, and that if people were equally concerned about a disaster in their own country and a similar disaster in Africa, they would give *more* to a representative African than to their own but that the Africans would receive *less* than their own compatriots. That they tend to give less to those in need who are far away indicates, of course, that people are less concerned about distant catastrophes.

Equal treatment for equal cases

A final important implication of this analysis is that individuals in 'like circumstances' should be treated alike. The meaning of 'like circumstances' is largely a matter of subjective judgement for the observer but analytically it can mean none other than 'imposing a like externality'.

Fig. 4.6

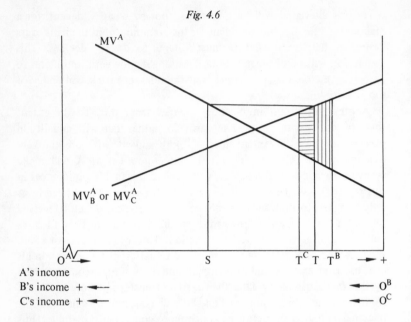

The normative implication that like cases should be treated alike can be derived with the help of Figure 4.6. MV^A once again indicates A's marginal valuation of his income in his own use and $M_B{}^A$ and $MV_C{}^A$ indicate his valuation of its use for B and C. If B and C impose a like externality — most likely when B and C are 'statistical' individuals (e.g. single pensioners with no savings of their own, unmarried mothers or fathers, *etc.*) and are not known personally to A — then $MV_B{}^A$ and $MV_C{}^A$ are identical. Social Welfare is then maximised according to the Pareto criterion where $MV^A = MV_B{}^A = MV_C{}^A$, i.e., where A transfers O^BT to B and O^CT to C, with $O^BT = O^CT$, himself sacrificing $2(O^BT)$ or $2(O^CT)$, retaining O^AS for his own use. If A transferred, say, O^BT^B to B and O^CT^C to C, it is readily seen that by equalising the transfer he would gain the vertically shaded area and lose only the horizontally shaded area. The same principle applies when there are large numbers of persons such as A and more recipients than merely two. The main complication in the large number case is that the A-types are not likely to feel the same externality (compassion) for the proposed recipients, though each will prefer every recipient to be treated equally. The methods by which the A's agree among themselves through collective action will, however, have to await the analysis of chapter 7.

NOTES

1. Some readers may be confused by our various discussions dealing alternately with households, families and individuals. In this chapter, individuals are the basic unit of analysis because individuals make choices, either alone or in groups. Since it appears to be the case that prime concern is over redistribution of incomes between *families*, one is really asserting that individuals are concerned more about the economic status of families rather than other individuals. For *analytical* reasons it is highly convenient, nevertheless, to treat families *as if* they were individuals. In empirical work, however, families must be carefully distinguished from individuals – if our presumption is correct that individuals are concerned mainly about families.
2. *The Economics of Welfare*, p. 89.
3. *Some Aspects* . . . , p. 10. In fact, this was not an application only of the law of diminishing marginal utility since this law alone said nothing about the *relative* marginal utilities enjoyed by different people.
4. 'Distributional Equality and Aggregate Utility: Reply', cited in the further reading.
5. *A Critique of Welfare Economics* p. 59, cited in the further reading.
6. The coercion referred to is not that coercion which may be readily agreed to by the generous in a Hochman-Rodgers world as a solution to the free-rider problem, they will face (see pp. 33–36 for a reminder of the nature of this problem). It is the imposition of the will of one section of the community upon another section.
7. *Economic Theory of Political Action* . . . , p. 137, cited in the further reading. The Downsian theory does not require politicians to turn with the political wind like weathercocks on every occasion. A politician may be successful simply because he is a sincere believer in particular causes and is consistent in his beliefs. He may also be successful in getting votes by *leading* opinion rather than by merely following it. Either way, however, there are tendencies for politicians who do not 'please the people' not to win votes and hence to have a lessened influence on policy. All politicians must seek one or another way of avoiding this contingency save those possessing those monopolies known as 'safe seats'.

FURTHER READING

A. C. Pigou, *The Economics of Welfare*, 4th Edn., London, Macmillan, 1932, for a comprehensive pre-Welfare State analysis of the role of the State in promoting 'economic' welfare.

Hugh Dalton, *Some Aspects of Inequality of Incomes in Modern Communities*, London, Routledge, 1920, for clear statements of the 'neo-classical utilitarian approach' and some worldly wisdom.

Abba P. Lerner, *The Economics of Control*, London, Macmillan, 1944. This classic book developed the welfare economics approach of Pigou further and is a milestone in thinking for intellectual socialists. Particularly notable for its uncertainty argument for equality.

William Breit and William P. Culbertson Jr., 'Distributional Equality and Aggregate Utility: Comment', *American Economic Review*, Vol. 60, 1970.

Abba P. Lerner, 'Distributional Equality and Aggregate Utility; Reply', *loc. cit.* These two articles further develop the Lerner argument.

I. M. D. Little, *A critique of Welfare Economics*, London, Oxford University Press, 1950. A sophisticated onslaught upon the logical foundations of the 'new' welfare economists, including Lerner.

W. J. Blum and H. Kalven Jr., *The Uneasy Case for Progressive Taxation*, Chicago, University of Chicago Press, 1953.

Harold H. Hochman and James D. Rodgers, 'Pareto Optimal Redistribution', *American Economic Review*, Vol. 59, 1969. The *locus classicus* for this approach.

Paul A. Meyer and J. J. Shipley; Richard A. Musgrave; Robert S. Goldfarb; Harold H. Hochman and James D. Rodgers, *American Economic Review*, Vol. 60, 1970, for a discussion of the original Hochman-Rodgers piece.

Anthony Downs, 'An Economic Theory of Political Action in a Democracy', *Journal of Political Economy*, Vol. 65, 1953 – the pioneering statement of Downsian theory, more fully developed in: Anthony Downs, *An Economic Theory of Democracy*, New York, Harper 1957.

G. J. Stigler, 'Director's Law of Public Income Redistribution', *Journal of Law and Economics*, Vol. 13, 1970.

James M. Buchanan and Gordon Tullock, *The Calculus of Consent*, Ann Arbor, Univ. of Michigan Press, 1965. The logical foundations for the Tullock theory, which is further developed in:

Gordon Tullock, 'The Charity of the Uncharitable', *Western Economic Journal*, Vol. 8, 1970.

On distributive justice, consult:

J. Rawls, 'Justice as Fairness' in P. Laslett and W. G. Runciman (Eds) *Philosophy, Politics and Society*, Oxford, Basil Blackwell, 1962.

J. Rawls, 'Distributive Justice' in P. Laslett and W. G. Runciman (Eds), *Philosophy, Politics and Society,* Oxford, Basil Blackwell, 1969.

J. Rawls, *A Theory of Justice*, Oxford, Clarendon Press, 1972.

On inequalities of wealth holdings, consult:

A. B. Atkinson, *Unequal Shares*, London, Allen Lane, 1972.

J. E. Meade, *Efficiency, Equality and the ownership of Property*, London, Allen and Unwin, 1964.

J. R. S. Revell, *The Wealth of the Nation*, London, CUP, 1967.

J. R. S. Revell and J. Moyle, *The Owners of Quoted Ordinary Shares*, London, Chapman and Hall, 1966.

A. Roe, *The Financial Interdependence of the Economy 1957–61,* London, Chapman and Hall, 1971.

5   Income Maintenance Policy in Britain

Poverty in post war Britain

The student of the British Welfare State can scarcely begin in a better place than William Beveridge's report *Social Insurance and Allied Services* which became the lodestone for post war social policy. As Beveridge himself wrote during the war 'A revolutionary movement in the world's history is a time for revolutions, not for patching'. Five giants were seen by him to be barring the road of reconstruction: Want, Disease, Ignorance, Squalor and Idleness. Post war policy against ignorance and disease was to be enshrined in the 1944 Education Act and the 1948 National Health Service Act. Poverty was to be attacked primarily by 'full employment' policy (about which we say very little in this book), by social security with flat rate contributions and flat rate benefits and adjustment of benefits to 'family needs' – i.e. making allowances for the number of children in a family, together with a fall-back system of means-tested National Assistance (later Supplementary Benefit) for those with special needs not covered in statutory categories. The fundamental Beveridge aim of a minimum guaranteed *subsistence* income for everyone (though he was by no means the first to propose it) was firmly entrenched in post war legislation.

The search for the minimum subsistence level of income in any technical sense has proved unproductive. Even for fundamentals such as food, individuals' requirements for 'efficient' work depend on the nature of the work, their age and a diversity of other factors. The analysis of the previous chapter suggests, however, that even had it been possible to identify technical 'needs' in this way, and to administer the exceedingly complicated schedule of benefits that would have resulted, these 'needs' would not necessarily have been the subsistence level that society would, in the event, have accepted for its minimum standard. To be sure, such information would have been of help to people making up their minds as to what the level ought to have been, but the truth is that a technological (or biological) approach to what is a *social* problem is not, of itself, enough. The resolution of a social problem depends upon the resolution of conflicting views (values, if you like) of what and how much *ought* to be done to alleviate hardship. In short, it depends upon (a) the heights and shapes of the MV curves in figure 4.5 and (b) upon the weights placed on different persons' MV's.

Suppose we made the assumption that everyone's MV counts as much as everyone else's (one man, one vote) and that the political system works in a Hochman-Rodgers way so as to signal a Pareto optimal 'subsistence' transfer, so that no-one could be made better off (in a total welfare sense) by further redistribution without at least one person becoming worse off. The latter is, perhaps, a tall order, but if we just suppose it to be true, then it becomes possible to infer that whatever level of supplementary benefit has been decided by the government is one unambiguous measure – but not a technocratic one – of the 'subsistence' level. We should admit at once that this will leave many individuals (non-recipients of benefit) unsatisfied. For example, the kindly people will almost certainly think it too mean, while the mean ones will think it too generous. Unfortunately, or fortunately, it is a feature both of democracy and Paretian economics that neither the virtuous nor the sinful have a monopoly of political or economic power. Some compromise is both necessary and desirable. For better or worse, we shall take the Supplementary Benefit levels as defining the socially preferred subsistence line at any point in time. It has the signal virtue of having been revealed by the collective decision making processes of government.

The post war history of Supplementary Benefits (National Assistance) well illustrates the behavioural rather than the technocratic concept of 'need' or of 'subsistence'. Social security benefits under the Beveridge scheme were to be paid as of right and without (save for one major and several minor exceptions) a means test. The major exception was the means tested National Assitance Benefit but this was intended to cover any cases of hardship not covered by other benefit entitlements, such as unemployment, disability and retirement, and was expected to constitute a very minor part of social policy against poverty – it was the safety net. In fact, right from the start of the operation of the 1949 National Assistance Act, National Assistance

Benefits (including the allowance for housing) *exceeded* insurance benefits. This placed the means-tested element in the foreground rather than in the background of policy. Moreover, instead of the numbers of people in receipt of National Assistance dwindling, they have consistently increased since 1948.

Some estimates of the number of persons with incomes (including social security benefits) falling below the National Assistance level are provided in Table 5.1, though for various reasons they are likely to be slight overstatements of the numbers involved.

A variety of other estimates of the numbers 'in poverty' have also been made. Brian Abel-Smith and Peter Townsend estimated 3.8% persons and 4.7% households in 1960 (0.9% and 1.3% respectively had incomes below 4/5ths of the NA Scale). A. B. Atkinson has estimated 3.4% persons below the line in 1969. These latter estimates are all, due to their reliance on Family Expenditure Survey data, likely to be *underestimates*, being based on household units and a concept of 'normal' rather than current income (people out of work for less than three months are considered to receive their 'normal' income).

Table 5.1 *Families and Persons with Incomes below National Assistance Scales*

Year	Families with incomes below N.A. Scales ('000's)	%	Persons with incomes below N.A. Scales ('000's)	%
1954	3,800	14.8	6,294	12.3
1959	2,584	10.0	4,607	8.8
1963	3,103	11.7	5,077	9.4

Source: I. Gough and T. Stark, Low Incomes in the U.K., 1954, 1959 and 1963, *Manchester School*, June, 1968, Table IV and fn 1 on p. 179.

Note: Families are Inland Revenue Tax Units adjusted so far as possible to include the head, spouse and dependent children only – i.e. the 'nuclear' family.

The data of Table 5.1 are likely to be overestimates due to reliance on Inland Revenue data, despite being based on the nuclear family, because a number of assumptions had to be made about, eg, unchanging family composition during the financial year. The correct figure for 1969 is likely to lie between 5 and 8% of the population.

Although the secular evidence is not reliable, there is some comfort to be derived from the apparent fact that the proportion of persons in poverty is gradually, if unsteadily, declining. Moreover, changes in benefit levels (recall that National Assistance or Supplementary Benefit Scales change through time in response to changes in the *MV* schedules) imply that in *absolute* terms, many of the poor today are not so poor as they were after the war. Although there have been fluctuations, those in receipt of Supplementary Benefits have seen them kept at approximately the same proportion of gross weekly earnings for adult male workers and rising in real terms over the long run. Nevertheless, although the data do not include inter and intra family transfers of income (for example from grandparents to children and vice versa) the sheer absolute number of persons which, by any account, is to be reckoned as being the number in poverty is surely staggering. How is this possible after about a quarter century of the Welfare State?

Causes of the perpetuation of poverty

The reasons why poverty has continued at the scale it has are broadly two-fold. First there has been inadequate realisation of the reasons why people and families are poor. Second, and not entirely independent of the first reason, there are explanations deriving from the theories of government behaviour outlined in chapter 4 of why all that could have been done has not been done to alleviate poverty.

The first set of reasons for the continuation of poverty are generally regarded as three: old age, children and the wage-stop. Atkinson has estimated that in 1967 50% of households below the poverty line were single-person households (mostly retirement pensioners). Couples with children made up 12% of low income households but 31% of persons living in households below the line. Nearly one in five of all households with six or more children have fallen below the line. In each case the major reason has been that the National Assistance/Supplementary Benefit levels used to define the poverty line have been *higher* than pensions for the old and family allowances. Many families with children can be in poverty even with the father in full-time employment. The problem is not, however, restricted to families with large numbers of children but also includes low earnings families. In the case of old people, many have not received the Supplementary Benefits to which they were entitled because either they were ignorant of them, or they believed that to be in receipt of them was to 'take charity'[1] or because they were reluctant to submit to a means test. Many of the families in poverty were poor also because of the 'wage-stop'.

The wage-stop is a rule by which a temporarily sick or unemployed person is entitled to receive as Supplementary Benefit an amount of no more than his 'normal' (net) weekly earnings when at work. Consequently, the man at work with net earnings less than the Supplementary Benefit scale cannot receive the full Benefit when out of work – he is permanently in poverty (unless he can get higher paid work). The reason for the wage-stop – which appears to be entirely *in*consistent with the whole of anti-poverty policy – is that it has been felt desirable not to discourage persons from work. It is a hangover from the earlier notion of the 'deserving poor'. An obsession with the work-disincentive effects of income maintenance policies runs throughout the discussion of anti-poverty policy, as we shall see. It amounts to a policy attitude that may be concerned about individuals' and families' overall command of sources of welfare – *except leisure.* It appears, indeed, that the nature of the externality imposed on the rest of society by the relatively poor is such that the consumption levels of most goods and services *are* involved (whether in terms of general purchasing power, specific entities – such as health and education – or both) but not the consumption of leisure. In fact, the wage-stop implies a particular form of the externality that seems highly unlikely on theoretical grounds, namely that *any* increase in the consumption of leisure by the relatively poor imposes such an adverse externality of its own that it completely outweighs the external benefits of lifting such persons out of poverty. What would seem far more plausible from a theoretical point of view is that increased consumption of leisure imposes an adverse externality (though it is hard to see *why* it should) but not to such an extent that it implies any automatic cut-off point and perpetuation of the state of poverty. If this latter surmise is correct, then the political mechanism has been seriously at fault.

This observation brings us to the second set of reasons why poverty has continued in Britain, based upon the theory of the behaviour of governments. Independently of the reasons for the existence of government,[2] elected governments have, according to the theories we have outlined, an incentive both to increase expenditure and to reduce taxation. Where possible, it is rational for governments to create 'fiscal illusion' by which social benefits appear to be larger than they truly are and costs appear to be smaller than they are. Several characteristics of government are consistent with the creation of fiscal illusion. One is to concentrate relatively more on current than capital expenditure (the real benefits of capital expenditure flow over a longer time period than most governments – even the most optimistic – expect to remain in office). Another is to raise taxation in the disguised form of an inflationary monetary policy and then to blame the inflation on someone else (e.g. the unions, speculators, foreigners). Another is to introduce ear-marked taxes designed to contribute *part* of the funds for expenditure on specific items, the rest coming from general fund taxation (the portion of the national insurance stamp allocated to the health service is such a case). Thus the public may imagine it is getting a tremendous bargain for its money. Yet another method is to make benefits so complicated that they are (a) hard to identify in detail, though easy in aggregate (b) less likely to be claimed but nevertheless not actually denied to legally entitled beneficiaries. Such behaviour may appear immoral but it is not irrational in the vote-maximising model.[3] In each of these cases, other reasons to explain this political behaviour may, of course, be adduced. But surely it is not mere coincidence that each serves to promote the selfish interests of government? (Incidentally, of the sources of illusion mentioned, only the first is likely to produce any systematic pressure on the government from civil servants to change its approach).

It is to combat fiscal illusion, obscurity, the arbitrariness and secrecy of officialdom and hence, hopefully, poverty that many of the proposed reforms of the system of income maintenance have been advanced. We therefore turn to some of these proposals, their costs and the 'work disincentive' effects that, it is alleged, may accompany them. Before embarking upon the disagreements that divide the proponents of rival schemes it is perhaps worth noting that all seem agreed that *some* additional cost may be worth bearing to reduce poverty more successfully than we have to date. The reader, naturally, is not obliged to agree with them.

Reforms of anti-poverty policy

A number of reforms of anti-poverty policy have been proposed. In this section we shall discuss some of them using the framework of the analysis set out in chapter 4. Poverty is a terrible thing and it is not surprising that the language in which it is discussed is frequently colourful and even exaggerated. Certainly the subject raises passions both among reformers and among those who see nothing 'wrong' in the existence of poverty. Stripped, however, of the moralistic and political overtones that colour much writing on the subject (and motivate much more, if not all, of it) our analysis suggests that the reason why poverty is of grave social concern is because it imposes an adverse externality on broad sections of society including the non-poor. Specifically the externality takes two forms. First the poor do not consume as much of specific economic goods as others would wish them to. Second, they do not consume as much of goods in general as others would wish them to. The implications of the first type of externality are examined elsewhere in this book, for it provides the basic rationale for specific policies in, for example, education and health. In this chapter we concentrate on the second kind of externality − deficiency of general purchasing power.

The form this externality takes is of crucial importance. We have asserted, for example, that its form is such that the external harm suffered by the relatively rich is the really important form, i.e. that it is the concern of the relatively well-to-do that forms both the basis of the problem and ultimately defines what 'poverty' is. An alternative specification is that the poor suffer an externality from observing the consumption behaviour of the relatively well-to-do. To put it in an unfavourable light, they are 'jealous'. Now while this may be a plausible description of the externality relationship it is not one with which we shall be concerned here for two reasons. First, our welfare economics cannot handle it at all. To internalise a 'jealous' externality requires a transfer from the rich to the poor, just as the internalisation of a 'charitable' externality requires a transfer from rich to poor. But if 'jealousy' is the real externality and the transfer takes place, while the poor undoubtedly gain we have no way of comparing their gain with the loss (for that is what it must be) suffered by the rich. Consequently we cannot decide whether such transfers are for the *social* good. If, however, the rich voluntarily agree to transfer for the poor on the grounds of 'sympathy' and 'compassion' then both poor and rich unambiguously gain. Such transfers are therefore (at least up to a point) for the social good. Second, were the 'jealousy' of the poor the real foundation for current policy, it seems that the 'jealous' have done a remarkably bad job of promoting their own interests. (If the rich are 'jealous' of the even richer, they may vote for distribution to the poor from the very rich. While this may provide extra explanatory power for actual redistributions, once again we cannot evaluate it as unambiguously for the *social* good.)

One policy implication of our approach is that *generalised* transfers of purchasing power to persons who are not 'in poverty' do not internalise any general externality and can therefore have no justification in social policy on these grounds. (The same need not be true of specific transfer in kind. For example, even the rich may not educate their children as much as others would like.) This is the inescapable consequence of specifying the externality, as we have done, in terms of the compassion felt by one section of society for another. Provided, therefore, that our specification of the problem is correct, economic analysis suggests that some degree of what is (loosely) known as 'selectivity' is implied – unless there are other costs (for example, identification costs) of selective rather than universal transfers of generalised purchasing power. In short, the less poor you are, the less (in net terms) should you receive by way of generalised income transfers. This basic implication rules out some proposals for reform that substantially benefit the middle classes as being beyond the scope of our normative methodology though, as we have seen, several authors have examined such transfers using positive economics. It also rules out *uniformity* of incomes, compared with the setting of *minima* below which no one should fall. Another implication is that families in like circumstances should receive like benefits. Were this not the case the elementary geometry of the last chapter soon shows that society as a whole would gain if more were given to those less favourably treated and less to those more favourably treated.[4]

With this as background the proposals of current interest to be discussed here are a National Minimum Wage (NMW), a Social Dividend (SD), Negative Income Taxation (NIT) and the proper implementation of the Beveridge scheme, or Back to Beveridge (BB).

A national minimum wage

The proposals for NMW are really less for its introduction than for extending and raising the present arrangements in Britain that already apply in a number of industries (Wages Boards in agriculture and Wages Councils in some other industries such as Button Manufacturing and the Ostrich and Fancy Feather Industry). The objective is therefore to extend the NMW to all industries and to legislate it at such a rate that those families where the wage earner is in employment would have their income raised to the Supplementary Benefit scale. It is appropriate to assume that proponents of the NMW also advocate higher Family Allowances so that the NMW needs to be set at the appropriate Supplementary Benefit level for a one child family. Setting it at a higher level (for example sufficient for a four child family) would imply treating families in different circumstances (imposing different degrees of externality) in the same way, which is presumptively non-optimal. Moreover, this assumption reminds us that the NMW is only a *partial* solution to the problem of poverty — it does not tackle the problems of poverty in old age, among the self-employed, casual workers or the disabled, nor does it (directly) tackle poverty in families where the usual earner is unemployed. (There would be an indirect effect on the unemployed in Britain insofar as the wage stop rules would be applied at a higher 'normal' earning level than usual. In fact, if the NMW could be set at the right level and varied according to family circumstances, the wage stop would cease altogether to be effective).

Three effects of the NMW are worthy of special attention, all of them requiring a substantial application of positive, as well as normative, economic analysis. The first of these consists in the possibility that, because minimum wages are legislated in monetary, not real, terms (though the intention is, of course, to raise real incomes), the intention of the NMW will be frustrated, or partially frustrated, through its impact upon the general price level via raising production costs in general and through the reaction of other workers (and employers) raising money rates in an attempt to maintain their own real wages. If the NMW were to apply to female workers, for example, the impact on the price level is likely to be quite marked (as well as leading probably to substantial female unemployment). Insofar as the poor tend to consume relatively unskilled labour-intensive products, the effect will again be more pronounced.

The second consists in the incidence of the costs of financing the NMW. The costs will be borne, in varying proportions, by the producers and consumers of goods and services but the precise incidence of the costs will depend, among other things, upon the elasticity of substitution of minimum wage labour and other factors of production, upon product demand elasticities and upon the consumption patterns of different income groups in society.

The third consists in the fact that NMW concentrates its benefit upon those who remain in employment while, at the same time, tending to drive others out of employment or into low-productivity self-employment as efficient firms substitute other factors of production for higher cost labour and/or reduce rates of output. If, however, the NMW is applied *effectively* (i.e. set at a rate higher than current wages) only in some sectors, rather than in all sectors, (the more realistic case), while on the one hand there need be no long term unemployment (provided workers are prepared to move between industries) any gains made in the earnings of workers who retain employment in the NMW industries will be offset, in varying degrees, by losses to other workers and to workers who are compelled to leave NMW industries. For example, a National Minimum Wage in the relatively labour-intensive sector of the economy causes prices in that sector to rise relative to other sectors' prices, whose output will expand and that of the labour-intensive sector fall. The capital-labour ratio in the capital-intensive sectors must fall and the (marginal) productivity of workers in these sectors must fall thereby tending to make these workers relatively worse off than they would otherwise have been.[5]

The significance of the various factors discussed here for the desirability of the NMW depends crucially upon the size of the NMW relative to current low wages, upon the empirical assessment of the appropriate elasticities and upon one's evaluation of the fairness of the incidence of its costs. Even making the crudest assumptions that characterise some discussions of the NMW, e.g. that all elasticities are zero, so that only consumers of the products produced by NMW sectors bear these costs, some assessment still needs to be made of the extent to which NMW earners consume the products of their own industry.

Social dividend and negative income taxation

Social Dividend and Negative Income Taxation are, as we shall see, formally identical, so they are treated together. The emphases placed upon them by their various proponents have been, in a historical sense, however, slightly different so there is some virtue in regarding them as separate proposals. The SD is, in general, a scheme that guarantees a weekly payment (let us suppose, set at the poverty line) for *everyone* and is paid by the state. A proportional or progressive tax rate is then applied to family income (excluding guaranteed income) above some minimum exemption level. By building a basic floor below every family's income it is clear that SD is paid regardless of need. Consequently, it is more 'universal' than 'selective', though some selectivity in, say, the form of Supplementary Benefit would have to be retained in cases of special needs not allowed for in the basic guaranteed income needed by the 'average' poor. Nevertheless, it is characteristic of SD/NIT schemes that they seek to simplify and to make the basis of receipt of benefit unambiguous and clear, thereby reducing the scope for bureaucratic arbitrariness and fiscal illusion and so, presumably, making optimal transfers the more likely. Let us take a highly simplified example of an SD plan. Suppose every two-person family were guaranteed an annual income of £700 a year and a *proportional* tax rate is applied to *all* other income[6] at 33 1/3%. Tax payments would equal SD receipts for persons with incomes of £2,100, which is usually known as the break-even point. The relationship between the (proportional) tax rate t_s. guaranteed minimum income Y_g and the break-even point B are rather obviously seen to be

$$B = Y_g/T_s$$

The emphasis, in NIT, is placed upon the break-even point which, in the NIT literature, has tended to be equated with the exemption level of income E. If a person's income exceeds the exemption level he pays (say) a proportional (though it could be progressive) income tax If his income is below E he receives an income maintenance payment equal to some (usually constant) proportion of the shortfall between actual income and exemption income. This proportion t_n is the negative income tax rate. Thus, if his income is Y, he receives $t_n(E\text{-}Y)$ if Y is less than E. The exemption level and the tax rate together determine the level of income below which no one can fall — guaranteed income Yg. Obviously, if ordinary income Y is zero, then

$$Y_g = t_n E$$

The similarity of SD and NIT is obvious, for if the breakeven and exemption levels are the same ($B = E$) and the same tax rates apply ($t_s = t_n$), then

$$Y_g = t_s B \quad \text{or} \quad B = Y_g/t_s$$

By an appropriate choice of any *two* of these variables (for the third will then be determined) SD/NIT can be a very effective way of helping those below the poverty line — in the sense that net assistance could go to those with incomes at or below the poverty line and transfers (and hence total cost) reduced to those above it.[7]

The effects of NMW on employment and prices have, as we have seen, been the cause of much concern. With SD/NIT concern has chiefly centred upon the effects it may have on individuals' willingness to work and upon the periodicity of payment.

The *disincentive* effects that new taxes and benefits and changes in their rates can have seem mainly to be of concern for the odd and Puritan reason that the nature of the externality is that it is all right to raise the real income of the poor so long as they do not take their real income in the form of leisure.[8] Let us, however, as we have before, sacrifice personal predilections for the sake of an objective approach and suppose that any reduction in effort *is* to be regarded as a disadvantage to be weighed against the benefits of the schemes we are discussing. Disincentive effects fall into two broad classes: total and marginal. A total effect exists in the choice between whether or not to work at all. This choice must evidently be affected to some extent by the amount of income available in and out of work. A marginal effect operates in the decision to work more or to move to a higher paid job and here the marginal tax rate (the resulting change in tax divided by the causative change in income) is the significant variable.

Taking the marginal tax rate first, the initial remarkable fact is that rather few people know what their marginal rate is – and most overstate it – in Britain at least. The standard rate of income tax is frequently supposed to be the marginal rate and in 1967 this standard rate was 41p. The earning of an additional pound, however, implied the payment of an additional 32p because of the 2/9ths personal allowance on earned incomes. When a number of standard tax payers were asked what rate they thought they paid, however, 40% thought their rate exceeded the true rate but lay below 50p and 20% thought it above 50p (i.e. even above the standard rate!). This propensity to overstate marginal rates would be expected, of course, to reinforce the disincentive effect.[9]

Now it is the fact that many families in our present British welfare state do face exceedingly high marginal rates of tax, especially those families receiving means-tested welfare benefits. For example, whereas the marginal rate implicit in the provision of free school dinners is zero at £16 or £18 per week, it is 75% at £17 per week (three child family). For a variety of means-tested benefits, while the marginal rate of income tax was only 0.9% at £17, the aggregate marginal rate was 142.0%! For a wage-stopped family where benefits equal normal earnings, the rate is 100% (clearly affecting the total decision).

The standard economic analysis of the effect of tax payments (and/or benefits foregone) on incentives to work is that there is an 'income effect' and a 'substitution effect' usually working in contrary directions. The income effect reduces take-home pay and hence provides an incentive to work more to maintain living standards. The substitution effect reduces the price of leisure relative to the rewards of work and hence encourages more leisure.[10] Which dominates the other cannot be told *a priori* (the theory is mainly of use to counter those who argue *a priori* that increases in tax rates *always* have a disincentive effect). The empirical evidence on this point (see Further Reading) is patchy but gives no firm evidence that marginal tax rates have any serious disincentive at least for the lower income groups. It is tempting therefore not to worry about high marginal rates, at least from the incentives point of view. As for the *total* effect of guaranteed incomes on those who are not in work, one would expect to see a disincentive effect operate most keenly if the system were one that offered *both* a high level of benefit relative to earnings in employment *and* a high aggregate marginal tax rate on income. Once again, there is little evidence that the unemployed who are in receipt of benefit are reluctant to work (if they can find it, and if they are not otherwise handicapped).

We have so far failed to relate this discussion of incentives (assuming that they are in principle a rational source of concern) to the SD/NIT proposals. The reason why will now be clear. What little evidence exists suggests that in practice disincentive effects are not likely to be very important. The really interesting (and costly) exercise of testing the behaviour of people when faced with different benefit/tax opportunities – even of working out the theoretical probabilities in a comprehensive way – remains to be done in Britain. This is another stretch of the uncharted waters in the economics of social policy. Nevertheless, at least in principle, the implicit marginal rates in most SD/NIT schemes can be adjusted to avoid most of the sharp breaks that occur with many of the means tested benefits that are currently available in Britain.

In general, the unlikely featuring of 'leisure' in the true externality relationship together with the empirical evidence suggest that obsession with the incentives question is mostly misplaced.

Another area of controversy with SD/NIT proposals concerns the periodicity of payment of benefit. Clearly, to be effective, it is vital both that families in need receive their dues at the time of need (and not next year) and that their income deficiency be assessed on their current income (and not last year's). To tackle the poverty problem effectively while not placing a continuing heavy emphasis on the means tested Supplementary Benefits would imply a short accounting period – at least monthly and possibly even weekly. Those schemes (such as SD) which place the emphasis upon giving every family a guaranteed minimum *in advance* rather than (as in NIT) the difference between *expost* income and exemption (or breakeven) income are, on these grounds, to be preferred, though they may raise administrative costs substantially, and they also imply a greater throughput of finance through the public purse.

Another cause for concern relates to the definition of the income unit. While one of the chief advantages of SD/NIT is that it tackles the problem of poverty directly at its source (too little income) rather than according to circumstances (someone's notion of 'need'), it is a fact that the present income tax mechanism was not designed as a part of the welfare state. Thus, for example, tax is levied on individuals (rightly or wrongly) while benefits should be related to families (if the externality relationship has been correctly specified in this book).

Realistic policy choice (as well as efficient choice) of method must, of course, depend upon the administrative costs of the reforms. In the case of SD/NIT, for example, while reducing the staffing requirements for running Supplementary Benefits, and others, raising the Inland Revenue's coverage from about 20m tax payers to include everyone, and shortening the accounting period (NIT would apply only to individuals in the Pay-as-You-Earn income tax scheme) would add considerably to administration costs. How much it would add is an empirical matter dependent very largely on the details of any particular scheme and upon other accompanying changes such as the abolition of surtax. Whether the additional costs were worth incurring would depend upon the relative costs of alternative schemes, their relative effectiveness in helping the poor and upon the social valuation placed upon helping them. It is at least possible that the enthusiastic sup-porters of rival schemes place a far higher priority upon abolishing poverty than does society in general. Indeed, it would be rather remarkable if this were not the case. Consequently, society as a whole may prefer a cheaper scheme – even if it meant not dealing fully with its own concept of poverty.

Back to Beveridge

The final set of proposals to be discussed in this chapter relates not to some fairly fundamental reform of the approach to the poverty problem but to implementing fully some important aspects of the Beveridge proposals. It will be recalled that the emphasis in the Beveridge plan was placed on the suggestion that national insurance benefits and family allowances should be enough to guarantee 'subsistence' while Supplementary Benefits were really to be supplementary – and *not* set higher than the insurance benefits. The essence of the Back to Beveridge policy is: the reinstatement of social insurance benefits at higher levels coupled with the use of 'claw back' tax procedures to reclaim family allowances from those who are not poor; the abolition of child tax allowances (which do not assist the childless, and more importantly, non-taxpaying families); and the abolition of the wage-stop.

The BB proposals have the virtue of needing minimum change in the administrative structure. Unlike SD/NIT schemes, however, they do not tackle the problem of poverty across the board. Instead they focus, as does the present structure, on the 'needs' of categories of person (the sick, the unemployed, the retired) and require claims to be put in for benefit when a person changes category. This categories approach implies that there will still be a role to play for Supplementary Benefits (for those with special needs and for those in categories not recognised by the social insurance scheme). Moreover the BB scheme would not tackle the important problem of childless couples where the breadwinner is in paid employment – but at a very low wage. For this latter reason most BB proponents also advocate the introduction of the NMW, together with its attendant advantages and disadvantages.

A major flaw in the BB proposals is that their benefits are not confined (unlike suitably designed NMW and sliding scale SD/NIT schemes) to the poor but are given as of right to any one falling into the appropriate 'category' – provided he claims his right. This flaw, which amounts to internalising externalities that do not exist,[11] is intrinsic to the Beveridge scheme but is not necessarily decisive, however, if (a) the BB proposals are effective in eliminating poverty where it exists and (b) if its other costs are relatively low. For example, suppose that suitably designed SD and BB schemes effectively (or equally effectively) abolished poverty but that the SD scheme concentrated benefits almost entirely on the poor (at the same time avoiding stigma) while the BB scheme spread its bounty more widely. If the excess of the BB financing costs (including adverse effects of the NMW) over the SD financing costs were *less* than the excess of the SD administrative costs over the BB administrative costs, then it would be rational to prefer BB.

In surveying the various proposals (which have frequently been advanced with enthusiasm and attacked with vehemence) it is important to try to keep a cool head. One problem facing the conscientious student is that to date no one has attempted to compare the effectiveness of each proposal (or combination) in reaching a *common* goal (neither have we here). True cost-effectiveness can be assessed only if the 'output' of the rival programmes is, as nearly as possible, held constant. Another problem, should one already feel tempted to plump for one, rather than another, scheme is that those we have surveyed are not a complete set.

When discussing redistribution in chapter 3, discussion was restricted to the redistribution of *income*. We eschewed the important topic of wealth redistribution. This bias has been followed in chapter 4 and in this. While there has been a literature on wealth *taxation* there has not to date been anything at all like as much serious thought about tackling the problem of poverty by redistributing *wealth* to the poor. Here then is yet another relative lacuna in the economics of social policy and one worth attempting to remove before further passions are spent in defence of a favourite scheme for transferring current incomes to the poor.

Finally, a caution about the use of expressions such as 'universal' and 'selective' in the context of policy against poverty. It has become the fashion in some quarters[12] to describe SD/NIT as 'selective' though it guarantees benefits to all (with Supplementary Benefit as fall-back) and BB as 'universalist' even though it attempts to relate benefit to the specific needs of certain 'categories' of person (plus Supplementary Benefit again as fall-back). It would appear that these expressions are totally without value in describing the rival sets of scheme — even in describing their disadvantages. It is far more important to consider their *effectiveness* and *efficiency* at solving the problem of income deficiency rather than to pretend that an important social choice problem about the *means* is about the *ends* of policy. Since this pretence is to be found among reformers on both the 'right' and the 'left' the reader should fore-arm himself against it before tackling the literature on poverty.

NOTES

1. There is a literal sense in which they *are* in receipt of 'charity' – in the sense that state retirement pensions, for example, are not calculated on a strictly actuarial basis, though one pays contributions over one's working life-time, for no government can bind subsequent governments to a policy. They are strictly transfers from working workers to retired workers and their relations partly because of externalities of the (charitable) sort discussed in previous chapters, partly because it is in most workers' selfish interest to seek to perpetuate a transfer system from which one day they will ultimately benefit. Nevertheless, when in retirement, receipt of a pension is utterly dependent upon the goodwill of those generations who are currently financing it. Recipients benefit 'as of right' only so long as the rest of society *gives* them this right. To secure take-up, however, it is extremely important to hide from recipients this inescapable dependency situation.
2. Implicit in the theories we have discussed are two principal reasons: (a) the desire for society to have a controlled but dominant wielder of force (to impose and enforce, for example, common legislative procedures) and (b) to facilitate the efficient production of public goods by economising, through central representation, on what may be broadly termed the bargaining costs of rival interests.
3. We should, however, qualify this to the extent that successful politicians may also personally share the non-selfish aspirations of (some of) their electors. The existence of such individuals is (fortunately) consistent with the vote-maximising model, for they may be more effective vote-getters because of their manifest sincerity. Other things equal, such persons will be less inclined to promote fiscal illusion than other politicians.
4. Assuming that the administrative cost of making the transfer to each group were the same.
5. For a possible exception to this general expectation, see the article by Harry G. Johnson cited in the further reading.
6. In practice, progressivity is probably preferable and the taxation of small incomes is anyway very costly by comparison with the revenues obtained. Whether positive tax rates are applied to all incomes or only beyond an exemption income level does not affect the breakeven point.
7. The Family Income Supplement (FIS) is a form of NIT. In its original form it specified a breakeven point equal to the poverty line and paid a benefit equal to 50% of the difference between this and family earnings plus family allowances. By its construction, however, the arithmetic of SD/NIT implied that the income guaranteed (by FIS alone) was only one half of the Supplementary Benefit level. Moreover, it has to be claimed and is not received automatically, thus losing a major attraction of more thorough-going SD/NIT (especially SD) schemes.
8. See p. 95 above. An alternative specification of the externality such that taking more leisure would definitely detract from the welfare of the rest of society would derive from making the size of GNP the maximand of social and economic policy. The reader will not need reminding that in this book, the far more sensible maximand 'social welfare' is adopted, not social wealth, though our maximand includes wealth. So long as any reduction in effort is marginal to the economy as a whole, even though output must necessarily fall, social welfare will not.
9. See the article by C. V. Brown cited in the further reading.

10. A more complete approach treats the individual as combining *time* with other things to 'produce' consumption goods. For example, this leads to the complication that to enjoy leisure one must earn income to acquire the other things that make leisure different from mere idleness. See, e.g., Gary S. Becker, 'A Theory of the Allocation of Time', *Economic Journal*, Vol. 75, pp. 493–517.

11. Problem: define the utility function, and hence the nature of the externality, for a person who believes that benefits ought to be received in full by *everyone*, irrespective of income, without 'clawbacks' or inclusion of benefits in taxable income.

12. See the article by P. R. Kaim-Caudle cited in the further reading. So far as I am able to tell, the current usage of these terms implies the following unhelpful equations:

selectivist = right-wing or liberal, mean or generous
universalist = left-wing or liberal, mean or generous

In short, it depends upon what one means by 'right' or 'left' wing – always a tricky dichotomy, for the other man is always the 'right' winger!

FURTHER READING

General:

A. B. Atkinson, *Poverty in Britain and the Reform of Social Security*, London, CUP, 1969: A modern review of the pros and cons with a penchant for the Beveridge scheme.

A. B. Atkinson, *Unequal Shares*, London, Allen Lane, 1972. One of the few modern studies with proposals for wealth redistribution.

Sir W. Beveridge, *Social Insurance and Allied Services* (Cmd 6404) HMSO, London, 1942. The *locus classicus* of British social security.

M. Bruce, *The Coming of the Welfare State*, London, Batsford, 4th Ed., 1968. An introductory description of the history of the British Welfare State.

C. Green, *Negative Taxes and the Poverty Problem*, Washington D.C., Brookings, 1967. A clear and comprehensive discussion of SD/NIT schemes in the American context.

P. Townsend (ed), *The Concept of Poverty*, London, Heinemann, 1970.

Measuring Poverty:

B. Abel-Smith and P. Townsend, *The Poor and the Poorest*, London, Bell, 1965. An important booklet which had much to do with a resurgence of awareness that poverty is still a problem in Britain.

I. Gough and T. Stark, 'Low Incomes in the United Kingdom', *The Manchester School*, Vol. 36, 1968.

Ministry of Pensions and National Insurance, *Financial and Other Circumstances of Retirement Pensioners*, London, HMSO, 1965.

Ministry of Social Security, *Circumstances of Families*, London, HMSO, 1967.

A. R. Prest and T. Stark, 'Some Aspects of Income Redistribution in the UK since World War II', *The Manchester School*, Vol. 35, 1967.

B. S. Rowntree, *Poverty – A Study of Town Life*, London, Macmillan, 1901.

B. S. Rowntree, *Poverty and Progress*, London, Longmans, Green, 1941.
B. S. Rowntree and G. R. Lavers, *Poverty and the Welfare State: A Third Social Survey of York*, London, Longmans, Green, 1951.
T. Stark, *The Distribution of Personal Income in the UK, 1949–63*, Cambridge, CUP, 1972.
D. Wedderburn, 'Poverty in Britain Today: the Evidence', *Sociological Review*, Vol. 10, 1962.

Back to Beveridge
A. B. Atkinson, 'Policies for Poverty', *Lloyds Bank Review*, No. 100, 1971.
A. B. Atkinson, 'Income Maintenance and Income Taxation', *Journal of Social Policy*, Vol. 1, 1972.
M. M. Hauser and P. Burrows, *The Economics of Unemployment Insurance*, London, Allen and Unwin, 1969.
P. R. Kaim-Caudle, 'Selectivity and the Social Services', *Lloyds Bank Review*, No. 92, 1969. Like Atkinson, considers reform in the context of NIT-type proposals. Attempts unsuccessfully, however, to line up the schemes according to 'ideological conflict'.
T. Lynes, *National Assistance and National Prosperity*, London, Bell, 1962.

National Minimum Wage
Yale Brozen, 'Minimum Wage Rates and Household Workers', *Journal of Law and Economics*, Vol. 5, 1962.
M. R. Colberg, 'Minimum Wage Effects on Florida's Economic Development', *Journal of Law and Economics*, Vol. 3, 1960.
Department of Employment and Productivity, *A National Minimum Wage: An Inquiry*, London, HMSO, 1969.
Harry G. Johnson, 'Minimum Wage Laws: A General Equilibrium Analysis', *Canadian Journal of Economics*, Vol. 2, 1969.
J. Peterson, 'Employment Effects of Minimum Wages', *Journal of Political Economy*, Vol. 65, 1957.
G. J. Stigler, 'The Economics of Minimum Wage Legislation', *American Economic Review*, Vol. 36, 1946.

Social Dividend and Negative Taxation
C. V. Brown and D. A. Dawson, *Personal Taxation, Incentives and Tax Reform*, London, PEP, 1969.
A. Christopher *et al., Policy for Poverty*, London, IEA, 1970.
M. David and Jane Leuthold, 'Formulas for Income Maintenance: Their Distributional Impact', *National Tax Journal*, 1968, Vol. 21.
Milton Friedman, *Capitalism and Freedom*, Chicago, Chicago UP, 1962, ch. 12.
C. Green and R. J. Lampman, 'Schemes for Transferring Income to the Poor', *Industrial Relations*, Vol. 6, 1967.
R. J. Lampman, 'Approaches to the Reduction of Poverty', *American Economic Review*, Vol. 55, 1965.
D. S. Lees, 'Poor Families and Fiscal Reform', *Lloyds Bank Review*, No. 86, 1967.
A. K. Maynard, 'Negative Income Taxation: Problems and Possibilities', *Journal of Economic Studies*, 1972.
A. R. Prest, 'The Negative Income Tax: Concepts and Problems', *British Tax Review*, No. 6. 1970.
Royal Commission on the Taxation of Profits and Income, cmnd. 9105, *Minutes of Evidence*, Days 1–3, London, HMSO, 1954.
James Tobin, 'Improving the Economic Status of the Negro', *Daedalus*, Vol. 94, 1965.

James Tobin, J. Pechman and P. M. Mieszkowski, *Is a Negative Income Tax Practical?*, Washington DC, 1967.

Aggregate Marginal Tax Rates

A. R. Prest, *Social Benefits and Tax Rates*, London, Inst. Econ. Affairs, 1970. A pioneering British study of this important topic that actually calculates them.

Incentives

P. S. Albin and B. Stein, 'The Constrained Demand for Public Assistance', *Journal of Human Resources*, Vol. 3, 1968.

R. Barlow, H. E. Brazer and J. N. Morgan, 'A Survey of Investment Management and Working Behaviour Among High-Income Individuals', *American Economic Review*, Vol. 55, 1965.

M. J. Boskin, 'The Negative Income Tax and the Supply of Work Effort', *National Tax Journal*, Vol. 20, 1967.

G. F. Break, 'Income Taxes and Incentives to Work: An Empirical Study', *American Economic Review*, Vol. 47, 1957.

C. T. Brem and T. R. Saving, 'The Demand for General Assistance Payments', *American Economic Review*, Vol. 54, 1964.

C. V. Brown, 'Misconceptions about Income Tax and Incentives', *Scottish Journal of Political Economy*, Vol. 15, 1968.

D. B. Fields and W. T. Stanbury, 'Incentives, Disincentives and the Income Tax', *Public Finance*, Vol. 25, 1970.

L. E. Gallaway, 'Negative Income Tax Rates and the Elimination of Poverty', *National Tax Journal*, Vol. 19, 1966.

C. Green, 'Negative Taxes and Monetary Incentives to Work: the Static Theory', *Journal of Human Resources*, Vol. 3, 1968.

R. Perlman, 'A Negative Income Tax Plan for Maintaining Work Incentives' *Journal of Human Resources*, Vol. 3, 1968.

S. Rolfe and G. Furness, 'The Impact of Changes in Tax Rates and the Method of Collection on Effort: Some Empirical Observations', *Review of Economics and Statistics*, Vol. 34, 1957.

Royal Commission on the Taxation of Profits and Income, *Second Report*, Cmd. 9105, London, HMSO, 1954, Appendix 1.

H. W. Watts, 'Graduated Work Incentives: An Experiment in Negative Taxation', *American Economic Review*, Vol. 59, 1969.

H. W. Watts, 'The Graduated Work Incentive Experiments: Current Progress', *American Economic Review*, Vol. 61, 1971.

PART III

Social Policy—Essence and Environment

6   Are the Social Services Different?

With what should policy be concerned?

The answer to the question that forms the title of this chapter is 'Yes and No', which we shall elucidate. The reason for posing it is, however more obvious. We shall, in subsequent chapters be applying economic analysis to problems of specific social policies and social services and, in so doing, shall be treating the policy objectives and the services as economic goods. To do so implies the very reasonable question – is this valid? As an example of the kind of problem encountered, consider 'education' in university. Universities teach, they develop and preserve culture (they 'warm the air'), they train people for productive activity, they turn out 'good' citizens and so on. Many would take a more socratic view of what university education *is,* for example that it is essentially the pursuit of a universal object – learning – of intrinsic value as an end in itself, the other things being extrinsic accidents distinguishable from the essence and not necessarily associated with it. In short, is it not both naive and possibly dangerous to treat this phenomenon of education, of the profoundest concern to philosophers from time immemorial, as an 'economic' good? Does this not imply concentrating on the accidents and ignoring the essence thereby possibly destroying what is ultimately good about it?

Or, consider 'health'. What constitutes good health seems less of a philosophical question than the meaning of 'education' and yet the official definition suggested by the World Health Organisation – a state of complete mental, physical and social well-being – is evidently discussible in much the same terms as 'education'; though the view of 'education' which sees its essence as the individual pursuit of *universal* objects cannot readily be applied in health, for ultimately it is the individual who *possesses* health but no one can sanely claim to *possess* philosophy, history – or even economics!

Consider a tricky good that is less an end in itself than a means to the end of better health: human blood. There is clearly something abhorrent about considering this exceedingly useful therapeutic agent as an economic good – and indeed it has been asserted not to be one. *Ought* we therefore to apply our economic apparatus to it? More generally, ought thinking about social policy to be trammelled by cultural, as well as logical, constraints?

We are not, of course, always (perhaps, usually) aware of the cultural limitations of our thinking but if ever we are, then we fail to pursue the logic of our thought beyond the bounds of 'reasonableness' only at our peril. To say that education, health and blood are beyond the 'economic' is to say also that they are beyond the realm of social policy for only economic goods need to be allocated, whether according to principles of efficiency, or justice, or fairness, or anything else. It is to say that education – the pursuit, perhaps, of an ideal – cannot have policy decisions made about it. Since this is obviously false, we must find some reconciliation between the policy decision-making aspect and the essentialism that one feels inescapably drawn to when considering the nature of many of the social services.

It may sometimes be the case that the concern of social policy is *not* with essences but with accidents. For example, it may be of overriding concern to the scholar to establish the value *per se* of learning but social policy may be concerned principally with the *training* of qualified personnel. With blood, the principal concern may be less to do with its intrinsic (and symbolic) qualities as with ensuring its adequate supply in good condition as a medical life-saving input.

At the same time there is no general presumption that social policy is concerned solely with an instrumental view of education, blood and ethics. Social policy is concerned with *all* of the things that are of concern to society. This need not imply conflict (for example, the promotion of training is not necessarily inconsistent with 'education' – subjects pursued as ends in themselves are not necessarily useless for all other purposes) but it sometimes does. For example, an effective method of ensuring adequate blood supplies may involve buying and selling it which may discourage people from giving it – and acts of giving may be regarded as an essentially good thing in blood supplies.

In all this there is no division between the economic and the non-economic. Choices have to be made, priorities settled, means decided and so on. What is exceedingly difficult in the field of social policy is frequently the *quantification* of some of the most important characteristics which ought to shape policy. How does one quantify the output of the National Health Service? How does one quantify the values to be placed upon that output? How does one quantify the relationship between the output and the various costly inputs that create it? Some people argue that not only is quantification of such things impossible but also inherently undesirable.

As we shall see, these problems of quantification are receiving economic attention but even were it impossible to quantify the end outputs and their social value the scope for useful economic analysis would not be exhausted. We shall consider briefly some of the ways in which this is true. Later chapters will discuss some of these applications in much greater detail. One possibility in normative economics is to apply the techniques of cost-effectiveness in order to establish which of two alternative policies (considered to be, say, equally desirable in themselves) involve the least social cost. (Even if they were not considered equally desirable the costing of the options would reduce the area of uncertainty for decision takers.) A positive use would be to make assertions about the probable effects (i.e. based on economic prediction) of different policies or different organisational frameworks in terms of the direction in which important variables are expected to move. At the least such qualitative statements are useful in refuting naive prejudices. As we have seen in chapter 5 the economic analysis of labour supply to changes in tax rates does not unambiguously yield a disincentive effect, as is frequently thought.

The major danger with *any* public policy is that the perfectly proper public requirements of accountability and control may tend to give emphasis to those dimensions of social policy that are readily quantifiable at the expense of those, possibly more important, dimensions that are not. It is easier to calculate the social class of students attending university and to change the class composition of the undergraduate population than it is to measure its effects on 'education'. It is easier to cost a year's stay in hospital for a chronic mental patient than it is to measure the social value of keeping him there a year. It is easier to devise a new plan for paying for health insurance than it is to assess its cultural consequences in terms of the social environment. These dangers are inherent in the world we live in – a world of universal scarcity and partially delegated decision-making. They are, however, not inherent in economics. Indeed, as we shall see in the next chapter, economics has something exceedingly important to say about the form of institution that is appropriate for minimising these dangers.

Economists are frequently confronted with the charge that they try to 'add up' non-additive and highly disparate entities[1] and, moreover, that they try to extend this arbitrary adding-up procedure to *every* variable relevant to a policy decision by putting money values on everything. If anything, such strictures are more likely to be made in the context of social services than in that of, say, the siting of an airport. We should, therefore, be clear about what the economic (Paretian) approach really does imply.

First recall the vital role of compensation in the Paretian scheme. Compensation is the necessary evidence required to identify *unambiguous* improvements in social welfare. It is the basis upon which individuals manage to secure *voluntary* agreement to take certain courses of action. The problems really arise when money compensation does not take place – and, of course, it fails to take place most frequently in many of those areas of social policy where objections to 'adding up' are strongest.

As will be recalled from chapter 1, this is the point at which *potential* Pareto improvements become the limit of economic identifiability. In the Paretian framework, one cannot legitimately *recommend* courses of action identified as potential improvements. One must leave a final decision to the decision takers – usually government. Where compensation does not take place, there are both net gainers *and net losers* from any proposed course of action. The economist then seeks to provide estimates of the likely size of such gains and losses, based upon explicit value-judgements and knowledge about the facts. Thus if one effect of a policy is to increase leisure, proxy estimates of its social value may be based (a) upon the Paretian value-judgement that only the individual knows his own subjective value of leisure (b) upon the analytical implications of utility-maximising and its behavioural consequence that individuals try to adjust until the marginal value of time in leisure equals the marginal value of time in work, and (c) upon the extent to which existing (market) institutions permit a representative individual to make this adjustment. To the extent that, in a specific instance, it is judged that the market works well, the value of time in work (with additional adjustments suggested by analysis to allow for taxation, *etc.*) may be used to value leisure. Alternatively, if the market is judged highly imperfect, values may be postulated after discussion with government officials such as civil servants who are, via a hierarchy, accountable to responsible politicians who are in turn responsible to the public, an increase in whose welfare is postulated as being sought. Clearly, there is the necessity for judgements about which method (and there are others too that are consistent with the Paretian framework) generates the best figures. But there is no 'arbitrariness' about the procedure, save in the trivial sense that every systematic method of making choices derives from a set of assumptions that may be, in the technical sense, arbitrary.

Frequently, these estimated valuations have ranges of error attached to them – as they should do. That makes them less arbitrary than single, unique, values with no valid basis offered for presenting them as unique. They are also presented in terms of a common monetary measuring rod, which is arbitrary in one sense but more convenient than any other (such as peanuts?).

Thus, there is truth in the statement that economists seek to value the gains and losses from disparate sources of welfare – just as the individuals reveal through a market, more or less accurately as the case may be, their relative valuations of, say, cream buns and hours of toil on the shop floor. But it is not an arbitrary procedure: it is based on a theory of how marginal values become revealed by behaviour and of how effectively real world institutions permit these revelations to be made and, accordingly, how far we may wish to modify them or even discount them altogether as a basis of calculation. Chapter 8 contains a variety of applications of the kind of approach expounded here.

Returning, therefore, to the original question 'are the social services different': clearly they are different in the sense that pensions and health services are not the same thing as a violin recital or a ton of metallurgical coke. But they are not different in the sense that they require allocation and institutions to allocate them. Clearly they are different in the sense that they are allocated and often produced within the public sector – but coke gets produced in the public sector and recitals in the private. But they are not in the sense that *individuals* ultimately have to make the decisions concerning their production and allocation. Most important of all, they are *not* different in the sense that economic problems do not exist concerning their production and allocation, and in the sense that they are so disparate that only arbitrary methods exist of valuing their costs and benefits.

Attributes of health care

But this is not the end of the story, for having established the *prima facie* case for their not being different in the one important sense that matters for our purposes, there remains a set of specific attributes that is widely asserted to belong to social services either uniquely of more particularly than to 'other' economic goods.[2] Since these attributes have been held particularly to attach to the nature of health care we shall explore them in the context of health policy.

The reader should be warned that the context in which these attributes have been deployed is the question of whether or not it is better to organise medical care through an institution like the National Health Service or through markets, private hospitals and insurance companies. On the one hand it has been argued that because health care is *not* 'different' (as we have argued) there is no reason to treat it specially (i.e. outside the private-enterprise field of activity); on the other hand it has been argued that because it *is* 'different' (a view we have argued against) it *should* be treated specially (i.e. in the NHS, and not in the market). The view we shall come to here is that health care is not 'different' but that this implies *no* particular set of institutions for producing and allocating it. The final proof of this important result must, however, await some of the analysis of chapter 7.

The specific attributes that have been commonly alleged as differentiating health care, and other social services, from other goods and services fall broadly into three categories concerning the *rationality* of consumers of the services; the *information* available to them and the *indivisibility* and *irreversability* of the services and their effects on individuals. We shall consider each in turn.

Consider first the rationality of consumers of medical care. Since economic analysis is built up on the basis of individual rationality it is clearly important that at least *some* individuals be rational. By rationality, of course, we mean that the individual chooses entities consistently so as to maximise their value to himself. Now in health care many individuals, though sick, do not desire treatment. Many individuals are mentally sick which, in some cases, means that they are incapable of being rational in our sense. Moreover, they may pursue objectives that damage themselves. Finally, many individuals require emergency treatment and may not be in any position to make any choice at all, rational or otherwise (e.g. the unconscious victim of a road accident or heart attack).

Dismissing any individual, let alone whole categories, as incapable of making rational decisions is an activity obviously to be undertaken with caution. While, for example, some (but not all) mental patients may be incapable, it is far from clear that those who, knowing themselves to be sick, fail to seek treatment are being irrational. Nevertheless, it is certainly true that irrationality does exist. The question is how economics (or, come to that, social policy) can cope with it. As far as economics is concerned, if a person is genuinely irrational in the sense of 'inconsistent' (not in the sense of pursuing what someone else regards as foolish objectives) then the theorems of welfare economics simply cannot be applied to him — we cannot tell if, as a result of any policy, he is 'better off'. There is, however, a number of externality theorems which will certainly apply. The real social importance of irrationality is in the way *other* people (rational people) react to it. If one sees a road accident victim *other people* presume that it is in the victim's best interest to receive proper care. If a mentally disturbed person pursues ends (that are perceived — by others — to be harmful either to him or to others, even if he pursues them rationally!) then again *other people* are affected. In every case where other people are affected in these ways, whether they try to act in what they believe to be the individual's best interest, or in their own or others', the appropriate economic analysis is in terms of externalities. Now externalities, while fundamental to a proper understanding both of the role of social policy and to its improvement, are certainly not unique to health care or any other social service — they are all-pervasive in society. Hence, in this case, the social services are again *not* 'different'. What *is* required, however, is that the externally affected parties be rational even if the individual himself is not. Thus, provided that responsible citizens, friends, compassionate strangers, social workers and so on are rational, we can erect the basis for a rational social policy. We can discuss the most effective and efficient methods by which the externalities can be internalised. As we have already seen in the chapters on income redistribution, the internalisation of externalities is one of the principal foundations of the economics of social policy.

Consider next the problems raised in health care by absence of information. Many patients, though sick, do not know they are sick and therefore neither seek nor receive care. Even those who do seek care may not know in advance what care they need nor how much it would cost them; past episodes of sickness do not normally give them much guidance due to the great variability both in organic conditions and methods of treating them. Many consumers do not have the information necessary to assess, *ex ante,* the quality of the care they are likely to get nor, *ex post,* the quality of the care they have received. Finally, and frequently overlooked, there is often a substantial problem for the externally affected parties discussed above in deciding whether the action they may propose to take on another person's behalf is *truly* in that person's interest. The problem is, perhaps, at its most acute when contemplating euthanasia, but it also exists in every decision taken by an external party which affects the individual who has not, perhaps, even been consulted or been in a position in which it was possible to consult him.

Once again it is apparent that these problems are not, for the most part, confined entirely either to the health services in particular or to the social services in general. Absence of information about all things — one's own position, others' position, the implications of doing something, the future, and so on — is an intrinsic part of the environment we live in. One of the most fundamental economic problems of all is how to produce and disseminate information in the most efficient way. In practice, information has to be produced and in practice there is never 'enough'. In practice choices are made and always will be made in the face of uncertainty. In general the basic problem therefore becomes the problem of deciding the socially optimal amount and distribution of information — a problem that is very difficult both at the conceptual level and also in application. But at a crude level it is fairly easy to ascertain methods of changing both information requirements, the quantity of information made available and at a broad level to evaluate these methods in terms of their social desirability. One can also investigate methods by which uncertainty and risk can be perhaps left unchanged but shifted from one individual to another. For example, in health care, the uncertainty of an individual about the cost of treatment can be effectively removed by letting him have any care free of charge — the *ex ante* uncertainty about the cost consequences of an individual's case is replaced with a reduced uncertainty that the tax-payers will finance all such costs. Uncertainty can also be shifted by insurance. For a fee someone else will accept the cost consequences of an uncertain event occurring — the individual substitutes a more certain regular payment of a smaller sum for the uncertain irregular payment of a large sum.

Almost unique to health care is the fact that usually the service supplier — the doctor — knows not merely more than the consumer about the technical characteristics of the service (which most producers know more about) but also what service is most appropriate. Patients do not 'demand' (as they do with most products), nor do they 'instruct' (as they often do solicitors) – they *consult*. This, as well as the highly personal nature of an individual's state of health, makes the doctor-patient relationship rather special. It is, however, not easy to see that this relationship has any direct implications that make it unamenable to economic analysis, as we shall see in the next chapter.

So, do people know their own interest best in health matters or, indeed, in any others? The evidence certainly does not suggest that, given an uncertain world, they always take the best decisions – viewed *ex post facto*. The problem, however, is how to take the best *ex ante* decisions. Even massive and tragic calamities, such as the Thalidomide case, offer no conclusive evidence, for Thalidomide had been subjected to extensive experimental and industrial field testing and was pre-scribed by qualified doctors. Obviously, the texts were not extensive enough. But, in advance, what *is* enough? Whose opinion of what is enough ought one to take? The problem is far from unique to the social services – what testing is 'enough' for new models of motor cars? A solution does not necessarily imply government production, though it may imply government regulation to ensure that whatever consensus is reached on 'adequacy' is enforced throughout society. It certainly does not imply that *every* relevant piece of information will be obtained, or ought to be, for beyond the point at which the additional costs of information collection exceed the best guesses that can be made about the likely value of the extra information, further information does more social harm than good. In chapter 12 we shall investigate in some detail the case for having a social policy to control the consumption of illegal drugs where once more the problem of the interpretation of a person's best interests will be examined.

The third class of special characteristics that may make the social services in general, or health care in particular, 'different' is their indivisibility and irreversability. In health, the notion of indivisibility relates to the supposed technical characteristics of medical care but is, one suspects, largely the product of the awe in which we hold doctors (it is noticeably absent in the popular view of the teaching profession!). The point is that both the demand and the supply of particular items of medical care (e.g. a course of treatment) may be discrete – the diagnosis determines precisely what is wrong (demanded) and the treatment what is needed (supplied) to put it right as determined by medical tech-nology. In general, however, these things are not uniquely determined. Diagnosis, prognosis and therapy are all arts, dependent both upon the judgment of the practitioner and the reliability of techniques. Considerable uncertainty attaches to establishing whether something is wrong, what it is, what can be done and how effective the treatment actually is. Beyond the purely clinical choices about diagnosis and methods of treatment, even greater flexibility attaches to related decisions (e.g. length of stay in hospital) and paramedical ancillary services (e.g. amount of nursing, quality of hospital food, type of aftercare).

Were it in truth the case that an individual's condition were unambiguously and completely identifiable, that the course of treatment were likewise unambiguous, that it were unambiguously successful to a known extent and that every 'need', thus determined, should be fully met, then there would be no problem of choice for society. Clearly, none of these things is true.

The irreversibility of much medical treatment emphasises the importance of initially making the right choices and, so far as possible, of not committing oneself irrevocably to a course of action before it is absolutely necessary to do so. A more interesting aspect of the irreversability argument, however, which has not been much discussed, is that the treatment itself *changes* the patient. Similarly, much education is directed specifically towards *changing* an individual – his views, his modes of thought, his knowledge and his values. The effect of this process of consumption is, first to introduce a new kind of uncertainty – for the individual, who is *himself* an input in the process of production of some important social services, becomes at least in part a different person after the process has taken place. Moreover, the decision to 'change' the person is a conscious one on at least some person's part, if not the individual's own part (as is sometimes the case with medical treatment).

It would evidently be a very difficult thing to place a value on this change in a person – especially if it is a change in his values that may take place. On the one hand, many individuals do reveal the personal value they place upon education which has this effect, for they sacrifice other things they value in order to acquire the education. On the other hand, there is no obvious way in which society *in general* can place any explicit value upon it. It is not sufficient, for example, to state that individuals *ought* to have their values changed in particular ways partly because this may imply ignoring whether or not the individuals in question wish their values to be changed and partly because there exists no general consensus in society at large as to what constitutes 'good' ways of changing values and the importance of changing them. At one level, there may be a general consensus to treat, say, children's own values as unimportant. This we do in making education compulsory up to a certain level, partly in their interest (as we conceive it) and partly in ours – to turn them into responsible and sensitive citizens and to perpetuate our culture. At another level, we do not agree about the value of changing a person beyond certain elemental changes – such as making him more literate, nor are most of us prepared to ignore the preferences of adults with the consequence that, though they may be encouraged, they are not compelled, to do things they may rather not.

Fortunately, our society is still sufficiently liberal for these matters *not* to be of major concern in social policy. Indeed, it might be said to form a principle of current social policy that the extremely important questions involving changes in people's perception, values and humanity are still largely left to those individuals, to teachers, doctors, parents and so on. Social policy is left with ensuring, so far as possible, that a diversity of opportunities is available to suit the values of different individuals and cultures within the broader society.

In this chapter we have endeavoured to show that the social services are not, in any relevant sense, so 'different' from other goods and services, that important policy issues cannot be examined using the economic framework. This is not, of course, to say that they are not important – they are certainly more important than many other goods and services. Many people would say, and probably rightly, that the kind and extent of a society's social policy is an indicator of the quality of life in that society. Economics (but not, of course, economics alone) is supposed to help us to make the quality of life ever better, by focussing on the issues that have to be decided, the priorities settled and assessing the means to achieve the desired end. Specifically, the Pareto criterion for an improvement in social welfare is designed precisely to give an *unambiguous* indicator of improvements in the quality of life. It is also designed to preclude the opportunity of imposing one's own specific set of values upon either one's analysis or one's assessments. One is compelled to be democratic in allowing other people's values in on the act.

NOTES

1. A persistent critic is Peter Self. See 'Nonsense on Stilts: The Futility of Roskill', *New Society*, 2 July, 1970.
2. One approach, which effectively *defines* social services as being 'different' is the 'social rights' or 'welfare rights' approach used by some students of social policy and many social administrators. As we have seen in chapter 1, the arbitrariness of this approach is inconsistent with the Paretian method of analysis, for it permits statements such as 'I (Mr A) think Mr B ought to have a right to X and, moreover, Mr C ought to pay for it.' The actual preferences of B and C need not enter the picture at all. We argued in chapter 1 that while such utterances are perfectly legitimate statements of a personal viewpoint, they are unsatisfactory as the basis for a social science approach to social policy. However, our Paretian approach will include whatever benefit Mr A gets from transfers between C and B implied by giving Mr B some particular right. Beyond that, no matter how noble Mr A's motives are in one's opinion, we do not go. The 'welfare rights' approach accordingly finds little (academic) sympathy in this book.

FURTHER READING

Nature of Education
A. P. Griffiths, 'A Deduction of Universities', In R. D. Archambault (Ed), *Philosophical Analysis and Education*, London, Routledge & Kegan Paul, 1965, pp. 187–207.
J. H. Newman, *On the Scope and Nature of University Education*, London, Dent, 1915.
R. S. Peters, 'Education as Initiation' in Archambault, *op. cit.*, pp. 87–111.
P. H. Hirst and R. S. Peters, *The Logic of Education*, London, Routledge and Kegan Paul, 1970.

Meaning of health
H. E. Sigerist, *Medicine and Human Welfare*, New Haven, Yale U.P., 1941.
World Heath Organisation, *Constitution of the World Health Organization*, Annex 1, *The first ten years of the WHO*, Geneva, 1958.

Whether blood is an economic good
M. H. Cooper and A. J. Culyer, *The Price of Blood,* London, IEA, 1968.
M. H. Cooper and A. J. Culyer, 'The Economics of Giving', London, IEA, 1973.
R. M. Titmuss, *Choice and the 'Welfare State'*, London, Fabian Society, 1966, reprinted as ch. 12 in R. M. Titmuss, *Commitment to Welfare*, London, Allen and Unwin, 1968.
R. M. Titmuss, *The Gift Relationship*, London, Allen & Unwin, 1972.
This controversy is best read in its chronological order.

Whether health care is 'different'
A. J. Culyer, 'The Nature of the Commodity "Health Care" and its Efficient Allocation', *Oxford Economic Papers*, Vol. 23, 1971.

A. J. Culyer, 'Merit Goods and the Welfare Economics of Coercion', *Public Finance*, Vol. 26, 1972.

H. E. Klarman, *The Economics of Health*, New York and London, Columbia UP, 1965.

D. S. Lees, *Health Through Choice*, London, IEA, 1961.

R. M. Titmuss, 'Ethics and Economics of Medical Care', *Medical Care*, Vol. 1, 1963, reprinted in *Commitment to Welfare, op. cit.* chapter 21.

R. M. Titmuss, 'Choice and the Welfare State', *loc. cit.*

Office of Health Economics, *Prospects in Health*, London, OHE, 1971.

7 Institutions and Reforms

Public goods and public production

In this chapter we come closest to treading on the preserve of political science. We shall also be trying to search for answers that many students of social policy, drawing immediately upon their personal predilections, will – in their various ways – take for granted. Thus we ask, following the arguments of the last chapter, whether the social services are 'different' in such a way as to warrant, on grounds drawn from social science, government provision. We ask whether government provision is to be preferred to government financing. We investigate the fundamental reasons why government activity *in general* is warranted and, related to this, why it is and how it is that the behaviour of government and the behaviour of those who operate government institutions is different from the behaviour of individuals in general and of those who operate private institutions. By relating the answers to these questions to the objectives of social policy we shall then be able to make a consistent analytical critique of some of the controversies concerning current institutional arrangements and indicate a proper basis upon which students of social policy should seek answers to these weighty questions.

The traditional view has it that public goods will be produced at inefficient levels in the private sector, therefore they should be produced – or at least financed – by government. There are three elements in the argument: first, that private markets have an inherent inability to produce public goods efficiently; second, that government has characteristics which enable it to produce efficiently; third, that some meaningful distinction can be drawn between 'private' and 'public' sectors on *a priori* grounds (i.e. in terms of what they ought to be doing respectively rather than counting up what each actually does). We begin by showing that the usual form of the traditional argument has some severe shortcomings and then seek to establish a correct rationale for government intervention.

Free Riders

The standard argument for why the market 'fails' is that the nature of public good production is that it provides each potential consumer or client with an incentive (a) not to pay for the service and (b) to understate his own demand leaving it to others to provide it. In each case the individual would get a 'free ride' and since everyone faces the same opportunity of 'getting something for nothing'. Too little of the good will be produced — indeed none will be produced at all! Recalling the example of the village coach trip from chapter 2, the first incentive amounts to the villagers colluding to arrange the trip and then failing to pay the tour operator and the second amounts to each individual pretending he does not value the trip at all, leaving it to the rest of the village to provide it.

The incentive not to pay for the trip, however, is unrelated to the question of *public* goods but concerns the general enforceability of any contract between the providers of a service and demanders where delivery of the service and payment do not take place at *precisely* the same moment in time. If the market fails here it is because the law, custom, etiquette or moral sanctions do not enforce contracts. The problem exists whether the contract is between private individuals, between individuals and government or between governments. The answer lies plainly in the rule of law, the development of interpersonal agreements such as downpayments which make contract breaking unprofitable, and in the development of a moral climate in which obligations are recognised and honoured.

The second incentive is more subtle. The optimal length of a coach trip is determined by its marginal cost and by the sum of marginal valuations across the whole community. If one, some or all members of the community hide their true MV's, clearly a suboptimal length of trip will result. But why should individuals 'free ride' when its inevitable consequence is that they will each lose from such activity? Even if, in the village community, there existed one or two persons who valued the tour so much that they were prepared to pay for *some* trip regardless of what others did, free riders would still lose by virtue of the fact that, if the planned trip were too short according to the Pareto criterion, their own marginal valuations would exceed some potentially agreeable share of the marginal cost of extending the trip. There would be *some* distribution of marginal cost among 'free riders' such that each would benefit from a longer trip. Clearly, each person has an incentive to come to some agreement with his fellow villagers whereby these gains can be realised. In coming to this agreement, each may try to hide his own *MV* in order to increase his bargaining power and incur a smaller financing cost, but sooner or later the trip has to take place. If by that time agreement has not been reached such that the optimal trip is being provided then the 'free riders' will be 'punished' (along with everyone else) by the provision of a sub-optimal trip.

The true incentives in each case therefore work in favour of, not against, the provision of an optimal trip. In the first case it is in everyone's long term interest to have the rule of law or to invent ways of overcoming the possibility of contract abrogation. In the second case, while individuals may haggle over terms, *in the end* it pays them to reach an optimal agreement.

But, it may be objected, is not all this bargaining wasteful? Would it not be more efficient for the government, the local authority, etc., to impose the ideal solution thereby saving all this trouble — perhaps the resources saved from bargaining could be devoted to a longer outing for the children? If bargainers expected to gain from the imposition of ideal terms by a third party we should expect them to seek their services. People would voluntarily seek out the agency of such a third party. But where would the outside agent get the knowledge required to impose the ideal solution? In the real world, only individuals know their true *MV*'s. If they agree to reduce bargaining costs by inviting an 'imposed' choice from outside they will do so only if, in their experience, the third party can be trusted to act *on their behalf* and they will normally seek powers of control over him. In reality, the preferred solution will not be an *imposed* one at all but a *delegated* one.

Government and social contract

The real world is full of such mechanisms for delegated decisions. The profusion of clubs, charities and other private collective organisations bears witness to the variety of ways in which individuals, *in the private sector*, voluntarily seek to produce efficient outcomes in the production of public goods. Government, interpreted generally as the ultimate coercive force in a society, is neither necessary nor is it implied by any of the foregoing considerations. *Democratic government*, as a kind of club, however *is* so implied. The delegation of collective decisions to a government over which citizens have some control, is an extension of the general interest each has in getting public goods efficiently produced and is, indeed, the appropriate agent where the affected community is the whole community under the jurisdiction of a government. There is a general presumption that collective interests of a village — such as the children's tour — are most efficiently run by a local collectivity (e.g. the local Church, the Parish Council, the British Legion)[1]. Collective interests of a whole country — such as law and order, the health and education of the nation — are plausibly most efficiently implemented by a national collectivity (i.e. the central government). Clearly, depending on the nature and scope of the public good in question, there is a large variety of collective institutions that will be appropriate for different decisions. In every case, the delegation of decision making can be seen as a rational response of private individuals to the high costs of reaching agreements on every single issue involving public goods. In short, they are 'market type' reactions.

The usual dichotomy between 'the market' and 'the state' is misleading, implying either a dominant state which imposes its will regardless of the wishes of the community (which cannot be evaluated by our normative theoretical apparatus and is certainly not justified by it) or else some omniscient organisation, composed of superhumans, capable somehow of identifying community interests independently of their expression by the community (which is a myth). A preferable distinction is between individual and collective decision making — the latter being appropriate where it is in individuals' interests to delegate decisions. But to the extent that government power is wielded arbitrarily, or in the interests of a cabalistic few (whether they be saints or sinners) then the intervention of government in the decision making process can have no basis in economics.

It is curious that, despite the fact that much of economic theory has been founded on a narrow conception of self-interest (narrower than that adopted in this book), many students of the economics of social or public policy have failed to note that if the market 'fails' then it must contain within itself its own self-correcting procedures. To jump from the observation of market failure to the assertion that the government can 'do things better' is, however, a hopeless *non sequitur*. Sometimes it may. Sometimes it may not, for collective allocation can also, as we saw in chapter 2, 'fail'. Nevertheless, government intervention can be in the social interest. We must now examine more closely the differences that exist between decision makers acting on their own behalf and those acting on the behalf of others. The nature of these differences provides the fundamental rationale for some of the economic analysis of social policy to follow in the rest of Part IV. Moreover, since the foregoing arguments imply only that collective *financing* may be one way out of an efficient set of ways of making decisions we also seek to establish whether there may be additional roles for government to play – for example, not only financing but *producing* services (In our example the village *hired* the bus. It did not set up its own bus company.)

Governmental behaviour and its control

It is sometimes naively supposed that the individuals with executive and administrative functions in government are 'different' from such individuals as, say, consumers or businessmen, and for some this is a sufficient reason for transferring decision-making from one sector to another. This view cannot, however, be realistically sustained. Their behaviour may certainly be different, depending upon the function they perform but economics asserts that their behavior is different not because they are different *kinds* of people but because the *nature of the constraints* upon their behaviour is different. In particular, the costs of different choices will vary according to the constraints which govern those choices. The behaviour of persons working in a profit-seeking business, a non-profit charity, a public utility, a government department or a local authority will differ not because they are essentially different kinds of people but because the constraints on their behaviour differ.

What are these constraints? At the broadest level they consist of the range of rights owned by an individual in resources. They include not only the monetary wealth at his disposal (whether his or someone else's) and his time, but all other rights he possesses – rights to use, in specified ways, resources such as the air, rivers, office space, manpower, public parks *etc., ad inf.* Fortunately, it is not necessary to identify and measure the total constraint on behaviour for our purposes. It is sufficient to assume that there exists *some limit* to a person's rights (a realistic enough assumption); we then can investigate the consequences of changing the constraints — the rights structure — by using the fundamental implication of economic theory outlined in chapter 2: the higher the personal cost of obtaining any entity or engaging in any activity, the less will be acquired or engaged in during any period of time. The behaviour of a businessman who has effluent to dispose of will be different if the river by his factory is owned by someone else than if it is publicly owned or owned by no one (How?). The behaviour of a businessman working on his own account will differ from that of a similar businessman responsible to shareholders (How?). The behaviour of a businessman who can pay whatever wages he likes will be different from that of the businessman who must pay a minimum wage (How?). For our present purposes, however, the important distinction is between individuals who make decisions in the public or government sector, whatever activities may be included in it, and those who make similar decisions in the private sector.

Profit and non-profit motivation

An evidently frequent difference between organisations in the public and private sectors is that usually (though not invariably) the former are non-profit and the latter (again not invariably) are for-profit. This distinction is of great important in social policy. The question therefore is: why is it that public ownership suppresses the profit motive so effectively? The answer lies in two key constraining elements to the rights of the owners: non-transferability of ownership and non-convertability of revenues.

Transferability of ownership means that the *consequences* of one's ownership can be concentrated upon individuals. In a community of 1,000 with 10 separate organisations that are publicly owned but are nevertheless supposed to make profits (we assume), each individual has a 1/1,000th share in each organisation. The consequences of his actions to improve the profitability of any organisation will be that he 'gets' 1/1,000th part of the additional profit with the other 999/1,000ths going to the other 999 members of the community. Only if the others behave as he does in each organisation will he receive the full benefit of his product. By contrast, if ownership could be transferred, each person might have a 1/100th share of *each* organisation (still with 'equal' distribution of rights) and the benefits of an individual's actions would depend more upon *his own* activity and less upon the activity of others.

Divide each organisation into 100 smaller organisations so that each can have sole ownership and cost-benefit consequences of each individual's activity will be entirely concentrated upon that individual. If the objective was, as we assumed, to make profits, it is perfectly obvious that the ability to transfer and concentrate ownership will be more conducive to profit making — it only needs one person in the community who wants more wealth (and will work for it) for it to be worth his while to buy other people's ownership shares and more effectively concentrate the rewards of his own activity upon himself (also the consequences of his own mistakes) thereby relying less upon the wealth-seeking motivation of others to get his rewards and being less dependent upon their foolish choices. In a more realistic world where individuals have different managerial capabilities, different technical knowledge, different attitudes to risk and so on, the transferability of ownership will tend to be even more productive of profits. Conversely, non-transferability, or public ownership, will be relatively more effective in emasculating the profit-motive. This first argument thus shows why, even if publicly owned organisations are supposed to be every bit as profitable as privately owned organisations, they will tend in practice not to be so profitable, because the costs of not making profits are lower for each individual while the benefits of making more profits are less.

Even, however, if profits are not the objective, the cost-benefit consequences of decisions are less fully thrust upon owners which means that they will have less incentive to control closely the behaviour of the management of publicly-owned organisations. The absence of this incentive, or its weakening, means that other incentives are needed to replace those that are absent. In social policy, it is frequently the case that profit seeking leads to a neglect of some important social costs and benefits of the activities of an organisation. Public ownership is one important method of emasculating the incentive to make profits but, at the same time, if the incentive to operate in the social interest, more widely construed, is not also to be emasculated, additional constraints on the behaviour of management are required. The techniques of subsequent chapters in Part IV, such as output budgeting and cost-benefit analysis, are intended to provide precisely such a decision-making environment.

Non-transferability of ownership, while not unique to public ownership, is for our purposes its most important characteristic. Having thus weakened the profit motive it is a short step to prohibiting it *effectively* in social policy organisations. This done, the second element constraining the rights of public decision makers comes to the fore: non-convertability.

Non-convertability means that whatever revenues are brought into the organisation through its activity cannot be converted by the owners into personal wealth and is a constraint on owners of all non-profit organisations, whether publicly or privately owned. The inability of owners to take wealth out of the non-profit organisation means that other owners, customers, patrons and suppliers of funds (whether subscribers or taxpayers) are protected against the – possibly self-seeking – behaviour of any individual owner. But this constraint on owners implies that they will tend to seek other ways of increasing their wealth at the expense of the organisation. If they cannot do it by paying themselves agreed dividends or by selling their ownership there exist other, less open methods. An owner who happened to be a manager, for example, could pay himself (and his fellow managers) relatively high salaries; they could use luxury office accommodation; they could employ larger staffs than are strictly necessary. There are constraints on the extent to which these sources of wealth can be tapped, of course. For example, salaries cannot be 'unreasonably' high (i.e. so high as to be noticeably high) or the executive will be fired. But not all such activities can be easily monitored. For example, instead of paying themselves higher salaries, inadvertent profits could be invested in safe securities thus ensuring the management a more secure and long-lived salary – which is equivalent to a higher salary. Why should the not-for-profit form of organisation be chosen in view of these potential dangers? The reason is that whatever profits the organisation earns should be devoted *not* to the wealth of owners but to the well-being of those for whose benefit the non-profit organisation has been formed. It is a guarantee to clients and, more important, to the suppliers of funds, that the objectives of the organisation will not be changed at an individual owner's discretion. Hospitals, for example, are almost universally non-profit organisations and in Britain they are publicly owned as well. This guarantees that the costs and benefits of hospitals can be allocated in ways that are different from profit organisations. To be sure, the owners of a profit organisation could devote their profits to charitable purposes *at their discretion,* but if the discretion of a few individuals is thought to be unreliable, the non-profit form of organisation guarantees that the costs to manager-owners of taking out profits are raised. Moreover, if the institutions in question are publicly owned by the whole community, the policies of these institutions can be designed to serve the wishes of the whole community – for example to internalise community externalities.

Privately owned non-profit institutions tend to be formed to internalise externalities felt by the owners. Thus, free schools for certain types of children are or have been observed (e.g. for sons, sons of clergymen, daughters, Roman Catholic children, the very poor). Similarly, charitable hospitals have been operated, serving particular areas, illnesses or classes of patient. More generally felt externalities, however, are more effectively internalised by *publicly owned* non-profit institutions which discriminate among their clients on a less narrow and specific basis. Nevertheless, they will still have to discriminate (hospitals and universities, for example, have substantial excess demands for their services from clients legally eligible to receive them). The cost-benefit consequences of ownership rights on management are not such as to guarantee that they will operate *automatically* in accordance with the objectives of the organisation. Again, additional constraints will have to be supplied if they are to fulfil their functions properly (which patients should be assigned to hospital waiting lists and how long should they have, on average, to wait? Which of the many qualified students should be admitted to university? Would you trust doctors and university teachers to exercise their own discretion?).

Equality and the ownership of rights

Throughout this discussion we have not mentioned what, for many, is the major reason for state intervention through public ownership: to reduce inequalities in the ownership of wealth (and, thence, political power and influence). The reason for this is twofold. In the first place we have already seen that non-voluntary wealth redistribution (if that is how public ownership is to come into being) cannot be evaluated in the economic scheme we have set ourselves – it necessarily involves one set of members of the community imposing their values upon another. If erstwhile private owners are fully compensated, however, no effective redistribution takes place. Secondly, we have already seen that although public ownership does imply the 'equal' ownership of property by citizens, the rights in that property are not the same as the rights they have in private property – for example, the right to transfer ownership. Equality in ownership rights does not necessarily require public ownership, moreover, as we have seen in the illustrative example above, for rights to various types of private property may be distributed in a variety of ways. The view that 'property is theft' derives not from the nature of private property itself but from some historical point in time at which private rights were reassigned − perhaps some people had their property rights expropriated in what they thought was an unjust way (the Enclosure Movement is one example and the history of the British Empire provides endless examples of expropriated rights). There may well indeed be theft in a literal sense but this refers to the *allocation* of private rights, not to their *existence*.

What a system of transferable private property rights *does* imply, however, is that the rights will tend to become distributed towards those who value them most or can increase their exchange value most. For example, the most able managers will tend to acquire more rights over wealth than the less able; people who enjoy taking risks will, if they take risks successfully, collect more wealth than people who dislike taking risks. Exchangeable private property enables individuals to specialise in the kind of wealth management in which they have a comparative advantage. Thus, private property systems require a more or less continuous redistribution of rights of wealth if egalitarian objectives are to be pursued especially if the starting point is one in which there is already an unequal distribution of ownership rights. The need for this is absent with public ownership. Instead, one needs stringent controls over the stewards of publicly owned wealth and guidelines to indicate how best they might deploy publicly owned wealth in the social interest.

Whether, on balance, the constraints on the behaviour of private decision makers are more effective in promoting socially desired behaviour than the constraints on the behaviour of public decision makers is a moot point. Most readers will have a prejudice about it (and for many it will tie up closely with the view they take about 'freedom' and 'equality'). As professionals, however, the best view we can take is probably that in some circumstances the one method is preferred and in others the other. In addition one should be seeking continuously to find new ways of so altering the environment that constrains behaviour that decisions actually reached accord more fully with the social interest. In the public sector, with which this part of the book is concerned, some of these new ways include cost-benefit analysis and output budgeting. In the private sector, methods include the imposition of taxes and subsidies or reassigning − or assigning − private property rights, as we shall see when we deal with the problem of pollution (chapter 11). The political analogues to taxes and subsidies and reallocation of rights concern reforms of the democratic political system, for example to help voters more efficiently to express their wishes, to make politicians respond more efficiently to their wishes or to reduce the extent of 'majority tyranny'. Reluctantly, we shall have to draw back from an investigation of the economics of politics in this sense though, for the serious student of social policy, the insights to be gained from such a study are a rich diet – one not to be left unsampled.

Why organise social services through the state?

Before moving on to consider the use in social policy of some of these techniques for improving government choices some unfinished business remains from the preceding chapter. It was there argued that the social services are not different in the important sense that they are 'beyond', or cannot be usefully discussed in the context of, economic appraisal. They do not have any distinguishing characteristics that are intrinsically theirs and that differentiate their problems from other problems that are indisputably economic. The question we now take up, which has much exercised the ideologists of social policy, is whether there is any common element in what are regarded as the social services such that a particular institutional form of organisation is implied. It will be quite clear from preceding analysis that there are elements in all of the social services that require *collective* action if the economic problems of social policy are to be efficiently resolved because they all have, to a greater or lesser extent, degrees of publicness and produce identifiable (if hard to measure) external effects. Should the collective agency, however, be the government or a private one? In short, do the social services have technical characteristics that may assist us in resolving the 'market versus the state' debate? Again we return to the field of health – more of a *battle*field in this regard as the diligent student of the literature will have discovered. To dramatise the problem we examine the assertion that the British National Health Service is 'the best in the world' and compare the principle institutional features of the NHS with the principal institutional features of a privately organised market for health care.

Let us postulate the three characteristics which best describe the institutional setting of the NHS to be:

(a)   public ownership of all health care agencies
(b)   no user-prices
(c)   financing out of general taxation

None of these is a perfectly true representation, for private practice exists, some charges are applied and there is an ear-marked tax. Nevertheless, these three features describe the institutional form of the NHS as it 'ought to be', they are three features whose erosion would be strongly resisted by those who argue that the NHS type of organisation of health care is intrinsically better than any other. The market, we suppose, is likewise characterised by

(a)   absence of monopoly
(b)   efficient insurance as in chapter 2

In short we wish to compare, in the first instance, the 'ideal' NHS with the 'ideal' market.

Assume now a community of two persons (sufficiently general for us to derive some generalisations that would not be invalidated by a model containing more). A is a poor man (or myopic, foolhardy, over-optimistic); B is a rich man (or thoughtful for his future, prudent, pessimistic). In all other respects we assume them to be the same — especially as regards the state of their health — save one. This is that Mr. B is a generous person for whom the welfare of Mr. A is of concern.

Under circumstances where health care is needed the optimal amounts that should be received by A and B are such that

$$MSV^A = MSV^B = MSC$$

or

$$MV^A + MV_A{}^B = MV^B = MC$$

assuming that there are no external effects in the production of health care (i.e. $MSC = MC$). Figure 7.1 is an extension of Figure 2.1 and describes pictorially the conditions for optimal allocation. $MV^A + MV_A{}^B$ is the *vertical* sum of the two persons' valuation of care *for A*; MV^B is the social valuation of B's health care; $x^A + x^B$ is the horizontal sum of MV^A and MV^B and $x^{A*} + x^B$ is the horizontal sum of the *social* valuation curves.

If the private market failed to allow for the externality then only X_1 health care would be available for both individuals when they required it of which B would take $x_1{}^B$ and A, $x_1{}^A$. A would clearly receive too little care (in B's compassionate view) and the total amount of health care produced would be too small, for the ideal would be X_p with A receiving $x_p{}^A$. Even though we cannot, in the real world, observe all the points on these *MV* curves (which points *can* be observed?) we can nevertheless definitely infer that too little will be produced. If the 'ideal' NHS satisfied *all* wants at zero price, too much health care would *probably* be provided (at the expense of education, pensions, housing, etc.) — X_2 in total of which A would receive $x_2{}^A$ and B, $x_2{}^B$.[2] Certainly Mr. B would receive too much. More realistically, the NHS is, however, not going to produce X_2 health care because either Mr. A or Mr. B or both will press for lower taxation since, at X_2, the *MSV* of health care is zero while its *MSC* is positive. Whether they are able to adjust, through the political process, so that the amount available in total equals X_p is unlikely, though they will certainly be able to get it down below X_2. Whether, in practice, whatever is produced is so allocated between them such that *MSV*'s are equal depends upon the allocation procedures of health care providing agencies such as hospitals and general practices.

Fig. 7.1

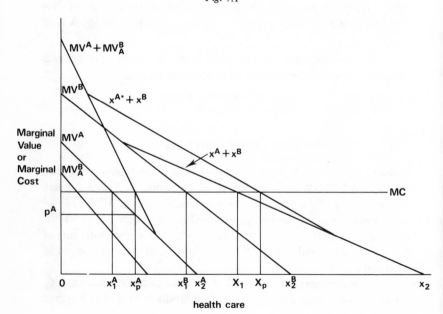

Likewise whether health care agencies in the private market produce enough in total depends upon how well B-individuals can organise 'charities' to subsidise health care for the A's; and whether the distribution between A's and B's is correct depends upon the allocation procedures of the charitable agencies.

If charges were to be used they would normally have to vary according to the type of patient being treated. In Figure 7.1, A should pay a (marginal) price of PA^3 and B should pay the full price equal to MC. In a more realistic world of many A's and B's it may be possible to identify fairly homogeneous classes of patient with similar MV^A's creating similar external effects (old soldiers may be an example) but otherwise a variable price would need to be charged in each individual case. Price discrimination of this type does occur in private markets for health care but whether it reflects an attempt of the medical profession to internalise externalities that are *generally* felt in society or to maximise their own wealth is not clear.

If zero prices are charged, additional rationing criteria have to be employed such as the medical urgency of the case. The advantage that the non-profit institutions of the NHS have over the non-profit institutions of the market-place is that if the nature of the externality is such that it is *community wide* and *community generated* and not associated only with specific patients (e.g. paupers, old soldiers, sons of clergymen, retired gentlewomen, cancer patients, maternity cases) who may be the concern of particular sections of society, it is easier, in principle, to exercise social control through a publicly-owned and centrally administered system through which common medical and social values can be identified and implemented.

Ardent NHS supporters frequently point to the 'chaos' of market provision. They bewail, for example, the pre-NHS distribution of hospital resources because it was a response to geographically local externalities while they themselves take a more societal view. The relevant question is not, however, what externality is experienced by one or another set of individuals but which form of the externality best represents the externalities experienced by the *whole community*. In Britain, in the absence of evidence to the contrary, it would seem that a community-experienced and community-generated externality does exist (though it certainly did not exist for most of the nineteenth century) implying that the NHS framework is more suitable, in principle, for internalising it.

For many reasons however, mostly deriving from the 'imperfections' of political and administrative processes analogous to market 'imperfections', there has been little systematic thinking about what the total allocation to the health sector should be and how it should be allocated among the competing claimants. It is pleasant to be able to record that economists have been among the pioneers in devising allocation devices in the absence of prices – how long should hospital waiting lists be; how long should patients remain on them; which patients; which treatments should be provided; what factors should be taken account of in determining lengths of stay; how are hospital costs related to inpatient and outpatient case-mixes; to mixtures of patient-care and doctor/nurse training; how can the output of general practitioners, dentists, medical social workers or hospitals be measured and monitored; how can overall control be most effectively exercised? In the more detailed application of economic techniques the reader is referred to the Further Reading for this chapter. The broader issues of efficiency, control and methods of financing are explored, however, in the following chapters.

To summarise the principal conclusions so far: neither the existence of externalities nor public goods justifies government production or financing of social services, though if the nature of the externality is such that it is both experienced by the whole community and generated by non-specific sectors of the community then both government collective provision and a fairly universal provision is the likely outcome – a *prima facie* desirable outcome – of individual wants. The corollary is that there is no automaticity in getting social wants translated into social action unless the behavioural environment in which the administrators and operators of social services work is specifically designed to promote socially desired behaviour. The economic techniques applicable to publicly-owned non-profit organisations are the same, in principle, as those applicable to the private non-profit organisations though in what is to come in Part IV, given the heavy public commitment in social policy in Britain, we shall concentrate exclusively upon the public sector. Choice between institutions – whether private or public – thus depends upon the nature of the externality, not the nature of the social service produced, and upon the effectiveness with which social control can be exercised over those who formulate and carry out policy.[4]

Most readers will be under no illusions about the efficiency of democratic institutions in improving social welfare. It may be the best form of government most can imagine but there is some hope that, as

more thought goes into devising better voting systems and as technology improves,[5] democratic government will undergo considerable
evolution and, in the process, become both more democratic and
participatory. We have, however, already revealed part of the hand that
is to be played in Part IV where methods of controlling collective
decisionmakers by output budgeting, cost-benefit analysis and related
techniques are to be discussed in the context of social policy.

Cost-benefit, cost-effectiveness, and output budgeting are essentially
ways of presenting information. They do not, as such, impel governments or government departments to act in the social interest. The
greater the degree of publicity associated with the techniques, however,
the more embarrassing it is for governments, officials and politicians,
not to act in the potentially better ways suggested by the information.
It is not, therefore, surprising that governments are reluctant to reveal
all the information used as the basis of a decision or plan. But even if
they did, the basis itself provides only a minor incentive for efficiency.
Its proper use is far too heavily dependent at the moment upon the
public-spiritedness of officials and politicians and upon the extent to
which they believe that they can make a career, or prolong their
political power, by advocating efficiency. Democracy is not so perfect
that it forces them to be socially efficient or socially just. While the
economic techniques are a step in the right direction one must not be
over sanguine about the extent to which it is in the private interest of
public decision takers to use them. Much further work remains to be
done in developing methods of ensuring a closer relationship between
official responses to their personal interests and appropriate public
policies.

Our final task in this chapter will be to indicate that there exists, in
some circumstances, an alternative to collective action where mere
individual action persistently fails to secure socially desired results.

Alternatives to collective action?

Much 'market failure' results in the creation of harmful external effects
simply because ownership rights have not been established in physical
things. Remember, no-one owns 'things', they own rights – if they have
any at all – in ways to use things. One does not, for example, usually
own the right to use one's property to destroy other people's property
physically. In America, forests were often destroyed because no-one

had rights in living trees — only in lumber. To establish these rights, forests were frequently destroyed and the cause of conservation may irrevocably have been harmed. No one bewails the disappearance of domestic cattle — they are not disappearing because they are owned — but the North American bison did not have the fortune to be owned by anyone. Nor did the dodo!

It is not coincidence that many of the most serious threats to our environment, a major problem for social policy, take place in 'property' that no-one owns or that is common property (i.e. owned and used in common). One is assailed by noise because property rights in the use of the air for transmitting sound waves are not usually established. One is assailed by smells and ugly sights (or the removal of beautiful sights) for much the same reason. Garbage and poisonous filth is poured out into commonly owned property, or non-owned property, at such a rate today that it is recognised that a social 'problem' now exists.

One method of solving the problem would be for the government to take over specific ownership of such property and to use cost-benefit type analysis to establish what the optimal rate of destruction of the environment should be by weighing the benefits of reduced environmental hazard against the costs in, say, lost production and lower money wealth. Many of the key variables required to make such an analysis more than merely an enumeration of points to consider — for example, the social value placed upon reduced noise from jet aircraft — are enormously hard, if not impossible, to calculate. The establishment of property rights where they do not exist and where external effects are the likely consequence[6] is a method that can sometimes obviate the need for immensely complex, costly and possibly inconclusive cost-benefit calculations. In chapter 11 we shall investigate two types of solution: one where property rights are established but cannot be negotiated (e.g. zoning laws) and the other where rights are assigned and are negotiable. The interface between law and economics is one of the most promising developments in social policy. In the chapters immediately following, however, we concentrate on the interface between economics and government administration.

NOTES

1. It is most unlikely that the citizens of Bradford would be prepared to pay for an outing for the children of Barmby Moor – though (perhaps because!) they are both in Yorkshire. Unfortunately, in a collectivity which included Bradford and Barmby Moor, Bradford would outvote Barmby many times over.
2. Why is the 'probably' there?
3. He need not pay this subsidised price for *all* 'units' of health care consumed (See the article by M. V. Pauly in Further Reading).
4. Note that the profit-maximising environment supplied by a competitive capital market (where ownership can be transferred cheaply) is one form of social control of managers and is appropriate where profit-maximising leads to socially desirable results – as it frequently does (especially where property rights are fully defined and are exchangeable).
5. The use of computers and mechanised voting procedures is in its infancy at present. In the not too distant future people may vote more frequently, on more specific issues, from their own homes!
6. An externality is *invariably* the result of absence of defined property rights but undefined property rights do *not* invariably result in externalities. Why?

FURTHER READING

On the structure of decision-making with public goods or externalities
W. Baumol, *Welfare Economics and the Theory of the State*, Cambridge Mass, Harvard UP, 1952.
J. M. Buchanan, 'Politics, Policy and Pigovian Margins', *Economica*, No. 29, 1962.
R. H. Coase, 'The Problem of Social Cost,' *Journal of Law and Economics*, Vol. 3, 1960.
H. Demsetz, 'Information and Efficiency: Another Viewpoint', *Journal of Law and Economics*, Vol. 12, 1969.
H. Demsetz, 'The Private Production of Public Goods', *Journal of Law and Economics*, Vol. 13, 1970.

On property rights and delegated decision making
A. A. Alchian, 'Some Economics of Property', *Il Politico*, December 1965. Easily the best, if rather inaccessible, basic – and pioneering – survey of the problem.
A. A. Alchian and R. A. Kessel, 'Competition, Monopoly and the Pursuit of Money', in *Aspects of Labor Economics,* Princeton, NBER, 1962. An application of the property right approach to business firms.
A. J. Culyer, 'A Utility-Maximising View of Universities', *Scottish Journal of Political Economy*, Vol. 17, 1970. The analysis applied to universities.
A. J. Culyer, 'On the Relative Efficiency of the National Health Service', *Kyklos*, Vol. 25, 1972. On the *a priori* efficiency of different institutional organisations for health care.
S. N. Cheung, 'Transaction Costs, Risk Aversion and the Choice of Contractual Arrangements', *Journal of Law and Economics*, Vol. 12, 1969.

T. D. Crocker, 'Externalities, Property Rights and Transactions Costs: An Empirical Study', *Journal of Law and Economics*, Vol. 14, 1971.

M. S. Feldstein, *Economic Analysis for Health Service Efficiency*, Amsterdam, North-Holland, 1967. Contains a behavioural model designed to predict hospital administrative reactions to changes in bed availability.

P. Jacobs, *Economic Theories of Hospitals*, unpublished D.Phil. dissertation, University of York, England, 1973. A comprehensive survey of existing theories with a more general theory of its own.

R. N. McKean, 'Property Rights within Government, and Devices to Increase Governmental Efficiency,' *Southern Economic Journal*, Vol. 39, 1972.

J. P. Newhouse, 'Towards a Theory of Non-profit Institutions: An Economic Model of a Hospital', *American Economic Review*, Vol. 60, 1970. Another non-profit theory of hospitals.

W. A. Niskanen, *Bureaucracy and Representative Government*, Chicago, 1971. A perceptive and instructive book by an economist with much experience of collective and delegated decisions.

O. E. Williamson, *The Economics of Discretionary Behaviour*, Englewood-Cliffs, Prentice-Hall, 1964. A classic development of non-profit maximising theory in the context of business firms.

On the nature of the externality and optimal price subsidies

A. J. Culyer, 'Medical Care and the Economics of Giving', *Economica*, No. 1971. Takes the view that the externality derives from the reaction of generous members of society to the plight of others.

C. M. Lindsay, 'Medical Care and the Economics of Sharing', *Economica*, No. 36. Takes the view that the rich seek to reduce their own consumption (of health care) as well as increase that of the poor.

O. A. Davis and A. B. Whinston, 'Piecemeal Policy in the Theory of Second Best', *Review of Economic Studies*, Vol. 34, 1967.

M. V. Pauly, 'Efficiency in the Provision of Consumption Subsidies', *Kyklos*, Vol. 23, 1970. These two articles explore the nature of an optimal policy for pricing to internalise externalities.

PART IV

Social Policy and the Government

8 Economics and Planning in Social Policy

One of the major implications of chapters 2, 4 and 7 was that while qualitative analysis can establish some of the *general* characteristics of an optimal social policy (e.g. equal treatment for equal cases) and can underline the inconclusiveness of mere *a priorism* in deciding between overall methods of organisation, its major use is in forming the theoretical basis for quantitative analysis of specific social problems. This and the next two chapters investigate further how this analysis can be used.

Until very recently there was very little planning based upon either the criteria or the methods implied by Paretian economics. Moreover, there has been substantial resistance to their introduction – though fortunately the techniques are being increasingly used today throughout the public sector and including social policy. Some of the resistance was based upon naive criticism of the basic theory. A hoary old example of this form of criticism is neatly summed up by the assertion that individuals and families are not precision calculating machines making explicit choices like 'Let's take Junior out of school – it's only yielding 8 % and we can get 9% on fixing Grandma's broken thigh-bone'. As Harry Johnson has expostulated, one might as well object to the law of gravity on the basis of seeing a feather float more slowly to the ground than a lead bullet. Such misconceptions are encouraged by textbook writers who teach their readers that individuals 'consult their preferences' before acting – as though there is an imaginary hobgoblin sitting on everyone's left (or right) shoulder. It is true that economic analysis assumes a fundamental kind of rationality in human behaviour but the basic theory does not purport to describe the *thought processes* that individuals go through. It asserts that they behave *as if* they went through these processes. And they *do* behave this way, though they

147

may actually follow rules of thumb, convention or copy their neighbours, for the conventions are successful conventions precisely *because* they produce results that are rational. A stupid convention is likely to be observed primarily in the breach. Sons' prior claims to education over daughters is not a stupid convention.[1]

The second kind of objection derives from the vested interests of selfish individuals with policy influence. No one likes being told he has been doing things all wrong (or partly wrong) and everyone would like, other things being equal, the basis of his policy decisions (especially if he is a politician) to be too obscure to be closely scrutinised. The techniques of this and the next chapters are supposed first to make public decision makers behave *explicitly* in accordance with the rational calculus of maximising social welfare and second to expose their decision framework to the public gaze so that elements that are largely matters of judgement can be seen as such and, if inconsistent with the general view, can be corrected by criticism and discussion.

The systematic use of welfare economics in social policy has been preceded by two basic alternative approaches to planning. One we shall term the 'arbitrary planning' method and the other is 'GNP fixation'. The unflattering labels indicate, of course, our disapproval.

'Arbitrary' planning

'Arbitrary' planning can easily be illustrated by the common practices of manpower forecasting in education or health. Clearly, it is necessary to forecast future staffing 'needs' in education or health if only because of the length of time it takes to train professional people. Likewise, it is necessary to make budgetary allocations each year to, for example, Teaching Hospitals in the NHS in order that they are able to meet their local 'needs'.

The first element of arbitrariness consists in the selection (or non-selection) of an objective. Manpower 'needs' and hospital 'needs' are meaningful only in relation to a policy objective. Government spokesman, planners and (alas) many social scientists speak of 'needs' — whether of industry or society — as if they were self-evident. All too often the use of the word 'need' is a veil to special pleading – an attempt to lend a spurious objectivity to a purely personal point of view. For, 'society needs', one should read all too often, 'I think society should get'.

The most accessible recent exercise in manpower forecasting in the health field is the study published in 1966 by Deborah Paige and Kit Jones (see Further Reading), in which they diagnosed a current doctor shortage and predicted a worse shortage in 1980, implying a 'need' then for nearly 9,000 additional doctors over the number projected actually to be available in 1980.

As with all economic problems there is a 'demand' side and a 'supply' side. Future supplies are dependent upon population growth, current students in training, future professional salaries relative to others both at home and abroad, facilities available abroad, and expected changes in the non-pecuniary characteristics of professional work (job satisfaction). Future demand depends upon population projections again, the demand for the services in which manpower is an input and the degree of substitution expected or planned between manpower and other inputs, affecting the productivity of manpower.

Characteristically, the 'arbitrary' forecasters go astray in their population forecasts – a hazardous task for the long term (and for mistakes here they cannot really be held culpable: one has to make the best guess one can) – mistakes about net emigration movements, failure altogether to consider substitution possibilities and arbitrary specifications of the targets or objectives in terms of doctor/patient or teacher/pupil ratios. One of the chief snags of targets of this sort is that they do not measure *outputs* of the services in question but a ratio of inputs to clients (who are *themselves*, in a sense, also inputs). But these ratios as such do not enter the social welfare function. Entities in the social welfare function certainly include good education and good health but there is no general reason to suppose that these will vary now or in the future in direct proportion with the input ratios. Moreover, the input ratios may be altered in a variety of ways not only leaving the real output unchanged, but even increasing it! There is firm evidence that this is true of health, let alone education. Due to technical progress, furthermore, the ways in which the ratios can alter themselves change. These factors make the specification of arbitrary needs in the future, based on current ratios, current technology and assuming current ratios to be 'efficient', completely meaningless.

There is no doubt that we are saddled with a substantial ignorance about the future, about the present and about the technical relations among inputs and between inputs and outputs. Strong assumptions have, no doubt, to be made. The corollary, however, is that they should not be stronger than they have to be and that substantial areas of ignorance can be removed by careful research. In this chapter we shall illustrate some of the detailed work that has taken place into producing outputs efficiently both now and in the future. The question of output measurement will be tackled directly in Chapter 9.

GNP fixation

'GNP fixation' attempts to assess the global productivity of education and health resources, usually in terms of its contribution to a nation's growth rate. While having the virtue of a clearly defined objective − increasing GNP − this approach is a highly restricted one. For a start, the objective of social policy ought not, at least as far as the values of this book are concerned, to be the maximisation of the growth rate of GNP. Secondly, such global estimates are not as a rule of any great help in the actual planning of health or education programmes, though possible exceptions to these judgments exist in poor countries, where public health programmes can have a major impact on real incomes per capita and where increases in per capita wealth may have a higher weight in the social welfare function than in more highly developed societies. Denison, a great innovator of the GNP technique, has shown that a 25% reduction in time off work due to sickness would raise the 1960−80 US growth rate by .05 percentage points, a 10% reduction in mortality would raise the growth rate by .02 percentage points and an increase of one year in the average period at school would add .07 percentage points.

One of the difficulties with this approach is that different assumptions about the aggregate production function (the relation between all inputs, technical progress and GNP) can have drastic effects upon the contributions that health and education are alleged to make to GNP. As far as we are concerned it seems far better to keep GNP firmly in its (important but subsidiary) place by treating the social services as having their own specific outputs rather than being mere inputs in the international game of keeping up in the growth rate league tables.

Microeconomic planning

The most fruitful approach to the planning of social policy appears, at least for the immediate future, to utilise the basic conceptual apparatus outlined in this book. The empirical techniques derived from Paretian microeconomics are commonly referred to as cost-benefit or cost-effectiveness analysis (with their corollaries, output budgeting and PPBS, which are investigated in chapter 9).

Cost-benefit and cost-effectiveness attempt to apply to public decision making the rational calculus of welfare economics: cost-benefit by comparing all the social costs and benefits of rival plans and selecting those that contribute most to social selfare; cost-effectiveness by comparing the social costs of rival methods of achieving a stated objective and selecting that which detracts least from social welfare. Clearly, the former is the more ambitious exercise since it attempts to evaluate community gains as well as losses, while the latter, especially valuable where the gains may be hard to estimate reliably, concentrates only on the costs of different ways of obtaining what is thought to be the same gain.

There exists an abundance of introductory material on these techniques (see Further Reading). It will be recalled that a major restraint (some would call it a strait-jacket) imposed on the social policy student in evaluating alternative methods of getting things done is that *he* should not judge changes from which some people lose and others gain as either good or bad in terms of *social* welfare (he can judge, of course, in terms of *his own* welfare). In practice this means strictly that only changes where losses are fully compensated can be evaluated. The working of market-exchange and costlessly operating, fully private property system provides the classic (but hypothetical) area in which the Pareto scheme can *always* be applied, for every loss imposed upon one individual by another individual will *always* be fully compensated, usually though not necessarily by the payment of a price.

In the real world, however, many losses are not compensated in this way with the consequence that, *if* one is to evaluate such changes, the (uncompensated) losses of some must be compared with the (uncompensated) gains of others. Any such comparison implies the use of the *potential improvement* criterion, which usually makes the assumption that each pound to each individual receives a weight of one. Thus, not only is the thousandth additional pound lost or gained by a rich man treated as of equal value to the tenth, but it is also treated as equal to any marginal pound gained or lost by a poor man.

The reasonableness of this procedure has been much debated. On the one hand it has been argued that this will be optimal since the prevailing income distribution must be the socially preferred distribution — otherwise why has it not been changed? — and therefore that the weights thrown out by this distribution are the ones that *ought* to be used in a Paretian analysis of policy. On the other hand it has been argued that a more egalitarian criterion should be used; for example by weighting gains and losses to individuals by the reciprocal of the ratio of their income to average national per capita income.

The Paretian method of this book suggests that neither of these two approaches is likely to be the appropriate one. The first is unlikely to be appropriate since, even if the distribution of incomes *is* Pareto optimal, there is no general reason why the income weights that are optimal in general should be optimal for the purposes in hand. It may be that there is no way of further redistributing incomes that does not make someone worse off in welfare terms, but everyone may agree that some special weights are appropriate in individual social investment appraisals. The second is equally unlikely in that it merely asserts a specific weights system that may be preferred by egalitarians (or may not), but which is not necessarily that preferred by society either in general or in specific cases.

In truth, it is not for the social scientist to decide what system of weights is socially preferred unless he has some means of knowing what society really does prefer. In practice, the choice of weights ought therefore to be made by democratic government. Analysts may experiment with some possible alternative methods of weighting gains and losses for different people, but if only one is to be used, pending a social (collective) decision about the proper weights, the simplest method is to select weights of unity. As such, they carry *no* normative significance. They are purely provisional. It may be, of course, that unitary weights turn out to be the ones preferred in a collective choice but this cannot be prejudged.

A second potentially important question of income redistribution in cost-benefit analysis concerns the fact that social investment itself changes the distribution of income. In some cases such changes may be sufficiently small for them not to be worth bothering about *as redistributions*. Even if they are important, however, it has been argued that the long term distributional effects of numerous investments will tend to be randomised, so that on average, it is as if distributional effects were neutral. If neither of these arguments can be realistically sustained then it may become necessary to choose between the socially correct system of weights *before* the investment and the socially correct one *after* it. In practice, however, few investments are so momentous in their impact that they cause such substantial redistributive effects.

It is, of course, unusual for the economic adviser of government to have the preferred set of weights presented to him for his use. In practice he must either force decision takers to make their own choice or else he might offer them a menu from which to choose, including a whole range of plausible possibilities. His professional status, however, gives him *absolutely no competence* to choose for them, only a certain faculty for inventing some possibilities for consideration.

The application of cost-benefit techniques

In the remainder of this chapter, we illustrate the application of cost-benefit and related techniques in social policy, explaining some of the more obscure whys and wherefores as we go along. Of the various problems that have been tackled and which well illustrate the methodology and its limitations the following are illustrated in the present chapter: A, the net social returns to education – how many people should we be educating? B, the cost-effectiveness of treatments of kidney failure – how should we treat renal failure? C, the cost-effectiveness of improving the housing stock – rebuilding or renovation? D, eviction from council houses – should tenants in arrears be evicted? E, implicit valuation of library services – do decision makers have the right priorities? As will be evident, this selection covers a wide variety of different types of social policy problem, of different degrees of importance and at varying levels of aggregation. In each case we assume unitary weights for individuals' gains and losses and that no substantial involuntary redistribution of income occurs as the result of the decision.

A. Social returns to education

One problem that has absorbed the energies of a number of British and American economists is the *social* 'profitability' of education. Granted that it will not be possible to measure *every* social benefit from education (for example, the purely subjective and even contemplative satisfactions it yields) if there is evidence that the return, *excluding* these benefits, exceeds the rate of return obtainable by spending resources on something other than education then one has very powerful evidence that the education sector *ought to be expanded*. Of course, if the measured return is below this level we cannot say very much because the true return – including the missed out benefits –

may, or may not, exceed alternative returns. The result would, however, suggest the question, 'is the difference in returns to be regarded as larger or smaller than the additional non-measurable benefits?', and hence provide some quantitative guidelines within which a decision maker or student of social policy can focus his attention upon the imponderables.

Before exploring some of the empirical studies actually done in this area it is as well to itemise some of the fundamental difficulties. The basis of the returns to education/investment in the *human* capital view of manpower planning is that the social return is the gross earnings differential between educated and less educated manpower as a proportion of the full social costs of the additional education of the more educated. This differential, if greater than alternative returns, indicates the desirability of expansion.[2] But, one may ask, surely earnings differentials affect much more than merely education received — what about innate ability, intelligence, social background, parents' education and other factors? Secondly, if the social benefit is to be reliably based on earnings, this must imply that a marginal person's earnings are equal to the value of his production, yet we know that in practice (especially in Britain) wages and salaries are set at levels determined by all sorts of conventional, statutory, administrative or monopoly rules.

Of course the better educated *are* the more able, they *do* tend to come from more favourable home backgrounds and so on. The important empirical finding for our purposes, however, is not that education, earnings and these other factors are all intercorrelated, but that the other factors are *not* sufficient to explain earnings differentials. If, for example, being born with a silver spoon was enough to explain the differentials then clearly the educational system cannot *at all* be used as an instrument for, say, equalising life-time opportunities. Fortunately, this depressing thought is not substantiated by the evidence. The fact is that some uneducated people earn large sums of money and the reverse, too, is the case. There is a dispersion about the mean because education is not the *only* relevant factor. For the purpose of deciding whether to increase the size of the education sector, however, we are interested — as general planning must be — with *representative* or average individuals and we are aware that the other factors, such as innate ability and social class, have proved remarkably constant over time and are not likely to be changed significantly by expanding the education sector (say at university level) by a further, say, 10 or 20%. Consequently, one should not be intimidated by those prophets of doom whose ultimate contribution is only to slow progress in improving the techniques we have and to return social policy to the vague fuzzy world of arbitrary assertion and counter assertion of causality and value-judgment without much attempt to test the validity of the former or the general acceptability of the latter. A rough drawing together of the the evidence suggests that years of formal education accounts for about 2/3 of the earnings differentials.[3] With this proportion about constant, as we have argued, the return to education can then quite readily be calculated.

The second objection has merit though it usually derives from a presumption that the so-called[4] 'marginal productivity theory' of wages is wrong. In a competitive economy the earnings of a marginal worker represent an exact measure of the value of his contribution to social output. If, for some reason, his earnings are forced *above* the value of his production, then use of earnings will overstate social benefit. If they are forced below they will understate it. Consequently, rather than throwing out the marginal productivity theory altogether, it is far more sensible to use it as a guide to making plausible adjustment to market earnings — the development of 'shadow' prices.[5]

The social returns to formal education can be computed as follows. Derive the time profiles of historical gross earnings (adjusted for market distortions if plausible adjustments are possible) for the more and the less educated age cohorts. Assess the total costs of the additional education (value of teachers', and administrators' time, of equipment and materials, of inputed rent on buildings, and of students' foregone earnings while being educated).

These data having been assembled, whether or not an expansion of formal education is socially worthwhile can be established by using formula derived in Appendix 8.1, viz.

$$P = \sum_{t=1}^{n} \left[\frac{B_t - C_t}{(1 + r)^t} \right]$$

to solve either for r, the internal rate of return, by setting $P = O$ (if $r > i$, the best alternative rate, or the 'test rate' for the public sector, expansion is indicated) or by inserting $i = r$ and solving for P (if $P > O$, expansion is indicated).

Table 8.1 indicates some of the results that have been achieved to date using these techniques in the USA and in Mexico.

TABLE 8.1: *Social Rates of Return*

| | (a) USA, males, 1949 | | (b) Urban Mexico, males, 1963 | |
Grade	Marginal Return (%)	Years of schooling	Marginal Return (%)
1–2	8.9	–	–
3–6	14.5	2–4	12.8
7–8	29.2	5–6	34.5
9–10	9.5	7–8	20.6
11–12	13.7	9–11	12.3
13–14	5.4	12–13	11.4
15–16	15.6	14–16	31.5

Sources: W. Lee Hanson; Carnoy. Both in Further Reading.

The Mexican data have been adjusted for family background. The USA data have not. Estimates for the UK have been made making the 1/3 allowance for native ability showing a rate of 12.5% in 1963 for secondary education for ages 16–18 and 6.5% on higher education. Comparable marginal rates for Indian males in 1960 have also been calculated yielding 15.2 for primary education (cf. illiteracy), 14.2% for middle education and 10.5% for matriculation.

Evidence on *private* rates of return indicates a persistent excess over social rates, indicating the subsidies inherent in all education systems and the lack of inclusion of external effects in the private rates. However, the social rates for higher education fall within the band of rates that represent likely estimates of the social opportunity costs of education. A major implication, however, is that the rate of return in Britain to secondary education is relatively high, indicating the potential social desirability of an expansion of the numbers staying on at school between 16–18.

B. *Choice of technique of treatment for renal failure*
While cost-benefit analysis attempts to compare rival projects, possibly of a very different nature, cost-effectiveness compares the social costs of attaining a particular objective and hence (since the social benefits will be invariant with respect to the means adopted) does not have to concern itself with benefit valuation. Clearly, to be validly applied, it is crucial that the 'output' which is not being valued really *is* invariant.

Cost-effectiveness has two primary uses. First, where an objective has already been decided (on whatever grounds) it can establish the socially least costly method of implementing it. This apparent cart-before-the-horse approach need not be as irrational as it sounds. For example, the objective need not be fully specified in terms of the *size* of output to be accomplished (e.g. patients treated) but merely in the sense that *some* will be produced (treated). Cost-effectiveness in this case might attempt the measurement of unit cost (cost per patient). Second, where benefits are extremely hard to estimate reliably, it is helpful to have cost data in order to discover the cost implications of obtaining some unquantifiable benefits. Suppose, for example, that it is not possible to value human lives saved.[6] The knowledge that it would cost say, £50,000 to give a patient an expected additional two years of moderately healthy life will give a framework for decision makers to place an *implicit* value on life (e.g. by saying 'it's not worth it' a life year clearly is valued at *less than* £25,000).

Chronic renal failure due to kidney disease can be treated in three basic ways: by kidney transplantation, by haemodialysis (blood purification) by an artificial kidney at home or by one in a dialysis centre. In the USA it has been estimated that a transplant costs $13,000, home dialysis $5,000 and hospital dialysis $14,000. Obviously home dialysis is the most cost-effective. Or is it?

To find out the answer a common 'output' unit has to be identified, for if there is a 50% chance of surviving a transplant for 10 years and a 25% chance of surviving home dialysis for 5 years, the outputs of the different treatments become important. Secondly, the flows of costs must be identified through time, so that those falling relatively more in the future (dialysis) are more heavily discounted compared with those falling mostly to the present (transplants). Thirdly, the treatments are not mutually exclusive. A rejected kidney can, for example, be replaced with another and the patient eventually be given dialysis. Finally, since relative costs vary through time, expectations of future costs must be included in the analysis.

In the study reported here, Klarman *et al* estimated the probabilities of patients starting with one treatment moving on to others, estimated the cost flow through time and used as the standardised output measure 'expected life years gained'. The objective became to select that initial treatment that had the least social cost per expected life year gained. An implicit value judgement in this was that one patient's life-year is as

TABLE 8.2: *Costs of Treating Chronic Renal Failure $'000*

Initial Treatment	Present value of Costs	Life Years Gained	Cost per Expected Life Year
Hospital Dialysis	104.0	9	11.6
Home Dialysis	38.0	9	4.2
Transplantation	44.5	17	2.6

Source: Klarman *et al* (see Further Reading)

socially valuable as any other's. Using a 6% discount rate the USA data led to the results in Table 8.2.

Thus, the final results differed substantially from the crude expenditure data. As a matter of fact, some adjustment was made for the superior quality of life enjoyed after transplantation but the differentials between the alternative methods are so sizeable that this element of arbitrariness and others, including omissions, are such as to be unlikely to alter the ranking of the three basic methods of treatment.

One important omission in the cost of the transplant, however, is the cost of acquiring the right organ at the right time. A major impediment to the wider use of transplanting is the chronic shortage of available 'spare parts' for suitable patients. This raises the interesting question of whether it would be a useful aid to policy to institute a system whereby living persons could be provided with incentives or compensation for bequeathing their organs at death for clinical purposes.[7]

In any event, the analysis established the *prima facie* superiority of transplantation and also indicated that machinery installed in a patient's home was less than half as costly as hospital dialysis. A shift to home dialysis would also reduce the cost of transplantation by virtue of the fact that a proportion of transplanted patients move on to dialysis.

C. Choice of technique in slum replacement

Most urban local authorities are the reluctant owners of sub-standard houses and slums. Local authorities have two means at their disposal for rectifying the problem — they may either demolish and build replacements at the socially approved standard or they may renovate existing dwellings. The socially optimal balance between rebuilding and renovation will be determined principally by the following factors: the density of redevelopment (scale economies are achieved when entire areas are dealt with); the direct costs of demolition and rebuilding or renovating; the expected life of new as against renovated dwellings; relative maintenance costs; and the relative value placed upon the services of each type of dwelling by tenants and the rest of society.[8]

Cost-effectiveness analysis can help in this difficult decision by incorporating the quantifiable elements of the problem into a single decision rule. The principal unquantifiable element is, of course, the subjective valuations placed upon the units by tenants, which includes the positive benefits of better housing as well as the negative ones associated with community and family upheavals. Let us assume that the external benefit to the rest of society consists in getting housing up to whatever acceptable standards are set — as is implied by externality theory. Then we may further infer that since both renovated and newly built accommodation meet these requirements, the rest of society is indifferent about which type is made available, ignoring costs. This leaves unsettled the problem of tenants' valuations. Let us leave them undetermined for the moment and return to them later.

Renovation will be a less costly method of providing accommodation than rebuilding if the discounted present value of renovation costs plus the present value of the cost of rebuilding in n years' time plus the present value of the maintenance costs is less than the present value of rebuilding plus the present value of maintaining the new dwelling.

In practice, this calculation would prove quite complicated in view of the relationship, for example, between maintenance costs and age of dwelling. Moreover, scaling factors should be applied when large scale redevelopment is undertaken and according to whether it is high rise or low density. For our purposes, however, the usefulness of the method can be illustrated with a simplified example of rebuilding or renovating a single three bedroom dwelling unit.

Ignoring the value of the quality difference to tenants, therefore, our decision rule says renovate rather than rebuild if the following inequality holds:[9]

$$M + R_M \left[\frac{(1 + i)^n - 1}{i(1 + i)^n} \right] + B(1 + i)^{-n} < B + R_B \left[\frac{(1 + i)^n - 1}{i(1 + i)^n} \right] \quad (1)$$

where:

M = the direct cost of modernisation, assumed to fall in the present year

R_M = annual maintenance costs of modernised dwelling, assumed constant in constant prices

B = the direct cost of demolition and rebuilding in constant prices

R_B = annual maintenance costs of rebuilt dwelling, assumed constant and in constant prices

i = discount rate

n = expected life of modernised property

Rearranging equation (1) we get this rule, modernise if

$$M < B \left[1 - (1 + i)^{-n}\right] + (R_B - R_M) \ \frac{(1 + i)^n - 1}{i(1 + i)^n} \tag{2}$$

In 1966/7 the average tender for a two storey three bedroom council house was £2,900 and the difference in maintenance costs between pre and postwar properties was £12. Assuming that the renovated property would last 15 years before requiring demolition and replacement ($n = 15$), the critical value for M works out (using a 10% interest rate) at £2,698 – so long as the cost of direct modernisation of such a property in 1966/7 was less than this sum, renovation was the more efficient method of providing improved housing (at 6% the critical sum is £1,807).

Suppose that it cost £1,500 to bring a dilapidated property up to standard. The appropriate consideration for the local authority becomes whether the additional amenity to the tenant, which has been omitted from the calculation, is worth more than £1,198 (£2,698–£1,500). Before jumping to the conclusion, however, that it is not and that there should be a massive switch to the renovation of substandard dwellings from new building recall that rational policy would involve renovating those properties that are cheapest to renovate first. Other things being equal, the optimal balance (ignoring tenant amenity) is where the marginal renovated dwelling of this type has risen to £2,698. Further housing improvements should then be made by rebuilding.

D. Should tenants in arrears be evicted?

Cost-benefit analysis can, as we have seen, be a useful exercise even though it is not possible fully to quantify every cost or benefit. A good example of a case where many effects cannot be quantified but where the technique gives quite positive guidance to social policy makers at the local level is in the treatment of council house tenants in arrears.

Arrears are frequently symptomatic of a far deeper social problem than irregularity of payment and this alone is sufficient for local authorities to exercise caution, before bringing in the bailiffs, by involving local social services departments at an early stage. An entirely different type of concern is also embodied in the Home Office and Department of Health circulars on this matter among which the potential burden on the rates of homelessness is one. The standard cost-benefit framework with its unitary weights system regards these, however, as purely interpersonal transfers – the tenant's benefit or the rate-payer's cost – which cancel out. The most plausible alternative assumptions about weights would normally place a higher value on the tenant's than the rate-payer's pound which makes one feel even less inclined to think that social welfare is much impaired by a shift of burden from tenant to rate-payer. A recent study in Reading, however, of the costs and benefits of eviction for rent arrears should make the problems raised by transfers clearer.

The number of evictions in Reading for rent arrears was small – six in 1966/67 with outstanding arrears of £670 from former tenants – and the total collectors' arrears owed by current tenants varied quite substantially around £2,000. The choice facing the authorities is simply between eviction, once tenants become persistently and seriously in arrears, and non-eviction.

The pattern of pure transfer payments created as a result of eviction is broadly as follows:

Rent of temporary accommodation for evicted tenants
Rent of vacated dwelling from new tenants
Supplementary Benefits
Rent of husband's lodging

Real resource costs and benefits are shown in Table 8.3, together with an item by item comparison of the net benefit (+ or −) of eviction compared with non-eviction.

Even though it was not possible to measure all the items, it is quite clear that, with the single possible exception of the care of the family (especially the children), eviction imposed net social costs upon the evicted family. Possible benefits not so far included are chiefly (a) the replacement of an irregularly paying tenant by a regularly paying tenant and (b) the incentive effect that eviction may have on neighbouring tenants. If eviction is to be justified at all, it will needs have to be justified on either or both of these two counts.

Previous analysis has established a fundamental point about the provision of social services: that the socially optimal quantity is where

TABLE 8.3: *Costs of Eviction and Non-Eviction (£)*

	Category	Policies		Net social benefit of Eviction
		Eviction	Non-Eviction	
1.	Direct costs of Eviction	25	0	−25
2.	Preparation for new tenants (redecoration)	5	0	− 5
3.	Allocation of new tenants	5	0	− 5
4.	Consumers' surpluses lost of temporarily vacant property	+	0	−
5.	Removal and storage of furniture	5	0	− 5
6.	Provision of temporary accommodation for one month	10	0	−10
7.	Social Services	10	0	−10
8.	Tenant's loss of earnings while searching for new accommodation	10	0	−10
9.	Effect on evictees	+	0	−
10.	Risk of permanent split in family	+	0	−
11.	Damage to tenant's property	+	0	−
12.	Care of family	−(?)	0	+(?)

the sum of all *MV's* is equal to marginal social cost. A second point, that the individual subsidies should vary (for income elastic services) according to income, will be derived in chapter 10 but is of relevance here. For our present purpose, the first of these conditions implies that the sum of *MV's* should be set equal to the *open market potential rent* of local authority housing, this representing its social opportunity cost, not to either per unit historical cost or per unit replacement cost[10]. If we assume an optimal stock of local authority housing in any area the differential between open market rent and the rent paid by tenants is the *MV* of the rest of society. If every tenant paid the same rent for the same type of dwelling any tenant falling in long term arrears would signal a permanent fall in his *MV* and, if there were no excess demand for the optimal stock of subsidised housing, would imply a case both for eviction, if it were costless, and a reduction in the subsidised housing stock. If the social costs of eviction are positive, as they are, the greater the shortfall of the tenant's *MV* (as indicated by arrears) and the *difference* between open market rent and the rest of society's *MV*, the greater the likelihood that eviction is a socially optimal policy. However, only if the social costs of eviction are zero does it follow that *any* permanent arrears require eviction.

Identical rents for all tenants implies, however, that all tenants have identical *MV's* − supposing subsidising policy to be efficient. The fact that *MV's* differ implies modifying the conclusion of the previous paragraph for an accumulation of arrears may now be evidence for the need for a larger subsidy to the family in question − especially if it is due to a change in the family's financial circumstances. Essentially, this amounts to an assessment of the comparative urgency of 'need' of the family in arrears and the family with the highest priority on the waiting list. Since in practice priorities on the waiting list are usually based on arbitrary criteria such as length of wait it seems unlikely that the new tenants would, on average, necessarily represent more urgent cases in the sense of imposing an externality on the rest of the concerned community than those who have got themselves into chronic difficulties with arrears. In such circumstances, the adjustment of rent would be a natural and consistent corollary, the case for non-eviction being strengthened by the positive social costs of eviction.

The incentive effect of eviction is mainly an empirical matter which we do not propose to explore in detail. The Reading study indicated that the effect of eviction on other tenants in arrears was small, was confined to tenants in the immediate neighbourhood and was, anyway, temporary. Viewed purely as an incentive effect eviction is almost certainly an inefficient policy. Given both the small number of evictions in Reading and the relatively small size of outstanding arrears it does not seem likely that even the *existence* of the eviction right supplies much in the way of an incentive to pay, especially by comparison with the many ordinary social pressures on tenants not to default on payments.

But implicit in the foregoing is a criticism of the standard treatment of transfer payments as merely cancelling items, for transfers, like prices, provide a measure (though frequently a very poor one) of individual and social valuations. If, for example, neither an individual tenant nor the rest of society is prepared to pay (possibly only implicitly in the case of the rest of society) enough to keep the tenant in a council dwelling in the public sector of the housing market, that is evidence for the potential optimality of either reletting the dwelling in the public sector at a suitable rent or for selling it.[11] In this way transfers can be used as the basis for shadow pricing to achieve both a socially optimal stock of local authority housing and a socially optimal mix of tenants occupying it.

E   What are library services worth?
Despite the fact that many outputs go unpriced, hence depriving decision makers of the most obvious *basis* (perhaps no more than this) for calculating social benefits, cost-benefit techniques are not necessarily rendered inapplicable, as we have seen. Nevertheless, it is frequently desirable to discover social benefits — or at least the marginal benefits (*MV's*). One method of discovering their likely order of magnitude is to derive the *implicit* values placed at the margin by decision makers, to make them *explicit* and then to ask them — the responsible deciders — whether what they are actually doing is what they thought they were doing or what they wanted to do.

A technique that has recently been applied to maternity services (see Further Reading) and to library policy (in universities) is that of inverse linear programming. Ordinary linear programming usually begins by asking, 'What do you want to achieve?', (What is the 'objective function'?) and proceeds to find the technically most efficient way of doing it. Inverse programming begins by assuming that what is being achieved is being achieved with technical efficiency and then asks, 'This is how you seem to value your different activities — do you think these really are the right values?' (An elementary explanation of the technique is in Appendix 8.2). Thus, at the very least, the technique can derive a range of relative shadow prices that are implicit in current and past decisions and compare them with what one may suppose to be true social priorities as established, for example, by policy statements made from on high.

Libraries — especially university libraries — illustrate the problems of benefit measurement well for not only do they not charge for any of their services but it is not altogether clear even what their services are. The first thing required therefore is to itemise as comprehensively as possible a mutually exclusive list of the most important outputs or services. Next the resources used in providing these services are

TABLE 8.4: *Outputs and Inputs of a University Library*

Outputs		Inputs	
(A)	new books per term (accessions)	(S)	senior librarians (man-minutes)
(OILL)	obtaining inter-library loans	(J)	junior librarians (man-minutes)
(LML)	user-hours of library material in library	(C)	clerical (man-minutes)
(LL)	Lending books on long loans (in book-fortnights)	(P)	porters (man-minutes)
		(£)	uncommitted money
(SL)	lending books on short loans (in half-day periods)	(St)	seats in seat-hours
		(Sh)	empty shelves (in feet)
(US)	user-services by senior librarian (man-hours)		
(UJ)	user-services by junior librarian (man-hours)		

itemised. For a university these two lists of outputs and inputs are presented in Table 8.4.

Given these categories the fixed coefficients showing how much of each input is used up in producing a unit of each output is derived. The 'technology matrix' for Durham University library was as shown in Table 8.5.

In addition to the resource constraints in the technology matrix (only the last two of which were, in actual fact, inequalities) three demand constraints were set such that in the following term user hours (LML), long loans (LL) and short loans (SL) must be at least equal to

TABLE 8.5: *Durham University Library Technology Matrix*

Outputs/ Inputs	A	OILL	LML	LL	SL	US	UJ	Resources Available
S	72	4	0	0.6	0	60	0	132,480
J	18	72	0.4	5	3	0	60	141,840
C	18	0	0	0	0	0	0	27,600
P	2	12	0.1	0.1	0	0	0	13,980
£	2.78	0.25	0	0	0	0	0	4,315
St	0	0	1	0	1	0	0	83,600
Sh	0.1	0	0	0	0	0	0	14,000

Source: J. Hawgood and R. Morley (see Further Reading) ch. 3.

the existing rates of these outputs to allow for certain externality effects.

With these data two further steps can be made. First, assume that library policy is rationally conducted. This implies that the *MV* of each service to library decision makers is equal to its *MC* and that, in turn the ratio of the *MV's* of any two services will be equal to the ratio of their *MC's*. Now the ratios of the *MV's* define the slope of the objective function implicitly used by library decision makers and hence the position they select on the production frontier. Since rational behaviour implies an equality between the ratios of *MV's* and *MC's*, by calculating the ratios of the latter the ratios of the former can be obtained and hence the optimal levels and blend of outputs.

TABLE 8.6: *Marginal Costs, Predicted and Realised Outputs of Library in next time period (term)*

	A	OILL	LML	LL	SL	US	UJ
Marginal cost	4.47	.89	.003	.045	.02	1.2	.44
Predicted output	1533	209	57,567	15,000	1,000	203	57
Realised output	1533	244	53,700	15,000	1,000	205	40

Table 8.6 shows the calculated average variable costs (assumed equal to marginal costs in *linear* programming) and the output levels predicted given the implicit ratios of *MV's*. Realised outputs are also shown for comparison with the predictions.

Assuming that the fixed coefficient, *MC* = *AC*, assumptions are reasonable approximations to reality, the rationality postulate is reasonably supported by these results – the principal discrepancies being in OILL and UJ.

The second step is to ask what ratios of *MV's* would produce exactly the pattern of outputs observed. The library decision makers could then be confronted with these implicit rates and asked – 'Are these *really* your priorities?' As the appendix shows, a variety of *MV* ratios may frequently produce the same output mix. The procedure here was to use the *MC* as the weight if it fell within the permissible range of weights and if not to choose the limit of the permissible weights nearest to the *MC*. Table 8.7 shows the results of the computer print out of these calculations. The reason for using one of the weights (*US*)

TABLE 8.7: *Implicit Weights and MV ratios*

	A	OILL	LML	LL	SL	US	UJ
Weight	4.05	.89	.003	.045	.02	1.2	.44
MV ratio using US as numéraire	3.4	0.74	.003	.037	.017	1.0	.37

in the first row as 'numéraire' for the second is, of course, so that we need not specify the units in which *MV's* are measured.

The interpretation of the *MV* ratios is as follows. If the university were presented with a choice between one addition to stock and four inter-library loans it would on average, according to current policy, add to stock. If presented with a choice between one addition to stock and four hours of user-services, it would choose the latter. If presented with a choice between an addition to stock and 1,000 user hours or 90 long loans it would add to stock. The library is run as if these were the relative priorities it set itself at the margin. Having got these relative priorities out in the open it is perfectly obvious that they need not correspond to what are generally felt (for example, by library users) to be the correct priorities.

The scope for applying this technique is obvious — it will almost certainly prove a useful source of dissertation fodder for graduate students of social policy. What implicit values are placed in your local library on fiction, travel, religion and art? What implicit values do local authorities place on the provision of different kinds of local authority housing? What currently hidden values exist in the present allocation of hospital beds — are they consistent with policy? Do maternity cases receive the kind of treatment regarded as most suitable for their varying needs by the experts (see Further Reading)? What set of relative priorities is implicit in current income subsidy schemes?

In addition, linear programming can trace out the consequences of changes in the resource constraints as input supplies alter and of changes in the technical coefficients as technical progress alters. And there are, of course, more sophisticated versions of the technique than that illustrated here.

The examples of this chapter illustrate the way in which the techniques of applied welfare economics can be used in tackling a variety of different problems in social policy. The further reading contains, however, an even broader range of applications which the reader who plans to muddy his hands in the dirt of the real world is well-advised to study closely. But those of a philosophical bent are also well-advised to do so for, as in other areas of social policy, many technical and rigorous refinements remain to be made. In view of the uneven quality of much applied work and the differences in conceptual approach that may occasionally be found it is as well, one should warn, to have one's critical wits well about one.

APPENDIX 8.1

The simple arithmetic of discounting

Costs and benefits accruing later are weighted less than those accruing earlier because early resources are preferred to later ones. A pound next year must be less valued by any member of society than a pound (of equal purchasing power) this year because it is always possible to keep this year's pound until next year, for one has a whole year between now and then to use the present pound. This latter set of options is not available if the pound is coming only next year. Therefore, on the fundamental principle that *more is preferred,* a future pound is always valued less than a present pound. In symbols:

$$P = F \times D, \qquad O < D < 1 \qquad (1)$$

where F is a future pound (next year), D is the fraction or *discount factor* by which it is discounted to get P — the *present value* of a future pound. Thus, if 100 pence next year ($F = 100$) are worth 75 pence today ($P = 75$), $D = 75/100 = \frac{3}{4}$. The relative values of P and F are $F/P = 100/75$ so the future value of the future pound is $33\frac{1}{3}\%$ higher than its present value, i.e. $F/P = (P + .33P)/P$ or $(1 + .33)$. $33\frac{1}{3}\%$ is the *rate of discount* or *rate of interest* (i). Obviously, therefore

$$D = \frac{1}{1+i} \tag{2}$$

which, since $O < D < 1$ implies $i > O$.

Substituting (2) into (1) we get

$$P = F[1/(1 + i)] \tag{3}$$

so the present value of a future pound can be found if the rate of interest is known.

If the pound is deferred for two years instead of only one, the formula can easily be calculated. The present value of F a year hence (F_1) was $F_1 [1/(1 + i)]$. Similarly its present value two years hence (F_2) is $F_2 [1/(1 + i)] [1/(1 + i)] = F_2 [1/(1 + i)^2]$. Deferred three years $P = F_3 [1/(1 + i)^3]$ and deferred n years

$$P = F_n [1/(1 + i)^n] . \tag{4}$$

If one receives a set of benefits *through* time, the present values of each are simply added up:

$$P = \frac{F_1}{1+i} + \frac{F_2}{(1+i)^2} + \frac{F_3}{(1+i)^3} + \ldots + \frac{F_n}{(1+i)^n} \tag{5}$$

If some benefit occurs at once (at time O) we amend equation (5) to:

$$P_0 = F_0 + \frac{F_1}{1+i} + \frac{F_2}{(1+i)^2} + \ldots \cdot \frac{F_n}{(1+i)^n} \tag{6}$$

To discover if an investment is worth undertaking all the social costs and benefits are expressed in money terms and the equation becomes:

$$P_0 = \sum_{t=0}^{n} \left[\frac{B_t - C_t}{(1+i)^t} \right] \tag{7}$$

where the B's and C's are benefits and costs and the t's refer to the time periods. Provided the correct interest rate has been selected, if

$$P_0 > O \tag{8}$$

the investment is socially worth undertaking in the sense of a potential Pareto improvement.

If $(B-C)$ is constant through time, equation (7) simplifies to

$$P_0 = (B-C)[1 + 1/(1 + i) + 1/(1 + i)^2 \ 1/(1 + i)^3 \\ + \ldots + 1/(1 + i)^n]$$

from which we derive

$$P_0 = (B - C)\left[\frac{(1 + i)^{n+1} - 1}{i(1 + i)^n}\right] \tag{9}$$

and if n is a very long time away, since $1/1(1 + i)^n$ becomes negligible we get

$$P_0 = (B-C)/i. \tag{10}$$

The internal rate of return r is found by calculating that rate of discount that makes $P_0 = O$, viz:

$$0 = \sum_{t=0}^{n}\left[\frac{B_t - C_t}{(1 + r)^t}\right] \tag{11}$$

and, provided the correct rate of interest has been selected, if

$$r > i \tag{12}$$

the investment is *sometimes* worth undertaking on the potential criterion.

The 'sometimes' is there because, as we have mentioned in the text, the internal rate of return rule is less reliable than the present value rule. The difficulty here can be simply illustrated. Suppose there are two projects, A and B, of which A yields recepits of £5 a year for ten years and B yields £1 in the first year, £2 in the second and so on up to ten years. Each costs £25.

INTEREST RATE %	PRESENT VALUES	
	A	B
3	42.65	44.84
4	40.55	42.01
5	38.60	39.38
6	36.80	36.94
7	35.10	34.73
8	33.55	32.68

According to the internal rate of return equation, A has an r of about 17% and B one of about 12.5% which makes A the more preferred option (so long as the interest rate is lower). The table above, however, indicates that at about 6%, A and B are about equally worthwhile and it is only at interest rates *higher* than this that A is to be more preferred. Thus, a ranking of projects according to the internal rate of return will not invariably yield reliable results.

APPENDIX 8.2

Elements of linear programming and its inverse

Suppose a management is responsible for the production of two outputs (X_1 and X_2) with three inputs (Y_1, Y_2 and Y_3). It is known that the amount of short run inputs available is $Y_1 = 3,200$, $Y_2 = 4,800$ and $Y_3 = 10,000$ and that with current technology the *minimal* amount of input required per unit of each output (whatever the output) is: for X_1, $2Y_1$, $6Y_2$ and $10Y_3$; and for X_2, $8Y_1$, $4Y_2$ and $20Y_3$. This information, summarised in Table 8A.1 (the technology matrix) is sufficient to establish the most *technically* efficient method of production for the management, given the (short term) constraints implied by resource availability.

TABLE 8A.1: *Technology Matrix*

Output/ Input	X_1	X_2	Total Available Inputs
Y_1	8.0	2.0	3,200
Y_2	4.0	6.0	4,800
Y_3	20.0	10.0	10,000

Figure 8A.1 shows the technically attainable levels of output for each input and the heavily drawn line ABCD indicates the maximum feasible production possibilities, given the amount available of all three inputs. Thus for an output mix of X_1 and X_2 along AB, only the Y_2 constraint is binding. Between B and C, neither Y_1 nor Y_2 is binding. Between C and D only the Y_1 constraint is binding. Given an objective (such as maximise the output of X_1 and X_2), known as the 'objective function', the most efficient point on $ABCD$ can be found – it can readily be seen, in this simple example, to be at B where the line EE with a slope of minus one is farthest from the origin, hence maximising output, given the inputs available, but not beyond the production frontier $ABCD$.

Formally, it is sought to maximise the objective function

$$Q = X_1 + X_2 \qquad (1)$$

subject to the following constraints

(Y_1) $\qquad\qquad 2X_1 + 8X_2 \leqslant 3200 \qquad (2)$

(Y_2) $\qquad\qquad 6X_1 + 4X_2 \leqslant 4800 \qquad (3)$

(Y_3) $\qquad\qquad 10X_1 + 20X_2 \leqslant 10000 \qquad (4)$

$$X_1, X_2 \geqslant 0 \qquad (5)$$

At B we see that the Y_1 constraint is not binding so the inequality holds (there will be some spare capacity) while the other two inequalities will, in fact be equalities. Solving the two simultaneous equations (3) and (4) we derive $X_1 = 700$, $X_2 = 150$ and $Q = 850$.

This result is not independent, however, of the *weights* used in the objective function (1). In the example just presented the weights are unitary – and the slope of EE line (the geometric version of the objective function) is minus one – the ratio of the weights. One way of interpreting these weights is to call them marginal values. For example, if X_2 were regarded as three times as important as X_1, it could receive a weight ($=MV$) of 3 with the weight of X_1 remaining unity. This means that instead of one X_1 being regarded as equivalent to one X_2, *three* X_1's are now needed to be equivalent to one X_2. The objective function correspondingly has a slope of minus three as in line $E'E'$, and the new most efficient point C is located.

It can readily be seen that if the decision makers produce in a technically efficient way (i.e. locate somewhere on $ABCD$) then it is possible to discover the slope of the objective function or, what is the

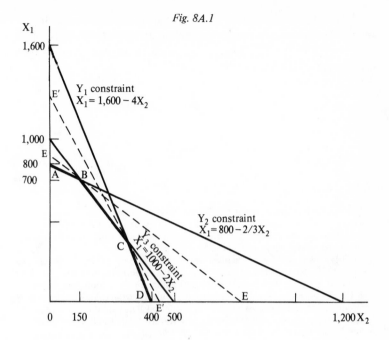

Fig. 8A.1

same thing, the ratio of implicit *MV's*. This method, known as inverse programming (the 'inversion of acriteria planning models') is used in the text of this chapter to make explicit the implicit values of decision makers who can then be confronted with them and asked if they really mean these. Likewise others — such as clients or experts — can see more clearly if current practice accords with the relative priorities they think ought to exist. Thus, if the decision makers have located at *B*, then the implicit ratio of *MV's* is between 3:2 and 1:2 (the limiting slopes set by the slopes of *AB* and *BC*). If they have located at *C*, the ratio must lie between 1:2 and 1:4; If they have located between *B* and *C*, the ratio is unambiguously 1:2, and one may reasonably ask 'Is it really right that we regard 1 of X_2 as equivalent to 2 of X_1?' The answer, of course, is up to the policy makers who, in a complex world, often without prices and other aids in establishing priorities, very, *very*, frequently have only the haziest notions of what is actually going on and whether it is consistent with their preferred policies.

Likewise, it is not surprising that in the real world where many managers and decision makers have to grapple with very many outputs and inputs, businessmen, for example, have found linear programming a useful technique for choosing profit-maximising output rates. In this case the weights in the objective function are objectively revealed, or subjectively anticipated prices. Using prices as weights gives equation (1) a very obvious interpretation.[12]

NOTES

1. But why use conventions at all? The answer in economics is implied by the answers to two additional questions — at what point should one stop 'considering' and *act* and how much information about two options is worth obtaining before one is selected?

2. Strictly, two analytical qualifications are in order. (a) A more reliable indicator is to take the present value of the differential less the education costs. If positive, this indicates the desirability of expansion (see Appendix 8.1). (b) Earnings of the less educated should be adjusted to the level they would be at if they worked the same (longer) hours of the more educated (see Lindsay, 'Measuring Human Capital Returns', cited in Further Reading).

3. See Blaug, *Introduction to the Economics of Education*, for a survey of this evidence.

4. It is not a theory of wages but of the demand for more labour time.

5. A related objection is that educational qualifications are mere 'union tickets' to employment, giving employers an easy way of discriminating among applicants but unrelated to productivity. An implication of this wholly unsubstantiated assertion is that firms would be equally profitable if they chose employees according to the colour of their eyes rather than the extent and type of their education — an improbable fact, to say the least!

6. Not true, however. See Further Reading.

7. The reader is left to devise a scheme which might increase the supply of organs while safeguarding the interests of donors, their relatives, and recipients. Note that one way of increasing the availability of suitable cadavers for transplants may be to increase communications between doctors and between hospitals. This need not be cheaper, however, than increasing the supply of suitable organs, even if many were not used.

8. Why does this list *not* include rents? The answer has something to do with our assumptions about the treatment of redistribution in cost benefit studies.

9. Why does the length of life of a new dwelling not feature in this equation? Why does not the initial value of the property being improved or demolished also figure?

10. Which is likely to be higher: open market rent, historical or replacement cost? Why?

11. The sale of council houses is *not* warranted so long as society's MV of a reduction in the need of the worst case on the waiting list plus that case's own MV exceeds the inputed monthly rental from sale.

12. What is it?

FURTHER READING

Techniques of Cost-Benefit Analysis
M. Dobb, *Welfare Economics and the Economics of Socialism*, Cambridge, CUP, 1969.
T. A. Goldman, *Cost-Effectiveness Analysis*, New York, 1967.
E. J. Mishan, *Cost-Benefit Analysis*, London, Allen & Unwin, 1971: Easily the best extended introduction.
A. R. Prest and R. Turvey, 'Cost Benefit Analysis: A Survey', *Economic Journal*, 1967.
Alan Williams, 'Cost-Benefit Analysis' in A. Cairncross (Ed), *The Managed Economy*, Oxford, Basil Blackwell, 1970.
Alan Williams, and H. G. Walsh, *Current Issues in Cost-Benefit Analysis*, London, HMSO, 1969. An excellent, lucid and *short* entrée to the arcane mysteries.
Alan Williams, 'Cost-Benefit Analysis: Bastard Science? And/or Insidious Poison-in the Body Politick', *Journal of Public Economics*, Vol., No. 2, 1972. A blistering attack on the naive critics of cost-benefit.

On the Choice of Interest Rate in the Public Sector
D. W. Pearce, *Cost Benefit Analysis*, London, Macmillan, 1971. Chapter 6 of this introductory text provides a neat survey, which is not hard going, of this controversial issue.

On the Treatment of Redistribution in Cost-Benefit Analysis
J. T. Bonnen, 'The Distribution of Benefits from Cotton Price Supports' in S. B. Chase (ed), *Problems in Public Expenditure Analysis*, Washington DC, Brookings, 1968.
C. D. Foster, 'Social Welfare Functions in Cost-Benefit Analysis', in J. Lawrence (ed), *Operational Research and The Social Sciences*, London, Tavistock, 1966.
C. M. McGuire and H. Garn, 'The Integration of Equity and Efficiency Criteria in Public Project Selection', *Economic Journal*, December, 1969.
B. Weisbrod, 'Income Redistribution Effects and Benefit-Cost Analysis', in S. B. Chase, *op. cit.*

Techniques of Linear Programming
R. Dorfman, P. Samuelson and R. Solow, *Linear Programming and Economic Analysis*, New York, McGraw-Hill, 1958. The best introduction for the not-too-numerate.
G. Hadley, *Linear Programming*, Reading, Mass., Addison-Wesley, 1965.

On Valuing Human Life
M. Jones-Lee, 'Valuation of Reduction in Probability of Death by Road Accident', *Journal of Transport Economics and Policy*, Vol. 3, 1969. Reprinted in M. H. Cooper and A. J. Culyer, *Health Economics*, Penguin Books, London, 1973.
E. J. Mishan, 'Evaluation of Life and Limb: A Theoretical Approach', *Journal of Political Economy*, Vol. 79, 1971.
T. C. Schelling, 'The Life You Save May Be Your Own', in S. B. Chase Jr. (Ed), *Problems in Public Expenditure Analysis*, Washington, 1967. Reprinted in Cooper and Culyer, *op. cit.*

Studies drawn on for illustrative material in this chapter
M. Blaug, *An Introduction to the Economics of Education*, London, Allen Lane, 1971. An excellent and well-balanced survey of most of this field.

H. E. Klarman, J.O'S. Francis and G. D. Rosenthal, 'Cost-Effectiveness Applied to the Treatment of Chronic Renal Disease', *Medical Care*, Vol. 6, 1968. pp. 48–54. Reprinted in Cooper and Culyer, *op. cit.*

L. Needleman, 'The Comparative Economics of Improvement and New Building', *Urban Studies*, Vol. 6, 1969.

Country Borough of Reading, 'Eviction from Council Houses for Rent Arrears' in P. B. Kershaw (Ed), *Cost-Benefit Analysis*, Institute of Municipal Treasurers and Accountants, London, 1969.

J. Hawgood and R. Morley, *Project for Evaluating the Benefits from University Libraries, Final Report*, Durham, 1969.

Manpower Forecasting

M. Blaug, *Economics of Education 1,* London, Penguin, 1968, Part 4 articles by H. S. Parnes, C. A. Layard, K. J. Arrow and W. M. Capron, and R. G. Hollister.

H. E. Klarman, 'Economic Aspects of Projecting Requirements for Health Manpower', *Journal of Human Resources*, Vol. 4, 1969.

D. Paige and K. Jones, *Health and Welfare Services in Britain in 1975,* London, Cambridge University Press, 1966.

A. T. Peacock and J. R. Shannon, 'The New Doctors' Dilemma', *Lloyds Bank Review*, January, 1968.

Education, Health and Growth

G. S. Becker, *Human Capital*, New York, NBER, 1964. The *locus classicus* for the investment in human beings approach.

M. Blaug, *Economics of Education 1, op. cit.* Part 1, articles by T. W. Schultz, H. G. Johnson, H. G. Shaffer.

M. Blaug and M. Woodhall, 'Productivity Trends in British Secondary Education 1950–1963', *Sociology of Education*, Vol. 41, 1968.

W. G. Bowen, "Assessing the Economic Contribution of Education: An Appraisal of Alternative Approaches', *Higher Education* (Robbins Report) Comnd, 2154–4, Appendix IV, pp. 73–96 (reprinted in Blaug, *Economics of Education 1, op. cit.*)

Robin Barlow, *The Economic Effects of Malaria Eradication*, Ann Arbor, Michigan UP. 1968.

E. F. Denison, *The Sources of Economic Growth in the United States and the Alternative Before US*, Committee for Economic Development, New York, 1962.

V. R. Fuchs, 'The Contribution of Health Services to the American Economy', *Milbank Memorial Fund Quarterly*, Vol. 44, 1966. Reprinted in Cooper and Culyer, *op. cit.*

R. J. Lavers, 'The Implicit Valuation of Forms of Hospital Treatment', in M. M. Hauser (ed), *The Economics of Medical Care*, London, Allen and Unwin, 1972.

C. M. Lindsay, 'Measuring Human Capital Returns', *Journal of Political Economy*, Vol. 79, 1971.

S. J. Mushkin, 'Health as Investment', *Journal of Political Economy*, Vol. 70, 1962, (Part 2 of No. 5). Reprinted in Cooper and Culyer, *op. cit.*

Housing

For some specific criticisms of cost-effectiveness techniques in housing consult

L. Needleman, *The Economics of Housing*, London, Staples Press, 1965.

E. Sigsworth and R. Wilkinson, 'Rebuilding or Renovation', *Urban Studies*, Vol. 4, 1967.

L. Needleman, 'Rebuilding or Renovation: A Reply', *Urban Studies*, Vol. 5, 1968.

E. Sigsworth and R. Wilkinson, 'Rebuilding or Renovation: A Rejoinder', *Urban Studies*, Vol. 7. 1970.

Miscellaneous applications in Social Policy

M. Blaug, 'The Rate of Return on Investment in Education in Great Britain', *Manchester School*, Vol. 33, 1965, (reprinted in Blaug, *Economics of Education 1, op. cit.*

M. Carnoy, 'Earnings and Schooling in Mexico', *Economic Development and Cultural Change*, 1967.

County of Essex, 'The Problem of Homeless Families' in Kershaw, *op. cit.*, which also includes a variety of other local authority studies of varying interest and quality.

A. J. Culyer and A. K. Maynard, 'The Costs of Dangerous Drugs Legislation in England and Wales', *Medical Care*, Vol. 8, 1970.

R. F. F. Dawson, *The Cost of Road Accidents in Great Britain*, Road Research Laboratory, 1967.

S. Enke, 'The Economic Aspects of Slowing Population Growth', *Economic Journal*, 1966, Reprinted in Cooper and Culyer, *op. cit.*

R. Fein, *Economics of Mental Illness*, New York, Basic Books, 1958.

M. S. Feldstein, *Economic Analysis for Health Service Efficiency*, Amsterdam, North Holland, 1967. A *tour de force*, using practically every trick in the economist's book.

W. Lee Hansen, 'Total and Private Rates of Return to Investment in Schooling', *Journal of Political Economy*, Vol. 81, 1963. Reprinted in Blaug, *Economics of Education 1*.

J. K. Mann and D. E. Yett, 'The Analysis of Hospital Costs: A Review Article', *Journal of Business*, Vol. 41, 1968, Reprinted in Cooper and Culyer, *op. cit.*

Office of Health Economics, *The Cost of Mental Care*, London, OHE, 1965.

D. Pole, 'The Economics of Mass Radiography', in M. M. Hauser (Ed), *The Economics of Medical Care*, London, Allen and Unwin, 1972.

J. J. Warford and Alan Williams, 'Rural Water Supplies and the Economic Evaluation of Alternative Location Patterns', in M. G. Kendall (Ed.) *Cost-Benefit Analysis*, London, English Universities Press, 1971.

B. A. Weisbrod, *The Economics of Public Health*, Philadelphia, Univ. of Pennsylvania Press, 1961.

On substitution in medical care

M. Reinhardt, 'A Product Function for Physician Services', *Review of Economics and Statistics*, Vol. 54, 1972.

K. R. Smith, M. Miller and F. L. Golladay, 'An Analysis of the Optimal Use of Inputs in the Production of Medical Services', *Journal of Human Resources*, Vol. 7, 1972.

9 Output Budgeting and PPBS in Social Policy

A case for output budgeting

In chapter 7 we noted the importance of rational decision making in the formation of social policy and also that there is no automatic tendency for public authorities to pursue the genuine objectives of social policy or to pursue them as efficiently as possible. Much of our political machinery is simply incapable of doing any more than ensuring a usually thorough financial audit of public activities and, as a consequence, bureaucracies – and politicians – are left with varying degrees of discretion in what they do and how they do it. The planning techniques of chapter 8 have as a prime rationale the task of imposing upon those who formulate and carry through various social policies the necessity for explicitness and openness and so do those of the present chapter. Less formal methods of policy appraisal – based on 'experience' or 'flair' – are basically *uncommunicable* and the 'truth' about social policy gets 'revealed' to but a few. Different programmes are not related to one another. Responsibility gets divided up in an arbitrary way. Democratic participation is minimised. The scope for the riding of personal hobbyhorses by administrators and policy makers is maximised. Cost-benefit analysis has the signal virtue of forcing the decision maker to concentrate (a) upon the objectives of policy and (b) upon the trade-offs between and within policies that necessarily have to be made. As a result relevant questions about policy are more likely to be asked (e.g. what information is needed to make a sensible decision?) and policy making becomes more open since the reasons for doing things (whether right things or wrong things) are more explicitly stated and hence discussable.

As we have illustrated, the scope for these techniques in social policy making is much wider than may be thought. Cost-benefit and cost-effectiveness can yield useful results even in the presence of substantial unquantifiables and without ignoring the unquantified factors or treating them as unimportant.

However, not only the presence of important unquantifiables (at least, currently) but also the behaviour constraining environment of decision makers and administrators means that frequently the information that is relevant to many decisions is simply never collected (e.g. earnings by educational attainment) while much that is collected is either almost entirely irrelevant (e.g. rental value of Crown properties) or is, from the point of view of rational planning rather than financial control, rather unsuitable if not downright misleading (e.g. conventional depreciation accounting, wages of otherwise unemployed labour). These factors limit the extent to which cost-benefit techniques can currently be employed. Because people have not been forced before to ask the relevant questions the relevant data are not available. But, in any case, the high cost of such exercises means that it is pie-in-the-sky to imagine their being systematically employed every time one of the innumerable policy decisions is taken, at whatever level, somewhere in the so-called administrative as well as top policy formulating ranks of the public authorities. *Output budgeting* is a technique that is designed to overcome some of these difficulties.

What is *output budgeting?*

The basic difference between output budgeting and traditional budgeting is that the former classifies costs (social opportunity costs so far as possible) according to the objectives for which they are incurred (outputs) while the latter classifies costs (financial costs) according to the type of resource purchased (inputs). It is for this reason that the term 'output budgeting' is used in this book rather than 'programme budgeting' − the same rose by a different name − for the former term really captures the essential distinguishing feature of the process. (PPBS stands for Planning-Programming-Budgeting-System). The reason for the input orientation of traditional practice is not hard to find in social policy. It is that markets do not usually exist for the outputs of social policy − frequently they have been deliberately withdrawn from the market. Consequently, the only 'hard' basis for assigning costs is on an input basis: budgets are divided up into capital versus current accounts, into wages and salaries versus equipment and materials, into administrative sectors such as hospital expenditure versus local authority health and welfare expenditure. In any case, administrative units demand cash for spending on specific resources and traditional accounting is designed to ensure that money is spent on those things for which it was given and on nothing else. Moreover the costs considered − given the necessity for financial audit and control − are only those 'costs' which appear as money flows within and out of the public sector. The earnings foregone by children staying on at school for an additional year are not *fiscal* costs so they do not appear in the accounts although they may be very substantial *social* costs and possibly larger than the fiscal costs (the fiscal costs may, of course, themselves be good approximations to *some of* the social costs of providing an additional year's education).

Major problems in output budgeting are likely to arise around four principal conceptual problems:

(a)   policy objectives need to be defined clearly.
(b)   output measures need to be devised to enable performance to be monitored and appropriate unit and marginal costs to be calculated.
(c)   genuine social costs only must be defined and measured.
(d)   the social costs need to be attributed as nearly as possible to the outputs that give rise to them.

In addition, since output budgeting is to be seen as a *routine exercise* − as routine as traditional budgeting − the decisions taken on each of these heads must be such that too great a detail is avoided to keep the cost of the exercise as low as possible. Output budgeting consequently indicates only the overall deployment of resources and provides a framework for rational choice. Cost-benefit techniques provide a vital back-up to output budgeting for more detailed examination of specific social programmes.

Policy objectives in education and health

Identifying policy objectives is equivalent to fixing the titles of social policy programes and sub-programmes and they should be sufficiently broad to be manageable but not so broad as to be meaningless. Thus, for example, broad programme heads for an education output budget together with some subprogrammes may be:

A. Compulsory Education
(Objectives: provide highest possible standard of education according to child's age, aptitude and ability during present period of compulsory schooling; increase equality of opportunity; improve staff/pupil ratio; improve standards of provision in Educational Priority Areas).

1. Maintenance of existing pattern and scale of provision
2. Improving teaching methods and curriculum
3. Changing availability of teachers

B. Nursery Education
(Objectives: assist educational development and social adjustment of children below compulsory school age; release mothers for work; raise proportion of children attending in Educational Priority Areas).

1. Maintenance of existing pattern and scale of provision
2. Change proportion of children attending and length of stay
3. Change availability of teachers

C. Education of the 16–19 year old
(Objectives: to provide education and vocational training for all these three age groups who wish it and who can profit from it; to meet projected qualified manpower requirements; increase proportion of children in full time, part time and day-release education) *etc*.

The identification of such objectives is itself an extremely valuable exercise. It highlights conflicts and potential conflicts between objectives (forcing explicit choices); it identifies logical interrelationships between objectives (some may be prior to others, others complementary); it compels the administration to think most carefully about the most useful way of classifying objectives. There is usually a variety of ways of classifying objectives and the 'best' method is usually that which is some compromise with existing classifications – which have the short term advantage of familiarity and for which data are often collected as a routine matter – but which will also reflect the major strategic policy choices that will be made in the foreseeable future. In the health and personal social services, for example, classification could be based upon client groups (e.g. maternity cases, children, the old) or in administrative terms (e.g. hospital services; primary – GP – care; local authority services), or some combination of these two. Within the hospital service, for example, a programme structure might be based upon either diseases, diagnostic groups, medical specialties, client age groups or client dependency. The last of these is not currently feasible and the first, though probably the most attractive from the resource allocation point of view, unfortunately contains several thousand elements. The compromise structure with which the Department of Health and Social Security is currently experimenting includes the following main programmes: general health; primary care; maternity; children and families; the elderly; the younger disabled; mentally handicapped; mentally ill; hospital surgical specialties excluding dental surgery; hospital medical specialties including paediatrics; dental services; ophthalmic services.

The sub-programme structure of the health and personal social services output budget would ideally carry through the basic client-orientation theme with each sub-programme representing a package of care. Unlike the educational system, however, where clients receive fairly homogeneous services according to their age and the type of institution at which they are studying the package of care received by a client of the NHS is almost infinitely variable depending on his condition, the judgment of the doctor or social worker and the locally available facilities. Thus, the elderly may receive a very wide variety of domiciliary and day care. As in the main programme structure again some compromise has to be made in order to make the budget manageable. One obvious method of doing this is to associate particular types of input with the basic programme structure and client groups. Thus, most main programmes in the NHS have the following sub-programme structure:

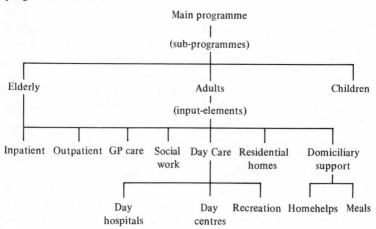

In addition, this procedure assists reconciliation with traditional budgeting conventions. Each input-element, for example, can be further subdivided into traditional expenditure categories such as recurrent gross expenditure, charges, capital expenditure, training and research.

Output measurement follows naturally from a clearly defined programme structure that corresponds reasonably well to policy objectives. The problem of output measurement is discussed at greater length later in the chapter but here we note the kind of problem that arises. On the one hand output measures are invaluable in monitoring the success of social policies and in helping decision makers to see and anticipate the consequences of increasing resource inputs or shuffling them around. On the other, it is only at the lowest level that one can normally discover easy output measures of any sort, where a low-level objective is naturally defined. Thus, for example, the number of pupils staying on at school after the compulsory school leaving age is a fairly 'hard' output measure for that part of the educational output budget to which it refers. Equally, however, it is on its own inadequate. A short list of other relevant output measures which would be useful might include: examination results; performance in non-examined subjects; pupils qualified for higher education; quality of social and sporting life of the educational establishment; quality of cultural life; employers' assessments of school leavers; increase in present value of lifetime earnings; output of school-leavers with specialised qualifications; level of 'citizenship' attained by school leavers. The difficulties confronting those who will be developing output measures in social policy are not easily overstated! Nevertheless the effort would clearly be worthwhile and even if some outputs defied all attempts at quantification, merely to identify the output and to classify costs accordingly reveals strategic policy choices that would otherwise be concealed from policy makers.

Treatment of costs

The costs in an output budget ought to be the true social costs of each programme. This implies incorporating costs that the organisation itself may not bear (e.g. foregone earnings; value of time waiting) and excluding genuine transfers.[1] In the initial stages, however, of setting up an output budget, rather traditional 'cost' or expenditure concepts may perforce have to be used until the budgeting system has developed sufficiently for the bases to be altered upon which routine data are collected. Nevertheless, even within the traditional cost concept in public accounting, the problem of allocating costs looms large. Because most programmes have a number of outputs and several programmes may share inputs there is no uniquely correct way of allocating total expenditures/costs. On the one hand, the marginal cost of expanding any one programme is the additional cost necessarily incurred, no matter where or by whom. One the other hand, total costs must necessarily be treated with some degree of arbitrariness. If one output dominates several others then it is sensible to allocate all costs to that output, treating the others, perhaps, as costless bonuses. Otherwise the usual practice is either 'slice-costing' – dividing total cost pro rata according to some measure of throughput or utilisation – or identifying a separate category of unallocated costs. While the former tends to overestimate the true costs the latter tends to understate them. A final possibility which might reduce the unallocable costs is to compromise the programme headings somewhat by, for example, shifting away from final *outputs* to *activities*.

Perhaps the most difficult problem in cost allocation concerns the proper allocation of costs *through* time. For an output budgeting period of one year the problem is how to allocate those costs (a) whose benefits flow over a longer period of time than that over which the costs are incurred and (b) those costs that are inescapably incurred in future budgeting periods as a result of a decision now. In short, the problem concerns the proper allocation through time of what are conventionally known as 'capital' costs.

The purpose of an output budget is to show either the present distribution of incurred costs among outputs or, if future budgets are being forecast, what future distributions are expected, *ex post,* to look like. Given this purpose, the question is how to allocate the cost of, say, a £1m building planned to last 50 years, whose building costs are to be incurred over the next 3 years. The cost of this part of a *programme* should be calculated in the way implied by cost-benefit analysis. For example, if the actual expenditure flows corresponding to the social value of resources used up were £500,000, £300,000 and £200,000, then the cost at time t_0 is

$$C_0 = £500,000 + £300,000/(1 + i) + £200,000/(1 + i)^2 - £x/(1 + i)^{50}$$

where £x represents the 'scrap value' of the building after 50 years. But this, it should be noted, is the cost of part of the programme not a cost of the *decision* to build. Building could always to stopped in the second year and thus costs inescapably incurred by a planned programme are not the same as those inescapably incurred by the decision to begin the programme, or subsequently to continue it for another accounting period. Output budgeting is concerned primarily with the costs of *decisions,* whereas cost-benefit analysis is concerned with the costs of *programmes* over their planned lifetime. Thus, for output budgeting purposes there is no need to include the present value of costs nor to calculate the annual annuity whose present value over 50 years has the same present value. At time t_0 the appropriate costs are, in fact, £500,000. At time t_1 the appropriate costs will be £300,000. At time t_4 they will be zero and time t_{50} they will be $-£x$ (if the programme is carried out as originally planned).[2]

This important distinction between output budgeting and cost-benefit analysis has led to considerable confusion by being not fully understood. Some output budgeting practitioners have even felt guilty about entering capital costs as they are incurred instead of, say, annuitising them over the life of the programme and have defended their decisions on grounds of practicability whereas they were, conceptually, perfectly justified in doing just that!

There are, then, a great number of problems to be encountered in setting up an output budget. They are, however, not really the problems of output budgeting but the problems of policy decision making itself. Output budgeting raises the problems in a highly explicit way – indeed it is designed to do just this, on the grounds that it is better to identify the elements in social policy choices as clearly as possible for *only then* can there be any chance that they will be systematically considered. Only then will the basis for social policy making be sufficiently exposed for greater public participation in policy formation. Only then are the key problem areas systematically identified for research teams to get to work on them. Only then, moreover, have we a system whose avowed intention is to enable tomorrow's decisions to be better informed and more widely discussable than today's.

With these general considerations behind us we turn to an illustration of how output budgets may be worked out in a specific area of social policy: output budgeting in the police force.

Output budgeting and the police

The allocation of expenditures in a police force according to conventional accounting is illustrated in Figure 9.1. It is readily apparent how unhelpful such a classification is in presenting police authorities, chief

Fig. 9.1: *Gross Expenditure on Police Force Distributed by Conventional Budget Categories*

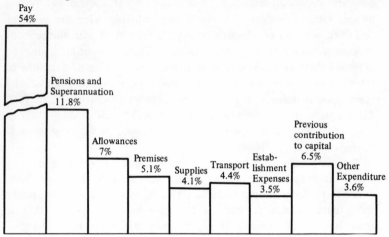

constables or the Home Secretary, with relevant information about policy options. The budgeting categories bear no relation at all to the activities of the police force, to their function or to the outputs they produce. What are these functions? A reasonable list might include the following:

1. Maintenance of law and order and protection of persons and property.
2. Prevention of crime.
3. Detection of criminals and interrogation.
4. In England and Wales (not Scotland) to prosecute, or not, as the case may be, persons suspected of criminal activities.
5. To conduct (in England and Wales) prosecutions themselves for less serious offences.
6. Road traffic control and advice to local authorities.
7. Duties on behalf of government departments, e.g. in respect of nationality questions.
8. A longstanding duty to befriend anyone needing help and to cope at any time with major or minor emergencies.

On the basis of such objectives for the police an entirely different budgeting system has been suggested. One such set of budget categories in a simple output budget identifying only major police programmes might be:

(a) Protection of persons and property from:
    (i)   criminal activities
    (ii) traffic hazards
    (iii) miscellaneous hazards
(b) Treatment of offenders:
    (i)   detection and apprehension
    (ii) process and trial
    (iii) training

Such an output budget is illustrated (in percentage terms)[3] in Figure 9.2.

Fig. 9.2: Output Budget for Police Force

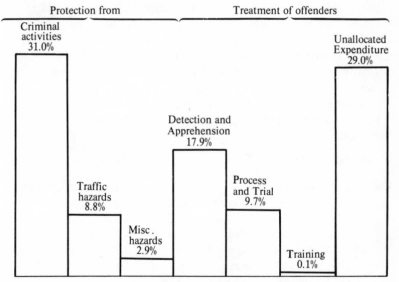

Each of the output categories in Figure 9.2 is drawn very broadly and within each programme head there would be, of course, a wide range of more specific outputs — classified, for example, by the severity of the criminal activity in the first programme. The advantages, however, of functional costing as against the more traditional budgeting are self-evident. What is, perhaps, less self-evident is the ease with which it becomes possible to link up the police output budget with other related activities both within and outside the Home Office. For example, in a comprehensive output budgeting system a non-police input into the protection of persons and property from criminal activity is the activity of the Criminal Injuries Compensation Board. In protection from traffic hazards, the Department of the Environment and the Welsh Office provide inputs, as do local authorities.

A difficulty that frequently arises with an output budget cast in strict output categories is that it is impossible to allocate all the costs meaningfully to a category, even using the rules of thumb outlined above. For example in Figure 9.2, which was based on the work in the Home Office of one of the most resourceful and imaginative practitioners of output budgeting, 29% of expenditure (assumed equal to cost) was left unallocated. Moreover, the strict output based budget poses the problem of output *measures* in its most challenging (intractable!) form. In the intermediate stages before output budgeting has become widely used and its problems and their solutions fully understood and worked out it is therefore sometimes desirable to effect a compromise based more upon activities than upon the ends those activities are supposed to attain. Such a programme structure is usually more immediately practicable, involves less intensive collection and processing of new data and conforms, as a rule, more closely to the managerial form of the organisation. Such a structure for the police may be:

(a) *Operational*

    (i)   Ground Cover
        1. Supervision and Administration
        2. Patrol
        3. Station Duty
        4. Extraordinary Events
        5. Vice Squad
    (ii) Criminal Investigation and Control
        6. Supervision and Administration
        7. Extraordinary Events
        8. General Investigation
        9. Specialised Investigation
      10. Investigation Support Services
      11. Crime Prevention
      12. Regional Crime Squad

(b) *Support*

    (i)   Management
    (ii)   Training
    (iii) Support Services

(c) *Overhead*

    (i)   Pensions
    (ii)   Accommodation

    (iii) Traffic Control
          13.   Supervision and Administration
          14.   Patrol
          15.   Road Survey
          16.   Traffic and Accident Information
          17.   Traffic Wardens
          18.   Road Safety
    (iv) Additional Services

Of these, the first four programmes are 'front line' activities corresponding quite closely with broad output categories and capable of intelligent division into sub-programmes. The output budget for major programme needs (more appropriately, the *programme budget*) resulting from this classification is illustrated in Figure 9.3.

Although this approach has some merit as an interim method it has the severe handicap that it is restricted to the police force's existing range of activities, while a genuine output approach identifies competing or complementary activities by other organisations and thus

Fig. 9.3: Programme Budget for Police Force

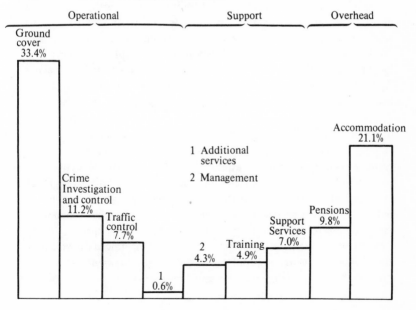

highlights the alternatives facing policy concerned with, e.g. road safety, punishment and care of prisoners, prevention of accidents. It has, moreover, been designed explicitly to avoid cutting across existing police organisational lines. Thus 'Ground Cover', for example, refers to most of the work of the uniformed branch and 'Crime Investigation and Control' to the work of the Criminal Investigation Department (C.I.D.). The strength of this method is that it avoids complicated cost allocations and is broadly familiar. Its weakness is that it may be too familiar to force radical thinking about efficient police activity and that it does not indicate what various police functions are costing since the various inputs relating to a given function are not brought together as a routine matter. It is as well, though, not to criticise these kinds of attempts too harshly so long as the properties of a good output budget are never lost sight of, for the necessity for the kind of compromise illustrated here is the result of our extensive ignorance of the workings of society in general and of having the results of appropriate criminological researches in particular. It is, of course, in areas such as this that interdisciplinary research comes into its own – economics posing the research questions but other disciplines contributing to, if not entirely providing, methods of answering them.

Enough has been said to show both the importance and the problems of introducing output budgeting systematically into social policy. The principal practical difficulty is to allocate (genuine social) costs to current decisions regarding programmes having clear and articulated outputs. The more detailed the output the more the 'overhead' problem looms and the more unsatisfactory one usually finds the existing organisation of the institutions whose budgets are being prepared. Not least of the many advantages of output budgeting is the clarity with which even an elementary exercise will indicate overlap between organisations (e.g. government departments) and many PPBS experts elevate the 'systems' part of their brief into a full-blown *systems analysis* whereby an attempt is made to identify objectives and to relate the organisational forms themselves to these objectives. These latterday Florence Nightingales, equipped with all the techniques of modern management science, are engaged upon essentially complementary activities to the cost-benefit and output budgeting experts.

Difficult though the problems of output budgeting itself are, they are as child's play to the problems of output *measurement*. We turn to these problems, under the guise of social indicators, next.

Social Indicators

There has been a growing tendency since the 1950's, especially in the U.S.A., towards the publication of books attempting to assess the 'state' of contemporary society — books such as Vance Packard's *The Status Seekers* or J. K. Galbraith's *The Affluent Society*. The authors may be social Pollyannas or Cassandras (usually the latter) and the features they seize upon in commenting upon the 'state' of society may accordingly be seen as vindicators or indicators. One thing, however, is clear and this is that, like the Paretian concept of social welfare, these authors emphasise that the accretion of material, and priced, wealth — the growth of Gross Domestic Product (GDP) — gives a wholly inadequate description of the welfare of a society — especially of the relatively wealthy societies. While the indicators used by these popular authors, and the interpretations put upon them, tend to reflect the particular values of the authors themselves the social scientist would seek a set of indicators both more comprehensive and whose importance might be more generally recognised. The 'social indicators movement', as it has become known, shares the fundamental belief that many of the most crucial areas for social decision making need to have a great deal more attention paid to them.

Just as output budgeting (or PPBS) was principally a development within the U.S. Department of Defense and was subsequently applied (rather too hastily for success) in a broad range of governmental activity, so the development of social indicators grew specifically out of another vast, costly and highly technological area of expenditure — the U.S. space programme. The social impact of much modern technology was recognised to be inadequately measured by the conventional 'economic' indicators such as incomes, prices and employment or unemployment rates. Exactly the same is true, of course, with many of the areas of social policy. We have in this book frequently noted the inadequacy of many prices as indicators of social value; frequently prices are altogether absent; we have also noted the difficulties inherent in conceptualising, let alone measuring, the output of many social policies. Sensible social policy would clearly be much improved if it were possible to measure more accurately (even if not perfectly) the social value of various policy alternatives, the 'real' consequences of social policies and the relationships between the means (inputs) and the ends (outputs).

Conceptual Approaches

The basic urge driving many members of the 'social indicators movement' is to measure things like 'educational deprivation', 'social inequality', 'health', 'need' or — most ambitious — Durkheim's notions of 'average morality' and 'individualism'. But this basic desire to make more rigorous any discussion or measurement of the dimensions of a social 'problem' or of social policy is not enough to enable one to proceed very far and can lead to peculiar results if careful thought is not put in at the fundamental level of designing *appropriate* indicators. It is not, for example, impossible to find accurate looking numbers among the social policy literature which purport to describe, say, the *urgency* of a social problem. Thus, studies exist which rank areas and regions along a scale which has been derived by adding such phenomena as numbers of unemployed, malicious woundings, occupied males in skilled and unskilled jobs, numbers of households with a density greater than 1½ persons per room, deaths from bronchitis and dividing all these by the population.[4] How could one use such an indicator of social deprivation or need? Why should the components of such an indicator receive equal weights? How would the indicator be affected by policies that are supposed to affect it? Is the indicator specific, or comprehensive enough? What social theory has been used to decide what to put into the indicator and what to leave out? Likewise, examples abound whereby the success of social policy is measured by the deployment of resources rather than by the impact of the resources deployed on the ultimate policy objective. *Input* measures (such as beds) or throughput measures (such as deaths and discharges) abound in the health policy literature and although they may be valid social indicators for some purposes they are not measures of output or of urgency of need or of effectiveness in meeting needs. These and related problems are evidently highly pertinent and must be answered before the measurement exercise ever gets under way. In short, a theory of the relationship of social indicators and social policy is required. One must be ever conscious that blind quantification — quantophrenia — may be as dangerous — and is probably more dangerous — than no formal quantification at all. We therefore begin, as usual, with the theory.

To make a rational choice in social policy, knowledge is required about the three key constituent elements in any social choice. Each of the three is necessary and together they are sufficient for rational policy making. These three are: first, a measure of the objective or *output* of a policy (or collection of policies). It is, for example, of little use to embark upon a set of policies designed to promote educational equality or equality of life opportunity unless one has some fairly unambiguous indicator which enables one to monitor the success of one's policies. The second need, in view of the multiplicity of the objectives of social policy, is the necessity to rank them in order of priority, to place social valuations upon them or 'shadow prices'. One has to be able to trade-off various objectives such as equality of educational opportunity and increasing the nation's health and to be able to identify areas where objectives are mutually complementary — where one policy increases two outputs. In short, one requires an indicator of *social need*. Finally, there is the need to understand the technology of policy — one requires a model which relates the increases in one objective to the necessary reductions in another. With either given or growing national resources it is equally necessary to know these 'production function' relationships, which set a limit to what *can* be done, which relate the real inputs in social policy to feasible outputs.

Although information is needed about only these three things, they are a formidable trio. The most fundamental of them in logic is the output indicator, for an indicator of need is naturally cast in terms of the output indicator: after all it is the output, or effects of the policy, that is needed. Similarly, production possibilities indicators relate one output to another. Output indicators are also, however, of importance purely for their own sakes in providing information about the state of society and the ways in which it is changing. It is in this sense that the term 'social indicator' has become most widely used, though it is a sense that can easily lead to misleading results unless the tryad of types of indicator is borne clearly in mind. For example, indicators of hospital throughput are sometimes proposed as measures of ill-health but they may vary as inputs in the system change. Thus, a planned reduction in psychiatric beds from around 2.5 per thousand population to 0.5 per thousand would falsely indicate an increase in the nation's mental health. This proposed indicator fails to make the kind of distinction emphasised here.

The relationship of this tryad to previous analysis in this book can be easily illustrated in a diagram. Figure 9.4 depicts our by now familiar conceptualisation of a social choice problem. The priorities indicator measures the social value of increments in the output indicator, and is equivalent to an *MV* schedule. The technical indicator measures what must necessarily be foregone of other outputs in increasing the

Fig. 9.4

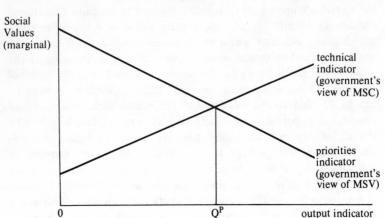

Social
Values
(marginal)

technical
indicator
(government's
view of MSC)

priorities
indicator
(government's
view of MSV)

0   Q^P output indicator

indicator in question. The money value of direct inputs in a programme
will normally be an inadequate guide to the height and shape of this
schedule for it is not merely the expenditure on, say, manpower in the
health service that is to be recorded here but the social value of that
manpower in its most socially valuable alternatives use — say, in
primary school education. This indicator is conceptually equivalent to a
marginal social cost schedule. For each of them one dimension is easily
seen to be the output indicator itself and the other is some numéraire
system by which numbers are attached indicating relative priorities —
money units are usually the most convenient. Clearly, the better the
information the more likely policy makers will be able to approach the
optimal programme size at Q^P.

Output indicators, in an ideal world, would correspond to the
programme headings of an output budget and would be more or less
aggregated according to the purposes of the output budget. For some
very specific purposes, not usually identified in a broad output
programme, one requires very specific output measures. To illustrate,
let us suppose that one is concerned with a cost-effectiveness study of
care for the elderly wherein one compares the effect of residential
homes or domiciliary care on the health and welfare of elderly persons.
Clearly, the required output indicator would attempt to measure as
accurately as possible the health and welfare of such persons. The
dimensions in which this can be done are, in principle, infinite and

include such aspects of their wellbeing as: ability to dress themselves; mobility; ability to feed; ability to cut toe-nails; mental state; and so on. Some of these dimensions will be highly correlated with others, enabling us to eliminate some of them. Expediency will also compel one to restrict the list and at this point the impossibility of leaving an entirely objective indicator becomes clear. Not only must a choice be made about which are the most important dimensions of 'output' for inclusion but those that are eventually included must be weighted according to one's view of their importance in contributing to a person's general state of wellbeing. For example, it is possible to score an elderly person's state of mind on a scale of, say, 1-3 and also his ability to cut his toenails, but it is obviously not possible for the scores to be added up as they are. Not only may they be not entirely independent of one another but one may be regarded as being much more significant than another. An element of subjectivity creeps in. Whose subjective values should be used? There can be no 'scientific' answer to this question. In practice it is likely that the values would have to be supplied by those experts who are doing the exercise though there is no reason why some control should not be exercised by those with more explicit public accountability and it is probably desirable that this should be so.

For more general purposes, output indicators may be more aggregated. For example, periodic surveys of the nation's 'health' may be taken which would be even cruder than specific output measures but which would raise essentially similar conceptual problems.

Outputs and inputs in health

The difficulties of devising reasonable output indicators are enormous. The most advanced work in this area to date has taken place in the health field. There has also been a long standing tradition (but mostly outside official circles) of measurement of the distribution of resources (but not much of the distribution of outputs). In the education field, however, output measurement has not yet got much beyond the crude basis of counting the heads of individuals in various stages of education – a throughput measure rather than an output measure. There has been no attempt to date to seek the ultimate outputs of education policy, to measure them and to adjust for quality. The reasons, of course, are not hard to find, for the task is very demanding. It may be that in some areas of policy, ultimate outputs will remain elusive and secondary indicators will always have to be used based upon some hypothetical relationship between the notional true output and its surrogate. In the short run the use of secondary indicators is inevitably more widespread for in many cases neither the conceptual nor the practical problems of final output measures have been solved. In short run compromises, however, it is of utmost importance that the long run objectives – with all their *organisational* consequences, should not be lost from sight.

The twin problems of developing usable short run compromise indicators while simultaneously tackling the long run development of proper output indicators can be illustrated by the problems confronted in health service policy. At present there is scarcely any information about the final outputs which measure the success of the health and personal social services in improving the nation's well-being, notable exceptions being in the maternity and general health programmes where the level of infant and maternal deaths and handicapping conditions arising at birth are known and the incidence of certain diseases subject to preventive measures is measured. Other output data are at best patchy or difficult to interpret (e.g. hospital inpatient waiting lists and times) or not based on random sampling (e.g. The Royal College of General Practitioners' morbidity surveys).

There does exist, by contrast, a relative abundance of secondary measures relating to:

(a)   numbers of cases treated
(b)   ratios of inputs (staff, equipment, expenditure, etc.) to clients
(c)   balance of care, i.e. the range and mix of services being delivered to different client groups.

Thus, it is possible by using these secondary measures to measure success in terms of the extent to which specific targets are obtained. But these secondary indicators – whose relationship with final outputs is far from clear – themselves need substantial improvement. For example even such a well-known throughput measure as the number of cases relates to episodes of sickness rather than to individuals – the same individual admitted twice, for example, to hospital counts as two cases. Outpatient events are not linked to inpatient events. It is not generally known whether the same elderly persons who receive meals on wheels also receive home help. A major improvement in these data will be to relate them to clients.

In an output budgeting context secondary indicators with a

satisfactory client base provide a valuable foundation for predicting future budgets – i.e. for forecasting future expenditures based on fulfilling anticipated health programmes. They also help to provide decision makers with an evolving picture of how policy in the health and personal social services is developing and help to identify problem areas worthy, perhaps, of special study.

Ultimately, however, the objective of health policy is not to provide certain ratios of inputs to outputs, to maintain or increase particular throughputs of clients or even to abolish waiting lists! It is to secure the optimal health of the population. The other factors are relevant only in so far as they help (a) to identify the real outputs (b) to locate their costs and (c) to enable decision makers to balance the relative (social) values of improved health as between different clients and enable higher decision makers to balance the relative value of improved health in general as against more education, higher pensions, less poverty, crime or broken homes. In short, the ultimate objective of genuine output measurement should never be lost sight of. Not the least important of the reasons for emphasising this is that only a genuine output-orientated approach can succeed in cutting across existing organisational lines and suggesting new ones basing organisation upon a more rational relationship with its end objectives. Programme budgeting, while better than nothing, remains only a halfway-house to genuine output budgeting.

Output of education

Difficult though even the conceptualisation – let alone the operationalisation – of an appropriate definition and measure of health output is, the output of education establishments is, if anything, even harder to come to terms with. Educators, like the medical profession, are understandably suspicious of the economic approach, fearing that it will tend to emphasise quantity at the expense of quality, the easily identifiable rather than the subtle, the short term effects rather than the long term, the financial rather than the cultural. However, many educators are inconsistent in their attitudes, especially when pay claims are in the offing. Then the assertion that the output or productivity (output divided by input) of schools and universities cannot be measured objectively is contradicted by their assertions that it has, in fact, increased since the last award.

As we have seen in the discussion of output budgeting in education, there is no single objective or output of the education sector. Therefore any measurement of educational output, at whatever level, must be multi-dimensional. At its broadest, education alters the individuals being educated and the purpose of output measurement is thus to measure this 'value added'. Standardised tests to measure the transmission of knowledge and other attainments of pupils and students, to test cultural awareness, creativity and moral or social values, have been devised by educational psychologists. Unfortunately systematic information, as compared with occasional experiments, has not been collected for any lengthy period of time or for the very long period (i.e. long term effects on those who have been educated). At the moment, therefore, such measures as these are not available for examining the secular trends in education or for measuring productivity and cost effectiveness.[5]

Some interim estimates of the output of secondary schools and universities in the UK have been derived by Blaug and Woodhall, based upon the crudest quantity indices, such as annual school leavers and graduating students. Since these basic measures manifestly fail to include any quality changes, methods of weighting the crude outputs were devised which went some way towards such an adjustment.

In the case of secondary education the procedure was as follows. The first weighting system tried was an 'economic' quality adjustment based on the assumption that, on average, differences in relative earnings after leaving school over working lifetimes reflect the vocational value of different types and levels of secondary schooling. Due to data deficiencies, only rough adjustments according to estimates of the present value of earnings were possible, leading to the time series of output in column 2 of table 9.1. The unadjusted number of school leavers is shown in column 1, showing that the adjusted indicator raised the annual growth rate of output from 2.0% to 2.5%. A second 'educational' weights system used the period of schooling on the grounds that this reflects an acquired taste for learning. If many pupils drop out of school at or soon after the statutory school leaving age output is considered, on this criterion, to be of lower quality than if they stay on. The result of this calculation is shown in column 3 of table 9.1, raising the annual growth rate to 2.6%. Finally, an 'academic' output indicator was devised where the weights were based upon 'O' and 'A' level examination scores. This indicator is shown in column 4 of table 9.1, and shows the fastest growth rate. Clearly, on all four

TABLE 9.1: *Indicators of Secondary School Output 1950–63*
(1950 = 100)

School Year	Unweighted No. of School-leavers	'Economic' Indicator	'Educational' Indicator	'Academic' Indicator
1950–1	100.0	100.0	100.0	n.a.
1951–2	97.2	97.1	97.2	n.a.
1952–3	102.0	102.5	102.3	n.a.
1953–4	102.5	103.6	103.2	100.0
1954–5	99.9	102.2	101.1	100.3
1955–6	95.1	n.a.	97.0	99.6
1956–7	102.6	n.a.	104.3	107.5
1957–8	109.4	n.a.	111.5	115.1
1958–9	116.4	121.9	118.9	124.0
1959–60	117.6	125.2	121.5	132.5
1060–1	119.9	128.7	122.6	136.7
1961–2	143.6	152.5	148.0	159.4
1962–3	134.9	149.1	142.0	161.8
1963–4	129.8	146.3	138.7	167.6
Average annual increase in output	2.0%	2.5%	2.6%	4.7%

Source: M. Blaug and M. Woodhall, "Productivity Trends in British Secondary Education", cited in Further Reading.

indicators, education output has been rising – and the quality of output (as measured by these three methods) has been rising even faster.[6]

For the university sector a similar exercise has been performed. The basic quantity unit was the number of students completing a course and this was adjusted by a similar 'economic' quality weights system and an 'educational' adjustment based upon the length of a course leading to a degree. The third method of weighting in this case was a 'cultural' adjustment which reversed the 'economic' set of weights and, in fact, used their reciprocal. The results are shown in table 9.2 for the three years for which data were obtainable.[7]

Perhaps the most remarkable feature of both exercises – especially in the case of universities – is the way in which the crude output data completely dominate the trends, the adjustments for quality add noticeably little to the overall picture. The reader is left to draw his own conclusions from these facts.

TABLE 9.2: *Indicator of University Output 1938–62*
(1952 = 100)

Year	Unweighted No. of Graduates	'Economic' Indicator	'Educational' Indicator	'Cultural' Indicator
1938	61	60	60	60
1952	100	100	100	100
1962	140	144	143	142

Source: M. Blaug and M. Woodhall, "Productivity Trends in British University Education 1938–1962," cited in Further Reading.

While the officials are currently busy developing programme budgets in many areas of social policy the scholars are increasingly turning their attention to the fundamental conceptual problem of social policy output measurement and to the design of practical experiments to test the reliability and validity of the conceptual measures. It is, as yet, too early to report on their degree of success for once again we come up against a frontier in the economics of social policy. This much is clear, however, that the questions being asked are the relevant questions and already a substantial quantity of obscurantism has been abolished.

NOTES

1. Transfers are, of course, important from the point of view of income redistribution.
2. Corresponding to these are present values of cost of
   at t_0:   £500,000 + £300,000/(1 + i) + £200,000/(1 + i)^2 − £x/(1 + i)^{50}
   at t_1:   £300,000 + £200,000/(1 + i) − £x(1 + i)^{49}
   at t_4:   − £x/(1 + i)^{46}
   at t_{50}: − £x
   which are the building costs of completing the programme at t_0, t_1, etc.
3. Note that these expenditure categories ignore substantial social costs such as foregone earnings of prisoners (if they are members of the society whose welfare is to be maximised), value of the time of witnesses, jurymen, etc.
4. We cite no reference and the example in the text is admittedly a parody — but it is not a grotesque parody!
5. Specific results are available, however, from some experiments. It seems, for example, that factors such as the level of teacher salaries, teacher experience, expenditures per pupil and library facilities are closely related to attainment scores in standard academic subjects, but the size of class, size of school and age of buildings are very much less closely related. For a general discussion of

these issues, see the articles by Blaug and Woodhall cited in the Further Reading.

6. However, productivity has been falling. See Blaug and Woodhall.

7. The reader who is interested in the detailed workings of the weights systems and some discussion of their meaning and relevance is referred to the Further Reading.

FURTHER READING

Output Budgeting

E. A. Collins, 'The Functional Approach to Public Expenditure', *Public Administration*, 1966.

Department of Education and Science, *Output Budgeting for The Department of Education and Science*, London, HMSO, 1970.

H. A. Hovey, *The Planning-Programming-Budgeting Approach to Government Decision-Making*, New York & London, Praeger, 1968.

Institute of Municipal Treasurers and Accountants, *Programme Budgeting – the Concept and the Application*, London, IMTA, 1969.

F. J. Lyden and E. G. Miller, *Planning, Programming, Budgeting: A Systems Approach to Management*, Chicago, Markham, 1968.

J. P. Martin and J. Bradley, 'Design of a Study of the Cost of Crime', *British Journal of Criminology*, Vol. 4, 1964.

D. Novick (Ed), *Program Budgeting*, Cambridge, Mass., Harvard University Press, 1965.

G. J. Wasserman, 'Planning Programming Budgeting in the Police Service in England and Wales', *O & M Bulletin*, Vol. 25, 1970, pp. 197–210.

Alan Williams, *Output Budgeting and the Contribution of Micro-economics to Efficiency in Government*, CAS Occasional Paper No. 4, London, HMSO, 1967.

Social Indicators

R. A. Bauer, *Social Indicators*, Cambridge, Mass. and London, M.I.T. Press 1966.

M. Blaug and M. Woodhall, 'Productivity Trends in British University Education 1938–62', *Minerva*, Summer. 1965.

M. Blaug and M. Woodhall, 'Productivity Trends in British Secondary Education, 1950–1963', *Sociology of Education*, Winter, 1968.

A. J. Culyer, 'Indicators of Health: An Economist's Viewpoint', in W. A. Laing (ed), *Evaluation in the Health Services*, London, Office of Health Economics, 1972.

A. J. Culyer, R. J. Lavers and Alan Williams, 'Social Indicators: Health', *Social Trends*, No. 2, 1971.

A. Shonfield and S. Shaw, *Social Indicators and Social Policy*, London, Heinemann, 1972.

D. F. Sullivan, *Conceptual Problems in Developing an Index of Health*, Washington D.C., Office of Health Statistics Analysis, U.S. Dept. of Health, Education and Welfare, 1966.

R. Rosser and V. Watts, 'The Sanative Output of a Health Care System', paper given at the O.R.S.A. Conference in Dallas, May 1971.

R. Rosser and V. Watts, 'The Measurement of Hospital Output', paper given at the Operational Research Society Conference in Lancaster, September 1971.

10 Financing Social Services

Questions concerned with the methods of financing pensions, education, housing, health, and so on have proved among the most controversial in a controversial area. Many people view finance as the area where economics is most to the fore in social policy, though the fact that it occupies only one chapter in this book should put its true importance, in terms of the contribution of economics, in perspective. Less widespread is the view that finance can be considered apart from the questions of priorities, planning and efficiency, after the administrators, doctors, teachers, and so on have had their say. Indeed it cannot, for methods of finance can have a profound effect upon the performance of institutions and individuals and upon the attainment of objectives. Hence, while financing is only a part of the economic problem it is a truly important part.

The problem of financing boils down to the questions of who should pay and how? These questions include the question of the share of the financial cost borne by the person who 'causes' the cost to be incurred, and the relative shares of the public and private sectors in financing any social service.

Earmarked taxes or general-fund financing?

Of the many choices facing society in the method of financing an important one, when programmes are funded entirely out of the budget, is whether the taxation used to finance them should be 'earmarked', i.e. a specific tax for a specific programme, such as a

202

'health tax' and 'education tax', or should be 'general-fund', i.e. programmes funded out of a common pool of tax revenue. The two methods would amount to the same thing if the government ran only one programme (obviously) or if the political mechanism operated in a perfectly democratic way in revealing individual voters' preferences. The importance of the distinction arises only because the political mechanism is not perfect and because governments, both central and local, run many programmes. The advantages of earmarked taxation are supposed to accrue to citizen-voters because it enables them to perceive more directly than otherwise the link between tax-finance and expenditure in the public sector. There is a presumption that the closer the 'control' the tax payer has over the activity of the public sector the more closely it will correspond to his preferences. But if the political mechanism worked perfectly, if politicians represented their constituents' interests perfectly, then political decisions based on general-fund taxation would produce precisely the same result.

In practice, of course, the political mechanism does not work perfectly so the question arises whether general-fund financing is to be preferred to earmarking, or vice-versa. In principle it would appear, with imperfect political revelation of preferences, that the earmarked system would lead to a greater degree of optimisation both in the size of public programmes devoted to health, income redistribution, *etc.*, and in their composition. And yet, for this really to be true, the information required by each individual voter-citizen to enable him to reach sensible decisions would have to be truly enormous – far more than one could reasonably expect him to cope with. Moreover, it would seem to imply a continuous series of referenda on every programme operated by the government. Given the likely size of these information and transaction costs, the general-fund system becomes more desirable, and the ultimate decisions about the size and structure of the programmes are taken by politicians. If they are to take them, however, they clearly cannot be constrained by the pre-ordained programme budgets implied by earmarking.

It is at this point that the corollary to general-fund financing comes in – namely that it ought to be complemented by the PPBS, cost-effectiveness type of analysis outlined in chapters 8 and 9, for the use of these techniques compensates, to a degree, for the remoteness of the political decision takers from those on whose behalf the decisions are reached. In a sense, one is trying to *simulate* the results that would come out of a 'perfect' democracy, rather in the way that the great democratic socialists have envisaged computers simulating market processes, though one retains a market sector to provide some of the basic benchmark values and quantities to be used in the simulation. The cost of the general-fund system as against earmarked taxes is that it reduces democratic *participation* in collective decisions. PPBS and related techniques attempt to force the administration and governments to think in terms of the outputs and inputs to and from particular client-groups, but they do not actually involve those client-groups in the formal process of decisions.

The remnants of earmarking persist in social security contributions, but in fact these contributions, in Britain, fall short of a sufficient collection to finance social security benefits, while that portion for health insurance contributes a minute proportion to the total costs of the National Health Service. As we have observed before, the main effect of these residual earmarked taxes is to create confusion among the contributors/tax payers and fiscal illusion.

Subsidies and rationing

Granted then that the general fund financing system suggests that government, both central and local, may make the decisions about the size and the composition of the programmes comprising their social policy, several important questions still remain. We do not here retread the uneven ground of public versus private *production* of services, but a choice still remains as to the methods by which particular *programmes* are financed. If the government is producing a service, one possibility is clearly that the service is financed directly and fully out of the budget. Other possibilities, however, include *partial* financing, with reliance being placed on client fees to recover the entire costs of sub-programmes (e.g. private hospital beds) or part of their costs (e.g. prescription drugs). They also include the possibility of *indirect* financing, whereby the government places purchasing power in the hands of the client group, tied specifically to a particular service in the form of tokens, coupons, vouchers, or grants, or loans. These latter possibilities in particular have created considerable controversy in the 1960's and 70's.

The present system by which housing is subsidised is a curious amalgam and illustrates perhaps the biggest tangle current in social policy of objectives and methods used to attain them. The externality imposed by inadequate housing appears to take two forms: first that housing expenditure should not be 'excessive' for any individual household and secondly that the quality of anyone's housing should not fall below a certain level. To this end the British government subsidises the improvement of privately owned and local authority owned dwellings; constructs new dwellings; subsidises local authority rents; regulates rents in the private sector; subsidises interest rates for purchasers using the mortgage option scheme and provides tax relief to owner-occupiers with house mortgages and tax exemption from imputed rents.

Tax relief to owner-occupiers (totalling about £225 millions in 1970) enables more individuals both to own houses and to own better houses than they would otherwise own, but not much of this sum can be said to internalise an externality, for the vast majority of currently subsidised owner-occupiers would not, it is reasonable to suppose, otherwise occupy substandard accommodation. This subsidy is surely one of the biggest anomalies in social policy. Similarly, some of the improvement grants to private owners are hard to justify.

The allocation of local authority rented housing contains no guarantee either that vacant accommodation goes to those in currently the worst housing or that, if household circumstances change for the better, households no longer in 'need' of subsidisation no longer receive it either by raising rents to an economic level, selling to tenants or terminating the tenancy.

Regulated rents have the effect of transferring income from owners to tenants (not obviously either efficient or fair redistribution) and of reducing the stock of private rented accommodation and the quality of the existing stock.

The principal questions which have to answered, in housing or any other sphere of social policy, concern the methods of ensuring that the externality is internalised, making sure that like cases are treated alike, that subsidies do not go to those who impose no externality (unless this is the most effective way of getting them to those who do), that sufficient overall service is provided and that the costs of the policy are equitably distributed. The principal issues of recent controversy in financing relate to whether the suppliers should make a service available at a subsidised price or the clients should be subsidised to enable them to pay (at least) the market price.

We consider first the extent to which the cost of a service is to be recovered from the client-group. The possibilities here are clearly that either part of the cost be recovered or none of it, and whether some cash should be paid *to* the client-group. One school of thought advocates a general policy of absence of user-charges on grounds of either equality of consumption or of equality of opportunity. In general, a policy of zero user-charges will attain these objectives only if (a) all individuals have zero MV's at the same level of consumption and (b) if individuals do not face different *full* costs at the margin. In *general* neither of these two conditions is fulfilled. First, as we have seen even in the case of health, MV's, at zero (or near to zero) prices, may vary a great deal while the values different people place on schooling vary notoriously. Moreover, MV's are also a function of individuals' incomes. For those services whose demand rises with income, the same consumption level will have a higher MV for those with higher incomes. Second, the full costs that are borne by clients include not only the price they pay for the service, but also the value of the time they sacrifice to obtain it (which varies from the relatively trivial hour or so it may take to claim a benefit, plus bus fares, to the overwhelmingly significant sacrifice of several years' earnings foregone by receiving schooling and education) among other things.

In addition to these factors, equality (whether of consumption or of opportunity) is only a *part* of the problem. Equal consumption, for example, should be equal consumption *at the right level*. Our externality relationships suggest that in general there is a unique level of consumption that is preferred by society. Moreover, it is generally the case that it is desired that everyone should receive *at least* this amount — for those dependent solely on the public programme, exactly this amount.[1]

These problems are illustrated in Figure 10.1. In this Figure, two relatively poor individuals, A and B are depicted. Suppose initially that they both face an identical price P and an identical (additional) subjective marginal cost C. The full price is $P + C$. If they faced this full price in, say, the market A would consume $Q_1{}^A$ and B $Q_1{}^B$, where we may suppose Q to represent years of schooling, or consumption of doctors' time — neither are equal but both are less than the socially ideal amount Q^P each. Abolishing price and making the service free confronts them only with C. A now consumes $Q_2{}^A$ and B $Q_2{}^B$. Once again they are not identical quantities and once again they do not correspond to the social ideal — in the diagram too little is still taken,

Fig. 10.1

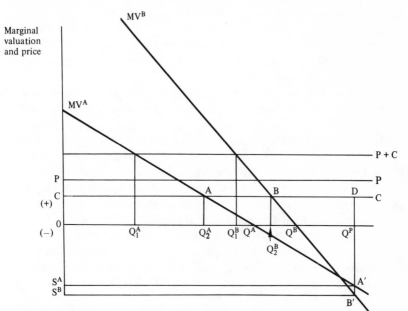

but it might have been too much. In education, for example, too little
tends to be taken even with zero price while in health, too much tends
to be demanded. In order to overcome these problems by manipulating
the costs facing individuals variable subsidies have to be given (where
too little is still taken). In the case of our two individuals, this requires
a (marginal) subsidy of CS^A to A and CS^B to B. Conversely, if too
much were taken, variable, but positive, prices should be charged. The
only reliable solution to the problem of too little being taken if
monetary means are impractical, or held to be undesirable on other
grounds, is to make a specified consumption level *compulsory*. In this
way, Q^P can be attained – e.g. education from five up to the age of
sixteen. Note, however, that even though the service may be provided
free of charge, unless *additional* compensation is given to these
individuals or families, they will *lose* from this arrangement. A suffers a
welfare loss whose money equivalent (to him) is the area ADA' and B
loses BDB' (to him). Consequently, though it is undoubtedly the case
that the rest of society gains from having A and B move to Q^P
(especially those who value education as such and those who earn their
living providing it) compelling A and B to move to Q^P from $Q_2{}^A$ and

$Q_2{}^B$ cannot be said *unambiguously* to represent an improvement in social welfare *unless* A and B receive compensation in addition to compulsory free schooling.[2] There *may* be an improvement, but we cannot tell, for the solution chosen is one that 'reconciles' a conflict of values by those holding one value-system imposing their (no doubt, superior) values on the others.

In the contrary case, where individuals consume *too much* at an effective personal cost of C, the non-financial method of ensuring optimal consumption is to impose rationing devices. In the case of health services, for example, these are left to the discretion of the doctors, operating with a given set of medical resources, who operate a system such that they evaluate the seriousness of patients' condition before recommending treatment (for example, suggest the wearing of a truss rather than admitting to hospital for herniotomy) or through the use of waiting lists. The welfare losses imposed by this solution, insofar as they exist at all, depend upon the method used. For example, waiting times imposed on people suffering discomfort and not able, perhaps, to work efficiently, tend to favour those whose subjective valuation of time is low, though everyone whose time is wasted – if it is wasted – suffers a loss.

The non-financial rationing systems for attaining the optimal consumption are thus imposed solutions, naturally supported by those who do the imposing and by those for whom an externality is internalised at a lower personal cost than may otherwise be needed, and equally naturally resented by those who are imposed upon and who may bear the costs. Such solutions depend upon who has effective power in the community to impose preferences. Unfortunately there is no scientific method for comparing the welfare gains of the gainers with the welfare losses of the losers. The identification of potential Pareto improvements depends upon estimating consumer surplus losses and gains such as ADA' and BDB' and there may be no reliable way of estimating the necessary sections of the MV curves. Moreover, even if there were, there are many who, on political grounds which are beyond the scope of this book, would object to the illiberal elements implicit to a greater or lesser degree in these rationing procedures (equally, many who regard their judgement as better than others would approve – so long as they themselves were being compelled to do only what they would do anyway).[3]

Where non-price rationing systems of the sort discussed are not used, predictable results are observed. It is not without reason, for example, that voluntary attendance at university is taken advantage of principally by the middle and upper income families, despite the fact that they normally have to pay more to support their children at college. Even if poorer families valued higher education as much as wealthier families, the sacrifices they would have to make would be, in real terms, far greater than those made by the richer (the difference between, say, £4,000 in family income over five years[4] to a poor family compared with £4,000 for a rich family). Using financial incentives would require *subsidies* to be given to low income households, not merely free education. If the non-price costs facing rich and poor could thus be brought approximately to the same level, then approximate equality of *opportunity* would exist.[5] Equality of *consumption*, however, would require further subsidies to those with low MV's. A longer term solution is to try to raise the MV's of low income households by making them appreciate the benefits of education more keenly, though proved effective methods of doing so remain to be established.

In university and higher education, where financing controversies have been engaged in most enthusiastically, the system in Britain is one in which the institutions are financed by direct grants from government (via the University Grants Committee, Research Councils, *etc*) and from fees charged by the institutions. The fees and student maintenance are financed in turn primarily by grants from local education authorities which are graduated according to parental income. While this system implies, on the one hand, a suboptimal level of consumption of university education from low income families,[6] the general principle of graduation is consistent with an approach towards efficient internalisation of externalities. Higher education is a superior good, the MV for a given amount of which rises as income rises. Assume that all parents have the same taste for educating their children — probably broadly true for most income levels save the lowest where the parents are likely to be educationally deprived. In Figure 10.2 MV^* is the overall community marginal valuation curve for *each* qualified student and MV^1, MV^2 and MV^3 are the MV's of three families with incomes in ascending order. Let Q^P represent the overall per-student ideal undergraduate course. MC represents annual tuition fee and maintenance cost. Clearly, for family 1 to send a student to university requires a per unit subsidy of OC (the rest of the community bearing the full tuition and maintenance cost), family 2 requires a per unit subsidy of AC (paying OA itself) and family 3 requires a per unit subsidy of BC (paying OB itself). Evidently, if each qualified student is to attend

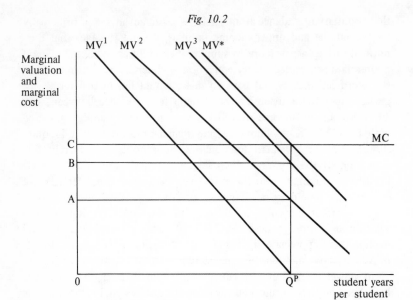

Fig. 10.2

university at least cost (minimum total subsidy) to the rest of the community, the per unit subsidy should vary inversely with family income.[7]

The present U.K. grants system in higher education — and, indeed, at all levels — has been criticised because it does not go far enough in discriminating in favour of the relatively poor on the one hand (by compensating them partially for loss of earnings) and because it does not discriminate sufficiently *against* the relatively rich.[8] Student fees in the whole of higher education account for less than 10% of recurrent expenditure, while in primary and secondary education, no charge at all is made. Consequently, at least so far as the relatively higher income groups are concerned, they are not very heavily discriminated against; indeed, once again subsidies are given to internalise externalities that do not exist. Of course, the full subsidies are not actually given in cash to the beneficiaries. Instead they are given to the institutions which then allow entry with nominal fees, as in higher education (these fees themselves being subject to the variable subsidy), or else with no charge at all.

One possibility, therefore, would be to change the current system so that the entire grant was given to the student (but graduated according to family income[9]) who received compulsory primary and secondary education and to those receiving voluntary sixth form or higher education provided they attended their institutions. Such a system could avoid both the gratuitous gift to those who impose no, or little, externality and the penalisation of those for whom even free places are excessively costly.

Education vouchers

A related, and much debated, proposal has been to give every family a lump sum payment for spending on education which would be normally sufficient to cover the full cost of an 'average' institution of a particular type for a specified period (presumably a term or academic year). A convenient way of ensuring that the cash is spent for its specified purpose is to award each eligible individual a coupon or, as it is popularly called, a voucher, entitling him to a prescribed money's worth of education. The purchasing power of the voucher could again be inversely related to family income and its maximum value in excess of the average cost of education – the balance being payable in cash.

The voucher is thus an earmarked benefit (not tax), and would necessarily (if the benefit is to be graduated) be supplementable out of family income. At the primary and secondary school levels, voucher proposals have also been coupled with the suggestion that they be used in both the private and public sector schools and that parents sending children to state schools should be able to choose whatever school they wish provided it meets the minimal educational standards implied by the externality. This complementary proposal implies according to its advocates that, in addition to efficient subsidising, there would be a greater variety of educational institutions (for example, placing different emphasis on scholarship, sport, discipline, free expression, social integration, religion, internationalism, political education); it would increase school responsiveness to parental values and concerns; stimulate competition among schools and hence quality; promote innovation; encourage parental initiative and, indeed, parental involvement in education; and finally, increase total resources spent on education.

The literature on vouchers is more to be noted for counter assertions about these claims and for counter statements of value-judgement than either for rigorous analysis of the plausibility of the implications of the scheme alleged by either side or by closer examination of the value-judgements that are involved. For example, the counter arguments run that variations in quality and of type of education are undesirable anyway; that parents would be the dupes of misleading advertising; that minimum standards would turn out very low; they would not promote common social values; social divisiveness would increase; that the cheapest schools would be ghettoes for the children of the very poor and for problem children; that the extra expenditure would go only to the children of the well-to-do and that, anyway, there may be no increase in the resources spent on education at all.

A little careful economic analysis can help us to sort out some, at least, of these conflicting claims. First, the question of variety, choice and common values. In general, if parents do have different preferences regarding the kind of education they would like for their children then any increase in choice enabling them to suit their preferences better would increase their welfare. At least the parties are agreed on the probable increase in diversity that would result from greater competition. The problem arises in comparing the welfare gains to parents who get their preferred choices with the welfare losses of those *other* parents (and non-parents) who do not approve either of the type of education chosen by these parents or of the fact that different value-systems may be inculcated in society by different types of education. In short, variety and freedom of choice *per se* impose an *adverse externality* on them. Now while the *existence* of this adverse externality is indisputable, its *status* is in doubt. Although we have not explicitly incorporated this point in our discussion of Pareto optimality – for it requires an additional value-judgement – it would certainly be in keeping with the spirit of Pareto to exclude some externalities from consideration in social welfare. For example, if I like my bedroom walls pink and you like *my* bedroom walls blue, provided you are not my wife, it would seem not unreasonable to suppose that the externality imposed on you by the offensive colour of my walls should be ignored – 'it's none of your business'. Perhaps the fact that I wish my child to have an education devoid of any religious instruction whatever but thoroughly imbued with the military virtues in an environment that excludes meat-eaters, while you do not wish *my* child not to have such an education, is such an externality that could be agreed, in a kind of 'social contract', not to be included in the calculus. If so, then the case for homogeneity and the inculcation of common values loses some of its strength. Remember, of course, that certain minimum standards are to be laid down in any case.[10] A similar argument could be made (or rejected) in the case of the 'ghetto' objection to vouchers. *If* it were the case that certain schools remained, as now, or more of them became ghettoes of a particular social class, ethnic group, or educational ability, it is at least not obvious that I should internalise the adverse externality I feel by forcing my middleclass friends to send their children there, even in the (unlikely) event that I shall send mine. In any event, should the ghetto phenomenon prove serious, it may be possible to avoid either side bulldozing the other side into accepting its values by taking appropriate measures to improve the quality of the education and environment in such schools by supplementary — and institutional — subsidies to these educational priority schools and areas.

The claims made by voucher proponents to the effect that total resources in education would increase are not unambiguous in theory. For example, if vouchers would produce a more optimal total expenditure (as they may do) it is not clear that this would necessarily be a *larger* expenditure than is current. It is perfectly possible for the education lobby, in the imperfect political mechanism, to have secured a larger than optimal quantity of resources. The extent to which wealthier families would secure 'better' or more education than others by supplementing their vouchers so as to make their total spending higher than the value of a maximum-valued voucher would depend upon a variety of factors including the basic voucher value, their taste for education and the minimum educational standards set. If, as seems likely, they would on average secure 'better' or more education for their children (as, indeed, they can at the moment by sending them to some of the better private schools) this would give them a welfare gain. If others resent this advantage they suffer a welfare loss and there is no obvious way of comparing these gains and losses to indicate an unambiguous direction of change in social welfare. Those, however, who would deny the exercise of this advantage to the rich (and to the not-so-rich who value a particular education so highly that they make great sacrifices to give it to their children) should recognise that in their view there can be *no* private sector education at all.

In short, once we get beyond the empirical implications that variety will certainly increase and that expenditure in total may or may not, the Paretian framework (unless modified) cannot help very much to indicate whether the voucher proposal is a good one or not. As professional economists we simply cannot say. The ultimate decision pro or con will go to those who can mount the most effective political power for since the one thing that is *not* agreed in this debate is to let each family 'do its own thing' one set of views must be imposed upon the other set. In this issue it is the liberal order itself which is in question. For some, liberalism must reluctantly be sacrificed to ensure that the educational values they so passionately hold be embodied in the society's educational system. For the others, liberalism and education are too inextricably intertwined for it to be possible to conceive that they do not go hand in hand.[11]

Student loans

While the voucher proposal is not inapplicable to the financing of higher education, concentration on new forms of finance in this area has been much more on the proposals for a system of loans for students. Objections to the present grants system are made primarily on externality grounds. If it is the case that inequality of educational opportunity in the tertiary sector imposes an externality, then the current system is inefficient twice over: first, because about half of the student awards go to students from families where the earning parent earns more than the average annual income and second, because the grants go to individuals themselves who have more wealth than average.

Since the latter proposition is not self evident, yet it forms the basis of the loans argument, we investigate it further. It will be recalled from chapter 8 that one of the effects of education is to enhance the earnings of those who have been educated. In present value terms, therefore, the relative *human* wealth of the educated exceeds that of the less educated. A loans scheme, it is argued, by which individual students were awarded repayable loans, would remove this inequity and would, at the same time, give low income households access to the same educational opportunities by relating credit-worthiness *not* to household current incomes (which may also be exceedingly unstable) but to the expected future income of the loan recipient himself. Moreover, in order to attain a Pareto-optimal flow of students through higher education, there is no reason why the loans terms should not be subsidised in a variety of ways (e.g. lower interest rates and delayed repayment) nor need adverse distribution effects be suffered by those making educational investments that turn out, for one reason or another, to be financially unprofitable, for repayment can be made conditional upon reaching certain post-education income levels. Thus, persons whose wealth was not increased by education would not be disadvantaged. In effect, then, the mechanism would take a roughly similar form to income taxation. Indeed, such proposals have earned themselves the tag 'a graduate tax'. (It is not hard to envisage a comparable 'owner-occupier tax' for those in receipt of subsidised house loans.)

Several arguments pro and con the graduate tax have been made. An argument against is that the present grants system has achieved an unparalleled (elsewhere) working class participation in higher education and the loans scheme would work against this achievement. Against this it can be argued (a) that the loans scheme would enable students to overcome some of the present discrimination against students from low income households and (b) that the proportion of working class students in British universities has remained about constant since the 1920's (at 25%) long before the present comprehensive grants system was introduced (in the 1960's).

For the scheme it is argued that it would increase the amount of resources devoted to education since it would eventually result in large sums being paid into the exchequer. Whether this is the case or not, however, depends first upon the scale of the loans scheme (covering, e.g. maintenance and fees or the full cost); second upon the extent to which the middle-class students, who presently gain a substantial bonanza from the current system, would find higher education less 'profitable' and whose relative numbers might fall; and third upon whether (a) capital sum repayments and interest payments were treated as an earmarked tax to be devoted entirely to higher education and (b) whether, even if they were, general tax funds were regarded as substitutable for earmarked funds. In general, there is no reason to suppose that the resources devoted to higher education would not remain largely discretionary to policy makers, as they are now.

Two fallacious arguments against loans are (a) that people who 'brain drain' would avoid repayments and (b) that those who do not emigrate pay higher income tax anyway – so we already have an implicit 'graduate tax'. The brain drain avoidance argument is easily met by modifications to existing reciprocal tax arrangements between Britain and several other countries – North America is the area that chiefly counts. The second argument confuses the general reasons for having a progressive tax system with those for making the beneficiaries from short term state assistance pay for it in the long term.

A final question may be discussed here in connection with loans. If it is the case that higher education is so very profitable, why has not the capital market already stepped in to provide facilities? The reasons are probably two-fold. First, since the future return is uncertain, capital markets characteristically require some collateral or security. In other areas this varies from the ability to participate in the control of a firm in the case of equity shares to the pledging of a life insurance policy as collateral. Low income households in particular find it difficult to use the capital market in general, as do some high income households, especially if they depend heavily on overtime earnings and want a mortgage. In the case of student loans little seems to be possible of this sort. Second, there has always been, in view of the externalities, a degree of charity in the financing of students. Even ignoring state subsidies, private individuals and institutions with an interest in education have made grants and scholarships – typically to the most promising students who have, presumably, the highest rate of return. Consequently, the 'cream' of the market has been skimmed off. Most of the loans schemes now proposed are not 'commercial' schemes. It is envisaged that they be either administered by the government or, if operated by private agencies, that the government would subsidise the terms of the contract.

Effects on efficient production and efficient rationing

The principles and problems associated with general fund and ear-marked taxation and with subsidies to reduce the market price (possibly to zero) or to place purchasing power in the hands of consumers in the form of cash grants, vouchers or loans are similar throughout the whole of the social services. The extension of the voucher system to health care – enabling individuals to purchase insurance against ill health – has, for example, most of the familiar pros and cons, value disputes and predictive disputes that characterise vouchers for education.

At least part of the general problem of assessing the relative desirability of the broad basis of approach – subsidising producing *institutions* which make services available at a lower price (possibly zero) or consuming *individuals* who buy at the market price, depends upon how one evaluates the relative merits of the two implied methods of discrimination between competing client groups. The use of market prices is advantageous to the extent that these prices reflect the true value of additional resources in their most socially valuable alternative use and to the extent that the subsidies in question can be strictly tied to the consumption of the externality creating activity and that once the additional consumption desired by society is secured it cannot be resold. In the health and education fields, while the latter two conditions are fairly easily met, it seems unlikely that the former (least cost production and, to a lesser extent, allocation to those who value the service most) are very perfectly met. Indeed, given the preponderance of *non-profit* institutions in these fields (even in the USA) where managements have relatively small incentives to be as efficient as they would have to be in a profit régime, it seems most unlikely. In housing, however, it is possible for all these conditions to be met.

The use of institutional subsidies is advantageous to the extent they are used efficiently to increase output and quality and to the extent that the shortfall in supply in zero price cases is rationed out according to principles consistent with the nature of the externality. If the subsidised institutions are not publicly owned, once again relative inefficiency is to be expected unless they are for-profit institutions. But if they are publicly owned, a far greater use of the economic tools of efficient organisation is required if their operation is to be markedly more efficient than non-profit private institutions. As far as discrimination between the excessive number of potential clients is concerned, unless *every* identifiable qualified individual is to receive the service (as in compulsory education), huge problems exist in defining who shall receive the service and in ensuring that those who carry out the day-to-day rationing procedures act in the social interest. High prices can always be overcome by giving the user enough resources to pay the price. Discretionary rules, however, are less easy to deal with and also place a great burden of responsibility upon those who do the allocating. How would *you* rank families on the council house waiting list? The practice varies enormously – from religion (in Northern Ireland) to length of waiting time and condition of present accommodation, weighted appropriately (how would you weight them?). How would *you* decide who ought to receive renal dialysis if you were a doctor in charge of a dialysis centre? The practice again varies, at least as regards non-clinical factors, from age and family responsibilities to first-come-first-served and trial by ordeal (= Giovanetti diet). How would *you* decide whom to admit to university? Again the practice varies, from 'A' level performances to parental occupation and random selection. In each case, supposing *you* were a highly conscientious person (a quite rare type[12]), how could you be sure that your priorities were also those of society?

These problems are not problems with value-judgments. They are empirical problems and the extraordinary thing is that having plumped years ago largely for a system that places enormous numbers of people in the position you have just been invited to accept we know very little about the rules that are actually used for health, housing and education (the rules for discretionary social security benefits are kept as secret as possible). What is even worse, however, is that we have only the rudiments of a theory to tell us what facts to expect (see chapter 7), and what to do about those facts that we do not like. Beyond the conventional financial accounting controls and ethical codes of professional practice (sometimes more in the interest of the professionals than their clients) we rely currently almost entirely upon the public spirit and good sense of public servants. It is not unreasonable to place the theory of how these people *actually* behave, and in response to what constraining factors, very near the top of the research agenda in the economics of social policy.

The public/private split and pensions financing

The financing of retirement pensions has long provided a battleground for the politicians and the ideologists of social policy. Although income maintenance and pensions policy has long been termed social 'insurance' as well as more suggestively, social 'security', its financing in Britain has never been insurance-based in the correct actuarial sense. Table 10.1 shows the current account position of The National Insurance Funds in 1971. In March 1971 the total National Insurance Funds stood at just over £1,000m earning interest (on government stocks only) of £70m. Rather than any insurance in the proper sense – with contributions based upon risk – the system is a social service financed basically by a poll-tax on employees, an indirect tax on employers and out of the general taxation of government, whereby the currently employed, employing and tax-paying make transfers to the currently retired, widowed, unemployed, etc.[13]

As we have seen in chapter 5 the original Beveridgean principle was to have flat rate benefits up to a subsistence level in return for flat rate compulsory contributions with an option for the individual to make further voluntary provision beyond this for himself in the private sector. In the event, benefits were not up to 'subsistence' level and supplementation by private occupational pension provision is wide-

TABLE 10.1: *Current Account of National Insurance Funds 1971*

Receipts	£m
Employers' contributions	1,312
Employees' contributions	1,212
Payments in lieu of graduated contributions	16
Grants from central government	494
Interest on Funds	70
Total	3,104

Expenditure on grants to personal sector	
Retirement pensions	1,953
Widows and guardians allowances	192
Unemployment benefit	218
Sickness benefit	393
Maternity benefit	44
Death grant	12
Injury benefit	30
Disablement benefit	72
Industrial death benefit	10
Other expenditure	145
Balance: current surplus	35
Total	3,104

spread (about half of all employees) though supplementation by earnings reduces entitlement to public benefit. Supplementary Pensions are claimed by about 30% of all pensioners — about 70% of all recipients of Supplementary Benefit. Minor modifications since the scheme was introduced in 1948, such as the graduated pension scheme (which introduced earnings-related benefits) and the old person's pension for the over eighties, have had little impact on the basic problem of ensuring that everyone receives the socially preferred minimum, though graduated contributions have eased the financing problem, and it is in this context that a controversy concerning the proper role of private occupational pensions has arisen which is another version of the universal/selective battlelines which are already familiar to us.

The solution to this problem that is currently (1972) being offered to the British public is a scheme with three basic components:

(a)   a compulsory state scheme providing benefits largely as at present, with inflation-proofing;

(b)   the encouragement of private occupational pension schemes for employees to make whatever additional provision they feel is appropriate;

(c)   the establishment of a State Reserve Scheme (SRS) for those retired persons whose arrangements under (b) — if any — are deemed to be insufficient to internalise the externalities of poverty in old age, which would also be earnings-related.

In essence, the scheme reverses the present arrangement whereby state benefits are invariate with respect to private pensions by permitting the reduction of state benefit down to the limit set by (a) as private provision increases. The alternative, 'universalist', solution would be to increase the standard retirement pension up to Supplementary Benefit level but this would, in the first place, involve very substantial transfers (about £1,000m per year) but would also mean giving a substantial subsidy to persons with adequate — or more than adequate — private arrangements, thereby internalising a non-existent externality. Indeed, it seems certain there exists *some* 'selective' scheme which would ensure a higher all-round minimum at the same cost in terms of compulsory contributions and exchequer funds as a universalist scheme.

Any system that seeks to economise on financing costs and to use the private sector requires an element such as (c) above in order to allow both for the tremendous range of private pension plans (currently about 65,000 different schemes are in operation) and for those employees whose employers do not (perhaps because they are too small) provide an occupational pension. Moreover, until recently, there was little evidence that private insurance funds were adequately inflation-proofed and the private funds have been frequently criticised for inefficient management and overcautious investment portfolios. A further major problem of the occupational pension — and especially of the non-contributory type — is that only limited transferability exists where it exists at all (it usually does not with non-contributory schemes) so that labour mobility before pensionable age is impeded or, alternatively, movement between employers, redundancy or long-term sickness is accompanied by substantial loss of pension rights.

The most effective pension system is, as a result of these problems, likely to be one which incorporates further features to those outlined as (a), (b) and (c). Thus, a condition for contracting out of paying contributions into the SRS should be that provision made under (b) must be at least as generous as that available under the SRS and, moreover, sufficient to ensure a minimum total pension equivalent to current Supplementary Benefit levels. In addition, if the 'right' to benefit from an occupational pension scheme is to be a meaningful right, not conditional upon remaining in employment with a particular employer, it is necessary to ensure either transferability of rights, the deferment of pensions, or the capitalisation of existing contributions for payment either to the contributor or into another scheme.

Are transfers costs, benefits or neither or both?

Pensions financing confronts us directly with a fundamental question that has been lurking beneath the whole of this chapter – what *kind* of social costs are financing costs, if any at all? Are they not identically equivalent to pure transfers which (if they are made at zero administrative cost) involve no net social cost at all on the assumption that, provisionally, a pound for A is of equal value to a pound for B. If this argument is correct, there can be no Paretian virtue in minimising financing costs. In health and education it may be agreed that real resource costs are involved – the cost of buildings, teachers' and doctors' time, *etc.* But these legitimate costs need bear no relation to financing costs. And in pensions, again assuming zero administrative costs, real resource costs of this type are *wholly* absent. We are left with pure transfers.

This argument has a superficial attraction and it is frequently put – especially by economists, who quite rightly try to persuade civil servants and politicians to look beneath public expenditures to the real social costs that are relevant for efficient decision. But it is wrong, for it uniquely identifies real resource costs with social costs. Social costs certainly include 'real' resource costs but they also include other costs than those obtained directly from real resources.

Recall that the fundamental economic reason (apart from a concept of socially just institutions) for making pure transfers (without a corresponding value of real resources flowing in the opposite direction) is that they *themselves* yield benefits to both recipient and contributor because of the presence of interpersonal externality relationships. The socially efficient internalisation of these externalities requires that the sum of the benefits exceed the sum of the losses by a maximum – and we have derived several qualitative characteristics of efficient schemes based on this requirement (such as a progressive tax structure). It is a fundamental premise of these arguments that, before a mutually agreeable redistribution from A to B takes place, A's pound in A's use does *not* have as much value *to A* as his pound in B's use.

So long as individuals can voluntarily agree to make transfers among themselves and in the process reveal that they are all moving to more preferred positions, no assumption about the relative value of marginal changes in different individuals' incomes is required to find an efficient solution. Some assumption is required only when these implied values cannot be revealed and individuals cannot make the moves they would prefer. Thus, with *involuntary* redistribution from A to B, since we have no obvious method of evaluating A's loss compared with B's gain, the *provisional* assumption of equal weights per pounds is made, with final weights to be decided by socially accountable persons. In short, the 'standard' economic approach to pure transfers is not so much an implication of economic analysis as a confession of the inability of analysis to discriminate.

This distinction accounts for two characteristics of our approach throughout this book. On some occasions we have imagined that the collective decision making process worked ideally and have used the Paretian apparatus to ask what characteristics would then typify social policy. One result, for income elastic goods, is that efficient internalisation of externalities requires subsidies that vary inversely with income. On other occasions, we have faced up to the fact that our collective choice institutions are not perfect and sought to discover ways that may help them to account for social benefits and costs more accurately. Both approaches clearly have their uses.

When it comes, however, to the *identification* of costs and benefits for the taking of specific decisions in the actual world in which the decisionmakers live, the judgment will often be reached that the institutions — public or private — do not reveal the necessary valuations accurately enough to be useful. Where real resources are involved it is quite often possible to impute shadow prices on a plausible basis. These imputations are often based on the money transfers (prices) that occur among individuals in the market as they compensate one another for services rendered, goods received and so forth. They are used as a basis because of the theorem of chapter 2 that holds that an individual will adjust his *MV* into equality with the (total) price he confronts. Under specifiable circumstances (e.g. no non-monetary dimensions to price such as waiting time) the price *reveals* the individual's *MV* of a real resource. Where pure transfers are involved, however, with no real resources being transferred, used up or produced, it is much more difficult to infer MV's from behaviour. This accounts for the conventional assignment of unitary weights to gains and losses per pound. This in turn implies that an administratively costless pure transfer will show neither a net social benefit nor a net social gain for the value of an additional pound *in terms of pounds, our chosen numéraire*, is a pound and can never be anything else.

The notion of pure transfer payment as being neither a social cost nor benefit in net terms is an artefact deriving from our inability to distinguish the different MV's of different pounds, which shifts the burden of responsibility for evaluation off the shoulders of professional economists to those of professional politicians. Quite obviously, the development of a technique that would enable more of this burden to be placed legitimately on the economists' shoulders would be a major contribution in an area where, presently, the economics of social policy has really very little to offer — save a statement of why it has so little.

NOTES

1. At least this is true for some programmes. For others, graduated benefits from some minimum seem to be preferred especially when the state takes on the task of providing a service *not* strictly required on externality grounds, such as pensions for the relatively well-to-do.
2. In fact some limited compensation does take place in the case discussed here. Local authorities pay maintenance grants to pupils staying on at school after the statutory leaving age but they are rather small (rarely above £70 a year in 1969), are given to few families and are, in any case, only *maintenance* grants. A loss of earnings of, say, £500 a year is by no means compensated.
3. For amusement, the reader may care to reflect on whether he would support enforced legislation to make his children (a) stay at school until 15, 16 or 18; (b) go to church every Sunday; (c) do five years' voluntary service overseas; (d) do two years military service.
4. Five years, because a qualification for three years' attendance at university is normally two years' attendance at school beyond the statutory leaving age 16.
5. But the costs would be very substantial. Whether the social benefits of equal opportunity exceed these costs is a moot point — £200 a year for all 5th and 6th formers coupled with a parental means test would cost around £100 million a year or, say, about 500 new nursery schools.
6. It may be argued that the existence of other institutions such as polytechnics and the Open University assists low income families since they may be either

less costly and/or less demanding in academic entrance requirements which themselves tend to discriminate against low income families.

7. Note that in Figure 10.2 the community's MV for university education is continuous and not kinked above Q^P or at each yearly unit. Consider the plausibility of this assumption and the consequences of assuming a kinked MV^* curve.

8. That surtax payers receive the minimum of £50 per year is a crude indication of the non-optimal tapering of the present system.

9. Including a negative 'tax' rate for those with family incomes below a certain level who would receive more than the total cost of providing a place in an educational institution to include at least some of the costs of taking that place up.

10. An alternative argument that recognises the admissability of this externality might be that the 'optimal' degree of freedom of choice will be determined – or ought be be determined – by the political process, with the gainers compensating the losers in terms of trading politicians' votes for public policies of one kind or another. See the discussion of log-rolling in, e.g., Buchanan and Tullock, op. cit.

11. Since much of the vouchers controversy is less economic and analytic than political and polemical, we have drastically excluded much that is fascinating (and important) in the debate. The Further Reading to this chapter contains most of the substantive material in this genre – but it is rumbustuous stuff!

12. Would you let your friend 'jump the queue'? How about your boss? How about someone you owed money to? How about someone you disliked intensely?

13. If it really were intended as an insurance scheme proper, it would be an exceedingly inefficient one. The reader may check for himself by reference to the discussion of risk in chapter 2 that efficiency requires that contributions (premiums) should be proportional to the risk for a given benefit.

FURTHER READING

Financing health care

British Medical Association, *Health Services Financing*, London, BMA, 1970.

J. M. Buchanan, *The Inconsistencies of the NHS*, London, IEA, 1965.

J. and S. Jewkes, *Value for Money in Medicine*, Oxford, Basil Blackwell, 1963.

D. S. Lees, *Health Through Choice, op. cit.*

H. M. and A. R. Somers, *Doctors, Patients and Health Insurance: the organisation and financing of medical care*, Washington, Brookings, 1961.

M. V. Pauly, *Medical Care at Public Expense*, New York and London, Praeger, 1971. The most comprehensive and rigorous discussion to date.

Financing education

M. Blaug, *An Introduction to the Economics of Education*, London, Allen Lane, 1970, especially ch. 10. A superlative summary discussion.

M. Blaug, *Economics of Education 1 and 2*, London, Penguin, 1968 and 1969. A comprehensive collection of readings.

H. Glennerster, S. Merrett and G. Wilson, 'A Graduate Tax', *Higher Education Review*, 1968.

S. E. Harris, *Higher Education: Resources and Finance*, New York and London, McGraw-Hill, 1962.

G. W. Horobin and R. L. Smyth, 'The Economics of Education: A Comment', *Scottish Journal of Political Economy*, Vol. 7, pp. 69–74.

E. J. Mishan, 'Some Heretical Thoughts on University Reform', *Encounter*, 1969.

A. T. Peacock and J. Wiseman, *Education for Democrats*, London, IEA, 1964.

A. T. Peacock and J. Wiseman, 'Economic Growth and the Principles of Educational Finance in Developed Countries', in *Financing of Education for Economic Growth*, Paris, OECD, 1968, reprinted in Blaug, *op. cit.*

Plowden Report, *Children and Their Primary Schools*, London, HMSO, 1967.

A. R. Prest, *Financing University Education*, London, IEA, 1966.

Robbins Report, *Higher Education*, Cmnd 2154, London, HMSO, 1963.

J. Vaizey, *The Economics of Education*, London, Faber and Faber, 1962.

E. G. West, *Education and the State*, London, IEA, 1965.

J. Wiseman, 'The Economics of Education', *Scottish Journal of Political Economy*, Vol. 6, 1959, pp. 48–58.

J. Wiseman, 'Rejoinder' (to Horobin and Smyth), *Scottish Journal of Political Economy*, Vol. 7, 1960, pp. 75–76.

Financing housing

J. B. Cullingworth, *Housing and Local Government in England and Wales*, London, Allen & Unwin, 1966.

D. V. Donnison, *The Government of Housing*, London, Penguin, 1967.

Institute of Economic Affairs, *Verdict on Rent Control*, London, IEA, 1972.

H. Gray, *The Cost of Council Housing*, London, IEA, 1968.

A. J. Merrett and A. Sykes, *Housing Finance and Development*, London, Longmans, 1965.

L. Needleman, *The Economics of Housing*, London, Staples Press, 1965.

A. A. Nevitt, *Housing, Taxation and Subsidies*, London, Nelson, 1966.

A. A. Nevitt, (Ed), *The Economic Problems of Housing*, London, Macmillan, 1967.

A. A. Nevitt, *Fair Deal for Householders*, London, Fabian Society, 1971

F. G. Pennance, *Housing Market Analysis and Policy*, London, IEA, 1969.

R. Turvey, *The Economics of Real Property*, London, Allen & Unwin, 1957.

Financing Pensions

R. W. Abbott, 'The Preservation of Pension Rights', *British Tax Review*, Jan-Feb, 1964.

T. E. Chester, 'Private Pensions or State Benefits', *National Westminster Bank Quarterly Review*, August 1972.

D. Cole and J. E. G. Utting, *Economic Circumstances of Old People*, Welwyn. Codicote Press, 1962.

T. Lynes, *French Pensions*, London, Bell, 1967.

F. W. Paish and A. T. Peacock, 'Economics of Pension Funds', *Lloyds Bank Review*, 1954.

A. T. Peacock, *The Economics of National Insurance*, London, Hodge, 1952.

A. T. Peacock, 'The Economics of National Superannuation', *Three Banks Review*, 1957.

W. Phillips, 'Making Pension Scheme Benefits Fully Transferable', *British Tax Review*, Jan-Feb, 1964.

M. Pilch and V. Wood, *Pension Schemes*, London, Hutchinson, 1960.

G. Rhodes, *Public Sector Pensions*, London, Allen and Unwin, 1965.

J. H. Richardson, *Economic and Financial Aspects of Social Security: An International Survey*, London. Allen and Unwin, 1960.

Strategy for Pensions, Cmnd. 4755, HMSO, 1971.

D. Wedderburn, 'The Financial Resources of Older People: A General Review', in E. Shanas, *et al., Old People in Three Industrial Societies*, New York and London, Atherton and Routledge, 1967.

J. Wiseman, 'Occupational Pension Schemes' in G. L. Reid and D. J. Robertson, *Fringe Benefits, Labour Costs and Social Security*, London, Allen and Unwin, 1965.

And, for an entirely different area of social policy:

A. T. Peacock, 'Welfare Economics and Public Subsidies to the Arts', *Manchester School*, Vol. 37, 1969.

PART V

Social Policy, Economics and the Law

11 A Farrago of Social Questions and Economic Answers

In this chapter we take up a theme that was initiated in chapter 2 and has appeared intermittently from time to time – the relationship between law and economics and its relevance for Social Policy. We explore first how economic analysis has been applied explicitly to the question of the best ways of applying the resources of crime prevention, detection and punishment to reduce criminal activity. Second, we apply the Paretian apparatus to ask what considerations lead to the conclusion that certain activities *ought* to be illegal – the example taken in both these sections will be the controversial one of drug 'abuse'. Finally we examine the role of social policy in providing the legal framework within which activities that pollute the environment are controlled (or not, as the case may be).

Positive economics of crime and punishment

The analysis of this section owes much to two fascinating and highly original articles by Gary Becker and Simon Rottenberg (see Further Reading) which both repay careful study in the original. The foundation from which policy implications are drawn is the (not unreasonable) assumption that criminals are essentially like everyone else – that is, that they are 'rational' in the sense of chapters 2 and 6. In deciding whether or not to commit any offence the potential criminal compares the (probable) benefits to himself with the (probable) costs including those of, e.g., imprisonment. By making some plausible assumptions such as an increasing marginal harm to society from criminal activities and an eventually decreasing marginal gain for criminals, Becker was able to specify certain optimality conditions relating to the 'supply' of offences and the socially ideal mix of punishments and resources devoted to raising the probability of criminals being caught and convicted.

It is more helpful for our purposes, however, if we concentrate on a particular type of criminal activity and the one we shall investigate amounts to a highly organised international industry — heroin trafficking (trade in LSD and marijuana is largely an amateur affair). We shall try to show that some quite elementary economic analysis can pinpoint some of the key variables upon which police and other detection and apprehension forces should concentrate and also that a policy that is to be cost-effective requires certain types of information about criminal activity that may not be normally thought terribly important.

The illegal organisations that distribute heroin, in the USA are monopolistic. The costs they incur are broadly of three kinds:

(a)   'normal' costs of production and distribution;
(b)   other costs associated with the avoidance of detection by the law;
(c)   the costs associated with detection — usually of a probabilistic kind with a probability of going to gaol or being fined of less than one. These costs easily outweigh type (a) costs for most, if not all, points along the illegal opium distribution chain. Those persons engaged in the trade require compensation if they are to incur these costs.

The length of the chain of distribution from the raw opium grown (usually) in Turkey (which produces only about 10% of world output) and converted there or in the Lebanon into a morphine base is long. The network passes through France and thence, or via Italy, Canada, Britain or Mexico to the USA. Once imported again a lengthy distribution network operates before the final sale of a small quantity of (much debased) product takes place between retailer and addict. The broad classes of dealer along the domestic line are the importer, the kilo-connection, the connection, the weight dealer, the street dealer and finally the juggler or pusher — the retailer. Why is this chain so long? The reason suggested by our model depends upon the probability of detection. Final sales are sales of small quantities. Other things being equal, the chances are that a one kilo heroin transaction is more likely to be detected than any one of 1,000 single gramme transactions. Since the retail end of the business is a high risk end, organisers of the traffic (e.g. importers) will lower their own costs (probability of detection) by lengthy distribution chains. Importers do not do their own retailing or wholesaling. The longer the chain of distribution the smaller the information available to each link about the other links, the smaller the value of the information of police and drug informants and the smaller the risk to the importers.

Of course, the risk is higher for individuals at the lower end of the chain. This explains why the traders' margins (and adulteration by adding quinine and mannite) increases as heroin is passed along the line.

The risk is also higher the longer stocks (incriminating evidence) are held and the larger they are. Consequently smaller stocks and a faster turnover characterise this illegal trade than characterise comparable legal trades.

This analysis suggests a number of important considerations for social policy, in particular relating to the organisation and deployment of detection forces and to the law itself.

The most obvious question which should be addressed is which points in the distribution chain are most profitably tackled by the police? On the one hand, the probability of making an arrest is clearly greatest at the retail end. On the other, the social value, in terms of the amount of crime removed, is certainly greater among the higher echelons. An immediate implication is that any system of rewards to police (say, in terms of promotion prospects) that is cast simply in terms of the numbers of arrests is unlikely to be the best policy socially. In principle, the optimal allocation of detection resources along the chain is where the social value of the information obtained at each link is equal per unit of additional resources expended — otherwise more valuable information in total could be obtained at less total cost in terms of police resources. One possibility in the absence of any detailed information about the value of information is clearly to concentrate relatively more on the middle links where the probability of detection is neither very high nor very low but the opportunity exists for generating information about both preceding *and* succeeding links in the chain whereas at the polar ends the option is for preceding *or* succeeding links. Secondly, however, this analysis suggests the great importance of establishing a scale of importance in the type of arrest made and the type of information likely to lead to an arrest. It seems likely that it would be socially profitable to offer quite substantial bribes or rewards for information likely to lead to the conviction of traffickers high up in the chain. Careful thought given to the pay of informers might yield substantial dividends. For example, in the USA a kilo of heroin retailed in excess of $300,000. The US Treasury Department (in 1966) offered $500 for information leading to the seizure of a kilo of heroin but would offer up to $50,000 for information leading to the seizure of other contraband of comparable value. This policy seems, on the face of it, irrational.[1]

A second line of attack hinges on the monopolistic nature of the illegal industry. Wealth maximising monopolists charge a higher price and trade in less than a more competitive industry. Hard addicts also commit crimes (mainly theft, sometimes robbery with violence – especially in the USA) to finance their addiction. While hitting existing operators and suspected organised routes and chains hard, therefore, it may pay the law enforcement agencies to concentrate less upon new entrants to the illegal industry, thereby encouraging more competition, for while a smaller illegal industry is generally preferable to a larger one, a smaller one, and a more monopolistic one (or one that is less hard for the major syndicates to cartelise because there are less operators to control), leads to higher prices and more crimes by addicts. Again, therefore, a particular and significant choice can be isolated for social policy-makers: a choice that depends largely upon the social harm judged to be inflicted on society by these various illegal activities.[2]

As well as concentrating upon the major criminal traders in hard drugs the criminal consumers of drugs are, of course, the object of policy attentions. We might, following Rottenberg, postulate three reasons for acquiring the drug habit:

(a)   they are told by an addict that the drug produces pleasant euphoric sensations – or they observe these apparent effects;
(b)   they admire the (say, artistic) accomplishments of a person they believe or know to be an addict;
(c)   they regard using the drug as a necessary condition for joining a community they find congenial.

Of these three plausible reasons (c) may include (a) and (b) but (a) and (b) do not include (c). Consequently group drug taking is more infective than individual drug taking in the sense that it offers a more powerful total incentive for non-addicts to take up the habit. Consequently, a unit of detection resources has a higher yield in preventive terms (as well as in identifying actual addicts) when applied to searching out group activity. Moreover, group activity is not likely to be more costly to detect than individual activity.

A second line of attack on the consumer side is to encourage (make cheaper) the availability of (a) cheaper and (b) less dangerous substitutes for hard drugs. This method is a rather obvious implication of the law of demand and is, consequently, much debated in circles concerned with the problem (Methadone is the most popularly canvassed substitute).[3] In Britain, there can be little doubt that the availability of drugs on prescription has resulted in relatively cheap sources of illicit supply with rather unattractive profit margins for the major racketeers.

As well as focussing on the supply and demand sides of the drug trade, the law enforcement procedures are highly relevant in social policy towards addiction. We have already seen how it pays the criminals to reduce the probability of detection and arrest. It will therefore be worth their while to attempt to corrupt law enforcement officers. It thus becomes important to consider ways in which the costs to susceptible officers are raised relative to the expected gains from connivance. One possibility is clearly to offer incentive payments to officers so that the ones who are active in getting successful convictions of important criminals receive higher rewards than those who are less active or less successful. A second, and more subtle approach is to minimise the opportunity that individual officers or squads of officers have to monopolise information about illegal activity. If one officer alone has some information about a criminal activity he may either report it to his senior officers (or act, correctly, upon it himself) or he may use the threat of action (of which he has a monopoly) to capture some of the monopoly profits of the criminal activity (he sells his 'silence'). Other things being equal, the greater the cost of his attempting the latter the less the probability he will in fact do it. A second, and related, line of attack is to increase the number of police officers who must be 'bought off' by criminals thereby increasing the cost to criminals of criminal activities. A system of organising police detection teams whose composition is not constant uses both lines of attack simultaneously: on the one hand it is harder for an officer to conceal what he is doing from his colleagues, there are more of them to persuade to join him in the connivance and to keep quiet and there are more among whom the spoils of connivance have to be divided; on the other hand the criminals themselves will find it harder to establish a regular relationship with an unfamiliar officer or team.

The reader will doubtless have discerned a number of additional implications of the analysis for himself. Many of these can be found more fully developed in the Further Reading, together with more sophisticated analyses than the introduction presented here. This is, indeed, a fascinating area of study in social policy and the recent application of economic analysis to problems of crime and punishment in general is producing a wealth of interesting and unusual insights into the problems as well as suggesting the kind of quantitative information that would be useful and the ways in which policy itself might be developed. If the analysis has been developed largely in an American context to deal with American problems the lessons are evidently not without value to a Britain in which it is primarily the trends rather than the absolute numbers that are of principal concern.

Should social policy concern itself with drug 'abuse'?

Social policy clearly does concern itself with drug abuse. In this section we seek, however, to ask why and to see if the answers to that question can be placed in the Paretian system and if so, how the reasons can be evaluated. Why *should* the law prohibit or seek to restrain the non-therapeutic use of drugs that act upon the central nervous system?

A little thought suggests that there may be six valid reasons for wanting to curb drug 'abuse' (the reader may be able to invent further plausible reasons). Each is a kind of externality:

(a) That an individual drug user's behaviour physically harms other members of society, for example, because users exhibit anti-social behaviour of one kind or another, perhaps becoming violent, perhaps committing crimes in pursuit of finance.

(b) That, sooner or later, the drug user may fall ill and require medical care and treatment which may be provided — indeed probably will be — out of the public purse.

(c) That other persons simply find such behaviour distasteful (disgusting, weak-charactered, shiftless, irresponsible, etc.) even though they may have no direct contact with drug users.

(d) That the drug user should be saved from his own folly.

(e) That an individual's behaviour may lead to a spreading through society of an undesired activity.

(f) That the drug-user is a less productive member of society and reduces Gross Domestic Product.

Physical harm to others. Crime and non-therapeutic drug taking are closely linked in the public mind. This is partly because to take narcotics may itself be illegal and also because addicts sometimes commit petty crime to enable themselves to continue to take drugs. An association between illegal actions (other than drug taking) and drug dependence is not firmly established causally so far in Britain save occasionally with cases of LSD (a non-addictive hallucinogen), with heavy doses of amphetamines which can induce aggression and, more frequently, with alcohol. In New York, however, from 55-60% of the income addicts require to support their habit is derived from burglary, robbery and larceny — a cumulative total 'cost' of about $1.3 billion annually. There is no known relationship between drug use and violent crime, though in about one half of New York murders either the perpetrator or the victim of the crime was a drug user. But even if it could be firmly established that particular types (or all types) of non-therapeutic use of drugs had harmful external effects of this kind, action could be warranted on this ground only if it could also be shown that the externality were Pareto-relevant at the margin. In short, society would have to decide not whether to cause the activity to cease altogether (we presume that total eradication would be far too costly) but whether, at current activity rates, the social benefit of a small or large reduction in the activity exceeded the social costs of implementing the reduction. Merely to establish the existence of a harmful external effect is not enough. One needs also to have information or guesses about:

(a)   the technology of harmful effects — how bad and for which drugs;

(b)   the technology of control — quantitative examination of, for example, the relationships discussed in the preceding section;

(c)   the costs of the nuisance and of the resources needed to reduce it.

One immediate possibility that may well be less costly than any other method in reducing the crime associated with drug abuse would be to legalise drug trafficking! A legal and more competitive — or even subsidised — industry could reduce the financing problem for addicts to trivial proportions. If this proposal is not acceptable the explanation must lie in one of the other reasons why drug taking is generally associated with social disapprobium.

Subsidised treatment. If society has taken a collective decision to provide care, as it has in the UK, at (almost) zero money cost to the patient it clearly has an interest in the state of every individual's health since the rest of society has an incentive to minimise the cost of care by taking preventive measures – of which the legal prohibition of drug taking for kicks may be one. The trouble with this argument is that, since pretty well everything affects a person's health, it can provide a general warrant for almost any kind of interference with the individual. For example, smoking harms smokers' health and the subsidised treatment argument could be – and has been – used to justify proposed restraints on smokers. Likewise, the logic suggests restraints on mountaineers, drivers, shoppers and many others, as well as on drug users whose health may suffer in particular through lack of proper hygiene in administering drugs and through indifference to general healthiness.

At best this argument implies either some degree of discouragement rather than making the activity in question illegal, or else a policy to ensure more suitable facilities for administering drugs, just as it may imply, in a less controversial area, encouragement for people to keep fit rather than compulsory keep-fit classes! We have in this book frequently come across the externality argument for subsidisation whereby externally affected parties may act to encourage the externality generating person to behave more in the way they prefer by compensating him. The problem with *forcing* him to do something is that we are unable to compare his welfare loss from being coerced with the welfare gain to the rest of society. Until someone invents a method of doing this (an unlikely possibility) we must either exclude the externality-creating person from our definition of society so that whatever happens to his welfare, as *he* sees it, is irrelevant to the social gain, or else we must drop the assumptions that the individual is the only judge of *his* welfare in favour of some form of paternalism, or we accept the Paretian rules of the game and conclude that the subsidised treatment argument is an argument neither for nor against forcing anyone into doing anything – we simply have no way of telling. As the reader will guess, the latter academic morality is the uncompromising position taken here.

Informational externalities. The importance of the 'informational' externality argument – that merely the knowledge that some person or persons behave in a particular way imposes an external harm (or benefit) – depends again upon the extent to which for normative purposes one wishes to use the Pareto criterion. If somehow you get to know about an activity by someone else that you either approve or disapprove then an informational externality exists. If the activity remained a secret from you, no externality would exist. If you dislike the colour of *my* bedroom walls (so long as you are not my wife) or the fact that I am black, or Jewish, or privately homosexual, there is a powerful argument for postulating that such external harms I impose on you should be regarded as irrelevant − as not detracting from social welfare. We simply disregard them. There may exist argument about whether to exclude some types of informational externality (e.g. your knowledge that I am poor, ill, ignorant) and which ones to exclude cannot be decided by any Paretian arguments. Essentially one is taking a high level 'constitutional' or political decision about whose welfare and which entities are to be counted in the social welfare function. The liberal approach would tend to exclude one set of effects and other, more paternalist, approaches would exclude others. Only the most ultimate kind of approach would require all such externalities to be efficiently internalised − and it would also include, for example, the welfare of children as perceived *by them* rather than by parents, teachers, etc. It is hard to imagine anyone (except children) in favour of so radical a position. Such extremism destroys one of the bases for adopting a Paretian ethical approach, by destroying the high probability of consensus about its basic value judgements.

In any case, as we have already observed above, even so radical an approach could not sanction *prohibition*, only compensated adjustment by one or other of the affected parties. The same is still true for drug users.

Merit wants. The merit want argument that drug users should be discouraged from the habit 'in their own interest' is usually regarded as the type of statement that cannot be evaluated by the Paretian approach which assumes that only each individual regarded as being a member of 'society' can know his own interest − and if imperfectly then more perfectly than anyone else.[4] More strictly, the approach implies that we have *no means of telling* whether one person's assessment of another's interest is better than his own, but presumes that it is not. If someone seeks to argue that he knows someone else's interest better than that person himself, one has only to ask him to prove it. Unfortunately the nature of a person's own 'interest' is so thoroughly subjective that such an objective proof cannot be discovered.[5] In practice, merit wants are just a fancy name for saying that you want to arrange someone else's life for him even though the behaviour in question affects neither your person physically nor your wealth. Had they been given the far more emotive name of 'bossy wants' it is unlikely that they would be taken as seriously in normative economics as they have been. No consistent practical policy attitude can be based on both the Paretian system and the merit want argument, so long as the persons whose behaviour is lacking in 'merit' count as members of 'society' (i.e. their welfare, as they see it, counts in social welfare). Thus, if drug users are to be counted as members of society and the Paretian apparatus used, the merit want argument for acting to protect *their* interest cannot be sustained. Even though one may be utterly appalled by the condition of drug users and addicts one is giving qualitative expression to *one's own* valuation of their condition, health, way of life etc., which is not the same thing as *their* valuation. Even if – and this may be hard to swallow – the drug addicts *themselves* later regret having become addicts this does not justify any current preventive action against the potential future addicts on the grounds that it is in *their* interest. The choice is simple and unambiguous: either their welfare counts in the same way as everyone else's or one decides that it does not. In the latter case, it must be one's own interpretation of their welfare that counts – the effect their behaviour, condition, etc., has on one's own welfare – and this is by definition an externality. The Pareto system does not help us to decide who shall have the franchise – though there is usually a presumption that exclusions need a strong foundation. The real question, then, is whether the foundation is strong enough in this case. Economics cannot answer this one, but the reader will have his own ethical views. Once this 'constitutional' choice is made, however, the Paretian apparatus can once more be brought into play, with the welfare of drug users as *they* see it either included or excluded from *social* welfare. For the purposes of this chapter, we include it.

Transmission of the drug habit. The methods by which the habit is spread among the drug-using sub-culture and the sub-culture itself is widened are partially known and in a general way have been hinted at in the first section of this chapter. Insofar as this is only a 'scale' effect it is not of substantive importance in the normative policy question with which we are concerned though it affects the social significance of any genuine social harm done and is, of course, of great importance in the positive approach to policy – implementing *effective* anti-drug policies.

The transmission effect is, however, of importance – of critical importance – in one respect, which is that it is the mechanism by which *minors* are exposed to the habit. Since the welfare of children for the purposes of this book is their welfare *as perceived by adults,* their protection is one of the most important aspects of any social policy towards drug use and the effect on children is certainly an externality that on any reasonable interpretation of Pareto optimality should be taken account of. To physical harm imposed upon others we may thus legitimately add a second factor in the Paretian approach to drug use control.

The output argument. The final set of arguments for legal intervention is based upon the effects that drug taking may have on the efficiency of the individual as a worker or on the length of his working life. These, however, are arguments that are related to *output-maximisation* not welfare-maximisation. They would be characteristic of someone with entirely materialistic values, who in a social sense might be exceedingly concerned over the rate of growth of GDP, but they are not characteristic of Paretian economics.

Insofar as individuals can affect their life-expectation they do so in a presumptively optimal fashion (from their own point of view), likewise the time allocated to work and non-work is also presumptively optimal. As far as the loss of GDP is concerned for marginal withdrawals from the labour force, this detracts from social welfare only insofar as wages do not reflect the social value of an individual's product. If wages are higher than this level the rest of society gains, in one sense, from the person's withdrawal. If they are less, then there is an inefficiency the removal of which the Paretian apparatus sanctions without additional arguments and which should be done. Policies to prohibit drug taking can, however, be justified on the output argument where there are *economic* shortages of labour which for some reason are permitted to persist. The empirical significance of such cases is not, however, very great in our present context.

Our conclusions as a result of these considerations is that the only arguments with genuine Paretian significance (so long as drug users' welfare is a part of social welfare) are related to physical harm to others and to the 'corruption' of minors. Any policy prescription based upon this analysis should strictly be based upon a careful cost-effectiveness analysis of the alternatives. Here, however, it is worth mentioning one policy which appears likely *a priori* to be very cost-effective. We have already indicated that legalisation of trafficking and more competitive production and distribution could in principle reduce the first problem substantially. No argument suggests that consumption *per se* ought to be illegal in a Pareto efficient social policy. Consequently, full legalisation for adults, together with 'zoning' regulations to protect minors from contact with adult users appears to be a probably efficient policy. Existing legislation concerning public consumption of alcohol provides a basic model for the kind of institutional framework appropriate. If you find this possibility unappetising you are probably disagreeing either with the Paretian framework or with the implied 'constitutional' definition of society and those entities to be included as relevant to social welfare. You may also have identified an externality missed out here but which may validly lead to alternative conclusions.

This controversial example illustrates well the kinds of normative policy inference and justification that the Pareto rules permit us to make. Similar arguments can quite easily be seen to underlie many of the most controversial social questions such as social and legal policy towards, abortion, censorship, homosexuality, prostitution, euthanasia and efficient types of punishment (capital, fines or imprisonment). Even if the reader does not find himself in sympathy with the Paretian value judgements it would be instructive for him to work through the Paretian *pros* and *cons* in some of these other cases. Those who are sympathetic will also discover how much they have to *supplement* the Pareto value judgements or substitute others in order to derive normative implications which they feel are consistent with their own pre-existing views on these questions.

In the last chapter of the book we shall return once again to the ethical status of the Paretian approach in the economics of social policy.

Pollution and the law

'Pollution of the environment' covers a multitude of sins against society ranging from pouring out filth, poison and noise, through congestion of roads and cities to the despoliation of natural beauty and wilderness and the depletion of fixed stocks of natural resources. Although we cannot hope to give an adequate treatment of the tremendous problems posed for social policy by these phenomena in the few pages available some of the key factors involved can be isolated, making our understanding of the basic problems clearer and hence the kind of policy proposals we invent more relevant.

One important clue to the source of many pollution problems was given in chapter 7 — the absence of enforced property rights. No-one owns, or has an incentive to enforce his rights in, clean air, clean rivers and clean seas. These are amongst the most polluted goods available to man.[6] The right to pass noise vibrations through the airspace surrounding other people and other people's property is not clearly owned by anyone. Again we get noise problems. Beautiful views are usually not owned by anyone and are consequently frequently destroyed by advertisement hoardings. The right to use a particular road space is not owned by anyone and it is congested.[7] The world's whales are not owned by anyone — until they are killed — and they get killed off too quickly. Frequently the only way one can acquire ownership over many natural resources is to drill them or dig them out. Stocks tend to run down very fast.

Unfortunately, our reaction to many of these problems tends often to be an all-or-none response. Either let the pollution rip or ban it altogether. Either make sure people are compensated for all the harm done them or not at all.

The second clue towards a sensible approach to solving some of these problems is not to take extreme sides but to recall that we have throughout this book discussed both the costs and benefits of different policies; in particular, the costs and benefits of some more or some less of the activity. Very rarely are we concerned — or should we be concerned — with all or none. In short, we need to devise social policies and frameworks within which individuals can act such that *optimal* rates of pollution occur. To stop it altogether implies that the social benefits of no pollution at all exceed the social costs of stopping it altogether and that there is no superior intermediate course, which is generally not the case. We could probably stop all pollution by stopping (probably we would need to reverse) economic growth, urbanisation and population growth. Such draconian measures almost certainly throw out the baby with the bathwater and we would be worse off than if we still had the pollution.

The first step in any solution to problems of pollution is the setting up of enforceable property rights. In using this term we do not mean only *private* property rights, but rights owned by someone, or some body of men, that define the uses to which resources — any resources — may be put. More specifically, property rights define (a) the uses to which the resources may be put (b) the uses to which they may not be put (c) the exclusion of others from use without the owner's consent and (d) the terms under which the rights may be transferred to others. These rights may be invested in individuals or firms (private property) or in clubs and other groups or in governments (common property).

Private property has tended to evolve in Western society where it can be reasonably cheaply enforced. It rarely causes pollution problems. Common property frequently does however, but before jumping to the (unwarranted) conclusion that common property rights ought to become invested in private individuals, pause to consider why common property exists. Usually there is simply no economical alternative. While, for example, it is possible to imagine a world in which the right to pass sound waves, smells and light waves over private property could attach to the private ownership of the land (up to what height?) and it is possible to imagine these rights being bought and sold, it takes very little imagination to appreciate the enormous costliness of the procedure, the costliness of policing and enforcing the rights and contracts made about them. Referring to the list of kinds of right given in the preceding paragraph while (a) and (b) are usually feasible, (c) and (d) frequently are not enforceable.

Two things in particular seem to change the kinds of right that are exercised over resources. One is the *value* of resources. If the potential social gains from an efficient use of resources are great then some rights are usually worth establishing and enforcing rather than none. The extension of national rights to the use of minerals under the ocean far away from previous territorial waters is an example of this process. Alternatively the costs of the pollution, despoliation or congestion can become so great that it becomes relatively worthwhile to establish rights by, for example, manning (or equipping) all entrances and exits of major roads for toll payments, or instituting smokeless zones in smoggy urban areas. A second factor is technology. Technological advances can make exclusion cheaper and hence the rights structure more complete — the impact of metering for road use has yet to be felt but it is now feasible and will, one day, make the rights system in road use more extensive.

The law does, indeed, frequently assign rights without including amongst these rights the right to transfer a right. You may not normally, for example, impose 'unreasonable' noise upon my residential quiet nor remove from my property access to a 'reasonable' quantity of natural light. In many matters, if my rights are in doubt, I can discover whether you are imposing a nuisance on me and, if you are, I can obtain an injunction against you. But I cannot usually sell some of the bundle of rights I thereby acquire to you so that we reach a mutually agreeable optimum – it is an all-or-none affair.

There are several questions that need to be discussed before we can derive social policy implications from the simple observation that exchange is fundamentally *not* about the exchange of 'things' but about rights to use 'things' in particular ways. To whom should the rights be given in the first place? Do different assignments of rights have *allocational* implications as well as *distributional* ones? Does our Paretian apparatus give any guidance in these matters?

Consider a homely example of dispute over a private right to pollute. A and B are neighbours and A enjoys using his power mower on Sunday afternoons just when B likes to enjoy a snooze in his favourite chair underneath his *Sunday Times*. Should A have the right to mow noisily or should B have the right to snooze. If A has the right costs are imposed on B, if B has the right costs are imposed on A. Naturally enough, every dispute over rights implies that one or the other party will lose, depending on how the rights are assigned. It is possible to imagine a world in which, at some point of time, rights were simply put up for auction by the government and allocated to the highest bidder. In this way the rights would go to those who valued them most but they would also tend to go to the rich and this method of assigning basic rights *ab initio* would generally be regarded as inequitable, just as rights seized by *force majeure* are generally regarded as inequitable. What assignment of even earlier rights has enabled the rich to become rich, one might reasonably ask? One is driven in a regress back to the assignment of the most fundamental rights of man about which economics has traditionally given little normative guidance (see, however, the brief discussion of justice in chapter 4). We may be influenced by the economic consequences of different fundamental assignments in our judgement but basically our judgement must be a purely political one based upon concepts of justice and equity. In our example you may decide, since A would be the active imposer of costs on B while B would be merely a passive imposer of costs on A, that B ought to have the right. But whichever way you decide you will get little guidance from any social science.

Suppose now that the rights are not merely to be assigned but that they are also exchangeable. Whoever is awarded the rights now acquires wealth that can be valued in the market place — if A has the right B can come along and offer to compensate him for shifting his mowing time to Sunday morning. If B cannot or does not value Sunday afternoon peace enough to offer enough to persuade A, then it is optimal for the noise to continue, and it will. If B has the right, A can come along and offer him compensation for making the noise. If A offers him enough B will accept and again it will be optimal for the noise to continue — and it will. The differences between the cases of no rights assignment, nonexchangeable rights assignments and the case of exchangeable rights is that only the latter affords us the opportunity of *testing* to discover whether the end result of any activity is socially preferred or not. The latter enables each party to adjust in the light of the behaviour and preferences of the other, so that each moves to a preferred position.

It is sometimes argued that the optimal result is the same regardless of who has the initial right except for distributional effects (clearly if A has the right B must sacrifice some wealth to buy A's right off him, or *vice versa*). This is, indeed, true if we may legitimately assume the unchanging measuring rod of value assumed in chapter 2 (p. 20). Unfortunately, however, this is a case where this assumption of convenience can lead one astray. If A gets the right B may offer him £5 to mow in the morning and, since A requires at least £6 to shift he will continue to mow in the afternoon. If B gets the right, A may be prepared to offer only £5 for the right to mow in the afternoon and B may not accept a penny less than £6. There is no necessary inconsistency here. If A has the right it is optimal for afternoon mowing to *continue*. If B gets the right it is optimal for afternoon mowing to *cease*. There need be no unique optimum since the rights assignment shifts the starting point of the negotiation. If B has the right he is better off than if he does not have the right and he may value his peace and quiet more highly in the first than in the second situation, requiring more money to forego it than he would offer to acquire it if he did not have it in the first place. Thus, the rights allocation can have allocational *as well as* distributional consequences though, provided rights are exchangeable, an efficient outcome will result.

The lesson we draw from this is that the exchangeability of rights is a necessary condition if the values placed upon different activities are to be revealed, even though unique optima may not exist. Where feasible, therefore, exchangeable rights are more conducive to social welfare than non-exchangeable rights. The initial assignment of rights may be made on grounds of equity about which economics as such cannot give any guidance (though voluntary *redistribution* of rights can be analysed in normative economics using analysis similar to that in chapter 4.)

It is not always possible, however, to have exchangeable rights. Where very large numbers of people are involved jointly in a public good or bad, exchangeability of rights in the way discussed is usually not possible. This is characteristically the case with common property in which governments usually fail to enforce rights[9] and is also the case with valuable resources that no one owns at all. Your factory may have discharged effluent into the local river for many years without having to pay or compensate anyone for the right to do so simply because the 'owners' of the river have not bothered to think about the efficient use of the resource – the river – or because those affected had no means by which they could force you to take account of the social costs you were imposing on them. It may be that your factory's gains outweigh their losses, but unless there exists some mechanism for finding out, there exists a ripe area for extensive social friction and discontent.

What then can be done about pollution and the 'exploitation' of natural resources? One possibility is clearly to ensure that private property rights are established. This is likely to work efficiently, however, only in cases where other persons are not affected by private exchanges and where excludability is feasible – without the former, private action is likely to be nonoptimal and without the latter it will not pay the private individuals anyway.

The more vexed problems concern the efficient use of common property – say a river – as between, for example, effluent producers, recreation activities and farmers. There are broadly three solutions: regulation, subsidisation and pricing. These are the three general solutions to all social problems.[10] By regulation, a target level of pollution reduction is set on some interpretation of the public interest and all polluters would be monitored to ensure that they have complied with the regulation. By subsidisation, either the government could set up a series of water purification plants of its own to ensure attainment of the target, or it could compensate individual polluters by subsidising their efforts to process their own effluent. By pricing, the government would charge polluters for the right to pollute and adjust prices (probably on a sliding scale) until the desired reduction in pollution was attained.

One's choice between these methods depends upon equity considerations in the implied rights assignments and upon the administrative and policing costs of each. In each case the government has to make a decision about the social value of clean water – about which cost-benefit analysis may be able to suggest some range of plausible numbers. But, most important, in each case there are social costs to be incurred in combating the pollution. With regulation, for example, an efficient policy would discriminate among the various polluters, some of whom were major polluters and others minor; some of whom would find it very much more costly to reduce pollution by x% than others; some of whom were already taking substantial voluntary measures to reduce their pollution. In practice this looks like implying a separate regulation for each polluter! The alternative would be not to discriminate which would economise on administration but would be unfair and would also mean that pollution would not be reduced in the most efficient (least cost) way.[11]

Similarly, to be efficient, subsidies to producers would have to discriminate and would also involve an extensive administrative and enforcement machine. A publicly-owned purification plant would avoid most of the latter and would probably also reap economies of large volume processing, provided its management had inducements to be efficient.

Pricing would involve less information collection about each polluter's pollution and his costs of control but would require experimentation with charges until the target global reduction in pollution was attained.

In each case, the incidence of the costs on taxpayers, polluters and consumers of the products produced by polluters would vary. The task of guessing at the qualitative changes in these cost incidences from method to method is left to the reader, as is that of inventing the hypothetically most efficient detailed scheme of each type.

Pollution frequently takes the form of a 'public bad' – the converse of a public good – but it is not usually a *pure* public bad, in the sense that it is impossible to exclude some people (at some cost) from its effects. This leads to the final possible remedy for some kinds of pollution, a variant on the regulation method discussed above – zoning, whereby some areas, times of day, *etc.*, are set aside for polluting activities to take place but they are prohibited at others. Zoning solutions[12] are quite frequently adopted in society already as in the case of smokeless zones, prohibitions on the sounding of motor car horns at night in urban areas, non-smoking compartments in public transport and green belts in town and country planning legislation. The analytical problems in zoning concern principally the determination of the optimal zone or, in alternative language, the assignment of pollution rights. Zoning has the disadvantage that the rights are not exchangeable but the advantage that in the many cases where exchange is not feasible it avoids the all or none solution whereby the non-polluting zone either extends to include all or becomes zero. In principle, even the polluted river could be subject to zoning – by ensuring that all polluting activities were located downstream from the clean water activities – but it will be obvious from this case that, in general, choice between zoning and other remedies depends upon the technology of the problem and the costs of running alternative schemes. In general, a cost-benefit appraisal of alternative methods is required if the social interest is to be served adequately by anti-pollution policy.

NOTES

1. I have not been able to discover comparable figures for the UK. Those mentioned here are instanced by Rottenberg (see Further Reading).
2. The question arises here – if addicts commit crimes because of the high price of heroin, why not *legalise* the trade on a competitive (even subsidised?) basis. Heroin consumption could remain illegal or, in turn, itself be legalised. We shall not discuss these possibilities here but return to them below as they are sufficiently important in the formation of social policy to warrant explicit attention in some detail.
3. An 'exception' to the downward sloping demand curve that is much beloved by some textbook writers is alleged to occur with drug dependence. The assertion is that the addict, craving for more the more he consumes, has a rising marginal valuation for the object of his habit. This arises from a mistaken notion of the role of time in the basic theory of demand. Our notion of demand is not one of sequential purchases through time, which the assertion implies – as well as many other textbook illustrations – but one about purchases during a period of time. The addiction phenomenon is a dependency relationship between consumption during different periods of time. Today's injection of 'H and C' (heroin and cocaine, the latter being supposedly non-addictive) may imply that tomorrow's shot has a higher marginal valuation but it does *not* imply that two shots today do not have a lower *MV* than one shot today. Addicts are not necessarily 'irrational' in economic terms.
4. The physiological and psychological harm measured in medical terms inflicted on themselves by drug takers is much in dispute. We are largely ignorant about the long term natural history of persons using drugs that act on the central nervous system including the extent to which use of so-called 'soft' drugs leads to 'hard' drug dependence or use. Pharmacological problems

exist too, such as the development of cheap non-dangerous analgesics analogous to morphine (derived from opium exudate) or pethidine (a synthetic narcotic).

Note that in this chapter the availability of subsidised health care to drug addicts is not in question. The analysis of earlier chapters applies here with only slight modifications if the concern of the rest of society for sick addicts is different from its concern for other sick people.

5. See, however, the article by Culyer cited in the Further Reading to chapter 6.
6. Note, however, that if someone does own a right and has an incentive to enforce it, pollution is not a great problem – for example anglers' associations or landowners own fishing rights which are successfully enforced.
7. Question – how does the over-crowding of roadspace differ from the overcrowding of families in slum tenancies?
8. No rights assignment invariably results in the victory of the 'active' parties causing a deterioration in amenity.
9. Some reasons why this is so – and when they may change their attitudes – may be derived from the analysis of chapter 7.
10. In education, for example, the optimal quantity could be obtained (a) by coercing every child between certain ages to attend school (b) by subsidising education and/or (c) by fining everyone (or their parents) who did not go.
11. For example, factory A already incurs costs in reducing its polluting effluent to 100 tons per year, to reduce it further would cost £20 per ton reduced. Factory B does nothing as yet and pours out 1,000 tons per year. A reduction for factory B costs £10 per ton. Non-discrimination in getting pollution down by 10% would cause social costs of, in total, £1,200. Discrimination entirely against factory B would cost society only £1,100.
12. Part of the solution to the drug problem posed above was essentially a 'zoning' solution.

FURTHER READING

Drugs, Crime and Punishment
G. S. Becker, 'Crime and Punishment: An Economic Approach', *Journal of Political Economy*, Vol. 76, No. 2, 1968.
J. Bentham, *Theory of Legislation*, New York, Basic Books, 1931. One of the earliest 'economic' approaches.
P. Burrows, 'On External Cost and the Visible Arm of the Law', *Oxford Economic Papers*, Vol. 22, 1970.
D. R. Cressey, *Theft of the Nation: The Structure and Operations of Organised Crime in America*, New York, Harper and Row, 1969.
A. J. Culyer, 'Should Social Policy Concern Itself with Drug "Abuse"?', *Public Finance Quarterly*, 1973.

F. Dawtry (ed), *Social Problems of Drug Abuse,* London, Butterworths, 1968.
E. Erickson, 'The Social Costs of the Discovery and Suppression of the Clandestine Distribution of Heroin', *Journal of Political Economy*, Vol. 77, No. 4, 1969.
R. E. Fernandez, 'The Clandestine Distribution of Heroin, Its Discovery and Suppression: A Comment', *Journal of Political Economy*, Vol. 77, No. 4, 1969.

J. R. Harris, 'On the Economics of Law and Order', *Journal of Political Economy*, Vol. 78, No. 1, 1970.

D. B. Louria, *The Drug Scene*, London, Corgi, 1970. A good general and well-balanced introduction to the drug scene.

E. J. Mishan, 'Pareto Optimality and the Law', *Oxford Economic Papers*, Vol. 19, 1967.

M. Moore, *Policy Concerning Drug Abuse in New York State*, Cronton on Hudson, New York, Hudson Institute, 1970.

President's Commission in Law Enforcement and Administration of Justice, *The Challenge of Crime in a Free Society*, Washington DC, Govt. Printing Office, 1967. The Taskforce report, *Narcotics and Drug Abuse*, is particularly relevant to this chapter.

S. Rottenberg, 'The Clandestine Distribution of Heroin, its Discovery and Suppression', *Journal of Political Economy*, Vol. 76, No. 1, 1968.

T. C. Schelling, 'Economics and Criminal Enterprise', *The Public Interest*, Spring, 1967.

G. J. Stigler, 'The Optimal Enforcement of Laws', *Journal of Political Economy*, Vol. 78, No. 3, 1970.

L. C. Thurow, 'Equity and Efficiency in Law Enforcement', *Public Policy*, Vol. 18, No. 4, 1970.

G. Tullock, *The Logic of the Law*, New York, Basic Books, 1971.

The Environment

A. A. Alchian, 'Some Economics of Property Rights', *Il Politico*, Vol. 30, 1965.

W. Beckerman, 'Why We Need Economic Growth', *Lloyds Bank Review*, October, 1971.

P. Bohm and A. V. Kneese (eds.), *The Economics of Environment*, London, Macmillan, 1971.

J. Culbertson, *Economic Development and Ecological Approach*, New York, Kuopf, 1971.

J. H. Dales, *Pollution Property and Prices*, Toronto, University of Toronto Press, 1968.

H. Scott Gordon, 'The Economics of a Common-Property Resource: The Fishery', *Journal of Political Economy*, April, 1954.

H. W. Helfrick (ed), *The Environmental Crisis*, New Haven, Yale University Press, 1970. Notable for the contribution by Kenneth E. Boulding.

A. V. Kneese and B. T. Bower, *Environmental Quality Analysis*, Baltimore and London, John Hopkins Press, 1972.

E. J. Mishan, *The Costs of Economic Growth*, London, Staples Press, 1968.

E. J. Mishan, 'Economic Growth: the Need for Scepticism', *Lloyds Bank Review*, October 1972.

C. A. Reich, 'The New Property', *Yale Law Journal*, April, 1964.

L. E. Ruff, 'The Economic Commonsense of Pollution', *The Public Interest*, Spring, 1970.

PART VI

Postlude

12　Rückblick

In this chapter we attempt to assess the stance adopted throughout the book by taking a final look at the old, old question of the relationship between economics and justice, equality and ethics and to size up the state of the art.

There are still quite a lot of students of social policy who regard the kinds of analysis and quantification, whether explicit or implicit, advocated in this book as intrinsically immoral. The view, so far as it is possible to understand it, is that there is some (rather elusive) sense in which the quantifying approach of economics – again whether actual or only implicit – somehow cheapens or debases the entities being measured. The only possible retort to this kind of value judgment is another, contrary, one that it does no such thing. The whole point of quantification is, of course, that it helps us to solve some of the social problems that confront us. We unashamedly treat it as a means to an end. Its validity and success are likewise to be judged in terms of its validity and success as a means. The incantation that 'people are not numbers' while literally perfectly true, of course, ultimately leads to the implication that we ought not collect the numbers of unemployed, the numbers of sick people: a patent absurdity.

The objective of this book has been to set out an economic approach to social policy that is a consistent, coherent whole rather than a rag bag of *ad hoc* techniques and value judgements. The object is to assist systematic analysis of social problems by whomsoever is interested enough to want to analyse them, and to assist policy makers to make choices. Note: *assist* not *dictate*. We have repeatedly drawn attention to areas in which analysis has not yet developed far enough for the economists to say a great deal and in many of these areas the policy maker's judgement has to be relied upon. As a consequence of this, we have also spent some time looking at the factors which determine the degree to which policy makers are likely to make choices that are consistent with the underlying value judgements upon which the normative economics of social policy is based.

We have explained earlier why it is that we made the particular value judgements we did, in particular why the objective of maximum social welfare was chosen. At that time, however, the logically prior question – why make value judgements at all? – was not asked. The answer is blatantly simple. In an ideal world it may be the case that the economist's role would be restricted to discovering the most efficient means of achieving (externally) given ends. He would be either an operations researcher or a cost-effectiveness analyst – and even then he would inescapably have to make value judgements. In the real world, however, policy makers and most other people who seek economic advice do not have well-articulated ideas of their objectives. One of the first tasks of a cost-benefit analyst, for example, is usually to seek to clarify the objectives – even to suggest some. For purposes of general exposition therefore, the Paretian system is an extremely handy method of developing a body of analysis with certain primitive value judgements built into it. For specific purposes it is relatively easy to insert additional value judgements (for example, about redistribution effects) as and where suggested (by the client). It is certainly easier (and therefore more economical) than starting from scratch each time one is presented with a policy problem.

The economic approach sometimes comes under heavy (and indiscriminate) fire: the analysis is too abstract, but the application too quantitative; the impossible is done by bringing all alongside the measuring rod of money, but too much is missed out that is of overriding importance; it is too subjective in its approach to valuation problems, but naively objective in its reliance on market-revealed prices.

Each and every one of these criticisms is wide of the mark. Of course the fundamental analytical framework is abstract – so is *any* basic analytical framework. Whether it is 'too' abstract must depend upon whether the framework can be *used*. Well, it can certainly be used and in using it one certainly quantifies. The dimensions of a social problem that need to be quantified vary in the complexity and ease with which accurate or reliable numbers can be attached. It is certainly desirable to estimate margins of error or to postulate qualitative degrees of reliability but this is not the same thing as restricting, or even abolishing, the need for quantification. We quantify in order to reduce dependence upon implicit and informal intuitive approaches to social problems. Economic analysis nails *explicitness* and *formality* to the masthead. No economist will object to the principle that discussion and argument may take place over *quantities,* but he may justly request those who oppose *quantification,* as such, to present their alternatives. They have yet to do so. Exactly the same point applies to the use of money as a measuring rod of social values (or ratios of money prices or shadow money prices which are, in fact, pure numbers). Unless one is prepared to tackle the task of expressing values in monetary terms, whether it is the value of an hour of labour time, the value of a life or the value of a beautiful view, there is no way of sensibly discussing priorities in an operational way. At least economics can present a rationale for basing policy recommendations in the social interest upon the revealed values of individuals. It can also suggest which circumstances make it unsafe to do so. Improving the numbers is a noble task; objecting in principle is to recommend an empty and emasculated obscurantism which defies not only analysis but even discussion. If things are 'missed out' of the economic analysis so much the worse for the *analyst* – but the analysis, a fundamental principle of which is that *everything* that has benefits or costs should be included, is left unscarred. What other methodology attempts to embrace all relevant factors and so enjoins its (all too human) practitioners? When an alternative is suggested, the criticism may begin to bear scrutiny.

A fundamental discovery of economics has been that subjective values can be translated – under certain conditions – into objectively revealed data. One (imperfect) mechanism for revealing these data is the market. Another (imperfect) mechanism is experts' imputation of shadow prices from other market revealed data. A third (imperfect) mechanism is the use of values implied by policy-makers' decisions. A fourth (imperfect) mechanism is to use directly explicit values postulated by policy-makers for the question in hand. Economic analysis of social policy does not depend upon any one of these sources of values, though choosing between them does present considerable difficulties which, at the current stage of the development of the analysis, are largely matters of judgement. The choice is, however, posed by the explicitness of the economic method of analysis. The method also invites the student to examine explicitly the reasons why some revealed values may be more subject to distortion than others. It also suggests a rather important point, that getting more information about values (or anything else) is not a costless activity.

Sometimes one may conclude that the additional information, or increase in reliability, is simply not worth it. Economists are far from mindless of the virtues of a cost-benefit analysis of cost-benefit analysis!

Underlying some of the suspicion about the ethical status of economics lies, perhaps, less a concern about the objective of maximising 'social welfare' as conceived in the Paretian framework as with the value judgements implicit in the definition of the 'social'. Certainly, a thorough-going application of the Paretian framework can sometimes lead to surprising results (recall the discussion of drug 'abuse' above in chapter 11). Throughout this book a very broad interpretation has been placed upon the 'social'. We have, for example, several times warned the reader off interpreting *his own* values as social values. However, as we have hinted from time to time, there is no particular reason why we should not moderate or restrict the range of entities that are to be counted in social welfare. There are broadly two ways in which this can be done. On the one hand one could restrict the *types of person* to be counted. For example, it is relatively uncontroversial to exclude the 'insane' and young children (suitably defined). As far as social welfare is concerned only their welfare *as perceived by others* would count, not, as for the rest of society, their welfare as they perceive it too. Perhaps more controversially one could exclude foreigners. Beyond this, however, it would be rather unconventional to describe the mode of analysis as 'Paretian', partly because of the likelihood of an increasing lack of consensus over the exclusion and partly because there are longstanding affinities between a Paretian and a liberal approach to social policy – though they are not quite the same thing.

The second type of exclusion is not of persons but of entities from which they get a benefit. Thus some externalities fall into this category – you may not like the colour of my bedroom walls but I can say that *ought* to be irrelevant (unless you are my wife). Some internalities also fall in this category too, however. A burglar may not, for example, be excluded as a person from the 'society' whose welfare is to be maximised, but we might choose to exclude the pleasure he derives from theft. Once again, however, a point comes when it is stretching the traditional use of language too far to describe the system as 'Paretian', though in logic there is no strict reason why one should not have even a Paretian dictator!

One seems therefore to be confronted with what is ultimately an arbitrary choice of which individuals and entities to include. While, however, the Paretian consensus approach cannot instruct us as to which individuals and entities to include, it does indicate a *method* of discovering which individuals and entities should be included. Ultimately the choice depends upon one's notion of justice or fairness and, as we have seen above (p. 75), a device for revealing what a fair or just set of inclusions would be is the *social contract*. By requiring a full consensus on what amounts to part of the 'constitution' of society, this device is also consistent with Paretian judgements.

What is required is for each rational person to imagine himself divested of the specific attributes he actually possesses in society so that he now chooses as if he did not know what wealth, position, intelligence, etc., that he would possess in society. In this frame of mind each individual is asked what rules he would frame for the inclusion or exclusion of individuals and entities from the social welfare function. At an obvious level it would seem rather likely for example, that a consensus would be reached that Jews or Negroes should *not* be excluded from the social welfare function, for anyone may turn out to be a Jew or a Negro – he would not yet know at the social contract stage. It seems highly likely also that consensus would be achieved that irrational persons should be *excluded*, for an irrational person would not seek his own welfare and might well jeopardise that of others. Likewise, a likely consensus would be reached that many 'informational' externalities, such as one person's preferences for the colour of the bedroom walls of another or for his reading or film viewing habits, would be *excluded* from the social welfare function.

It would appear that the set of individuals and entities for inclusion would correspond quite closely to those chosen (though not necessarily in a social contract situation) by persons having liberal/left values. Whether this is coincidental or not is something we shall not discuss here, however, for the case for this approach is not that it yields results that are related to someone's present general political views but that it minimises the subjectiveness of the fundamental value judgements necessary in a normative scientific approach to social problems: that which is just and good is that which people, under specified circumstances, would agree is just and good not that which one individual, with peculiar moral authority, tells us is just and good. In this sense, science demands a liberalism in morals.

Issues involving equality have often been regarded as lying beyond the normative capabilities of the sort of analysis we have used in this book. In the fierce controversies over health care (especially between the principal gladiators Lees and Titmuss) it seems to have been mutually agreed that the objective of equal consumption ('communism in health') is a major motive in many health service delivery systems, especially the British National Health Service. What has been less obvious amid the dust of the arena is that the desire for equality can be incorporated into the Paretian framework. To some extent this has been done in this book. A more thorough concept of equality has, however been introduced into the normative economics of health by Lindsay (see further reading to chapter 7). While there is a variety of ways of including such things in the analysis however, many of which have yet to be explored, one thing that the framework of this book does *not* permit is for the preferences of any one person, or set of persons, whether egalitarian or not, whether kindly or not, to be involuntarily *imposed* upon others. Whether you regard this as an approach that emasculates the policy potential of the economics of social policy or as one that constrains the professional student to a due humility is a matter of personal taste. It is clear that this author's personal taste favours the latter — as private citizens one's opinions may be what one likes but one's professional or academic knowledge and status does not, or at least should not, permit one to use it to lend additional weight to purely personal value-judgements. As 'experts' we may make certain limited value-judgements. We may also be called upon to exercise personal judgement because we have a certain expertise about what the facts, or the probabilities, are. But in a world increasingly dominated by the 'experts' it is right that a firm limit should be placed upon our competence. This is, perhaps, the most difficult lesson to be learn_d by the student of social policy, for 'Social reformers as a rule . . . fail to notice, or at least they disregard, the fact that individuals entertain different opinions with regard to utility, and that they do so because they get the data they require from their own sentiments. They say, and believe, that they are solving an objective problem: "What is the *best* form for a society?" Actually, they are solving a subjective problem: "What form of society best fits my sentiments?" The reformer, of course, is certain that his sentiments have to be shared by all honest men and that they are not merely excellent in themselves but are also in the highest degree beneficial to society. Unfortunately that belief in no way alters the realities.'[1]

Perhaps the reader feels emasculated by the austerity of this prescription — which we have rather harped on! And the end of this book is perhaps the right place to offer some comfort and solace by extending his freedom to pronounce and prescribe. There can scarcely be any student of social policy whose personal value judgements correspond exactly to those of the Paretian system. There is, moreover, a large number of social problems of general concern as well as of concern to the student upon which as a rational and concerned person he may wish to engage in advocacy going beyond the normative basis of the economics of social policy. Let him therefore not only feel free but *be* free so to advocate and so to engage in persuasion and controversy. The obligation he is under as an economist as well as a citizen, however, is that he make perfectly clear those conclusions that follow from economic analysis and those that do not. He should make perfectly clear those value judgements that (to the professional at least) are recognisably a part of the standard fare of academic economic policy analysis and those that are not. But let him not forget that his lasting contribution to the welfare of mankind is more likely to be made in the context of his scientific endeavour than his political activity. Always, his values and prejudices should be made explicit. Beware of statements including the words 'cost' and 'efficiency'. They are based upon value judgements. Beware of the word 'social'. Its definition hinges upon a value judgement. Beware of 'need' for which there are as many meanings as utterers of the word. Fortunately, the economic analysis of social policy, with its great emphasis on explicitness, renders it a little easier for the individual to separate his professional-status from his citizen-status.

The state of the art in the economics of social policy will have become pretty clear during the course of this book. We have repeatedly drawn attention to the great many *lacunae* in both analytical technique and in our understanding of how to adapt and apply existing techniques of analysis to problems of social policy. We have concentrated mainly on the application of basic analysis, having explained what the basic analysis is, and have foregone the indulgence of exploring the slippery slopes in the higher reaches of formal welfare economics. Our reason for this has not principally been that a discussion of, for example, formal general equilibrium analysis or 'second-best' theory, was out of place in an introduction to the field but that the more esoteric theoretical complications actually add very little to our ability to tackle the problems of the real world. 'Partial equilibrium' analysis or as someone once described it 'practical economics', can (as we have seen) take on a limited range of complications as and when they seem to be important. We have tried to restrict the tools only to those that help us to understand and improve the real world. In this sense this book has tried to occupy a place in the Marshallian tradition — in its best sense, viewing economics as a practical 'engine'. 'Man's powers are limited: almost every one of nature's riddles is complex. He breaks it up, studies it one bit at a time, and at last combines his partial solutions with a supreme effort of his whole small strength into some sort of an attempt at a solution of the whole riddle.'[2] Unless someone comes up with a persuasively explicit and practical alternative, there is little else one can do. Economics still awaits its Newton, let alone its Einstein.

One might reasonably ask whether social policy requires a peculiarly distinctive economics of its own. The message of this book is that it does not, but that it draws most particularly on a few analytical tools developed within the broad corpus of economic thought, and which are still being developed. The economic theories of externalities, human capital, public goods and collective action form the basis of the economics of social policy and their application within this area is likely to contribute to the progressive refinement and development of these 'engines of analysis'. The principal empirical developments needed in the coming years concern the measurement of outputs in social policy, the valuation of these ouputs and more accurate (and formal) statements of the relationships between inputs and outputs. Each of these presents daunting problems and it seems unlikely that perfect success is going to be attained in any within the foreseeable future. The important message for those who seek to improve the rationality, efficiency and fairness of social policy is not to let the perfect become the enemy of the good. The economic approach to social policy is, in general, more comprehensive than any other and, though it has many half-filled boxes, it has no empty ones. As a species of applied microeconomics there are adequate foundations both conceptual and empirical for building upon as well as extending. There is scarcely any area of public policy more important nor likely to be more important in the foreseeable future.

Only ten years ago the economists who attempted to apply their analysis to social problems could be counted on the fingers of one hand (at most two). They encountered much hostility and criticism both from the uninitiated and the unscrupulous. Those days are now largely past and the stage is set for economists to engage less in preliminary skirmishing and more in substantive and specialist analysis in which their skills can be seen rightly as complementary to those of sociologists, operational researchers and political scientists. To quote Mao Tse-tung, that was 'the first step on the 10,000 Li march'. In this book we have tried to signal future steps as well as trace the few that have already been taken all in the very firm belief that a rigorous science of social policy for a society of free and reasonable men can and should be developed, not in the interests of special pleading for special groups or special ideologies, but in the interests of a community of persons with different values and rival ambitions. That is the faith in which the subject has developed and this book was written. It is not a faith lightly to be discarded, in view of the alternatives.

NOTES

1. V. Pareto, *The Mind and Society, op. cit.* para 2145.
2. Alfred Marshall quoted by Milton Friedman in *Essays in Positive Economics*, Chicago, University of Chicago Press, 1953, p. 57.

Author Index

Subject Index

Addiction to drugs, 229ff
Arrears of rent, 160

Benefits of education, 153ff; internal, 26ff, 40n; of public expenditure, 50, 53; social, 27ff, 40n; supplementary, 91ff
Beveridge, W, 91, 105, 106; implementation of Beveridge Scheme or Back to Beveridge, 108
Brain-drain, 216

Capital, human, 45
Central Statistical Office, British, 53ff, 63
Child Poverty Action Group, 85
Collective action, alternatives to, 141, 142
Cost, external, 28ff; internal, 28ff; marginal, 21; output budgeting, 183; social, 28ff
Cost-Benefit Analysis, 10, 21; applications of, 153ff; of education, 153ff
Cost-Effectiveness Analysis, 203; and eviction, 160; and Renal failure, 156ff; and slum replacement, 158ff
Crime and Punishment, Positive economics of, 229
Crime Injuries Compensation Board, 188

Defence, U.S. Dept. of, 191
Demand, Law of, 21
Department, of Education and Science, 201; of Employment and Productivity, 109; of Environment, 188
Discounting, 168ff

Discretionary rules and allocation of social services, 217
Disincentive effects, 102
Drugs, abuse and social policy, 234ff; addiction and slope of demand curve, 247n; habit and transmission of, 238; illegal distribution of, 230ff; and subsidised treatment, 235

Education, Compulsory, 181; and Cost-Benefit Analysis, 153ff; Nursery, 181; and Output Budgeting, 180; Output of, 197; and Science, Dept. of, 201; Social returns to, 153; Vouchers, 211
Efficiency, economic, 22; and production, 216; and rationing, 216
Environment, pollution of, 240
Equality, of consumption, 209; and ownership of rights, 134
Equity, and rights allocations, 134, 245
Eviction, and Cost-effectiveness, 160ff
Externality, 25-30; of drug abuse, 234; informational, 236; see also Cost, Benefit, Public Goods

Family Expenditure Survey, 48, 53ff
Family Income Supplement (FIS), 107n
Financing, and Earmarked taxation, 202; General fund, 202; partial, indirect, 204; of pensions, 218
Fiscal illusion, 95
Fiscal residuals, 77

266